Trust and Rule

Rightly fearing that unscrupulous rulers would break them up, seize their resources, or submit them to damaging forms of intervention, strong networks of trust such as kinship groups, clandestine religious sects, and trade diasporas have historically insulated themselves from political control by a variety of strategies. Drawing on a vast range of comparisons over time and space, *Trust and Rule* asks and answers how and with what consequences members of trust networks have evaded, compromised with, or even sought connections with political regimes. Since different forms of integration between trust networks produce authoritarian, theocratic, and democratic regimes, the book provides an essential background to the explanation of democratization and de-democratization.

Charles Tilly is currently the Joseph L. Buttenwieser Professor of Social Science at Columbia University. He has also taught at the University of Delaware, Harvard University, the University of Toronto, the University of Michigan, and the New School for Social Research. He is a member of the National Academy of Sciences, the American Academy of Arts and Sciences, and the American Philosophical Society, and is a Fellow of the American Association for the Advancement of Arts and Sciences. Charles Tilly is the author of numerous books, including three recently published by Cambridge University Press: *Contention and Democracy in Europe, 1650–2000; Dynamics of Contention* (with Doug McAdam and Sidney Tarrow); and *The Politics of Collective Violence*.

Trust and Rule

CHARLES TILLY

Columbia University

CAMBRIDGE
UNIVERSITY PRESS

CAMBRIDGE UNIVERSITY PRESS
Cambridge, New York, Melbourne, Madrid, Cape Town, Singapore, São Paulo

Cambridge University Press
40 West 20th Street, New York, NY 10011-4211, USA

www.cambridge.org
Information on this title: www.cambridge.org/9780521855259

First published 2005

Printed in the United States of America

A catalog record for this publication is available from the British Library.

Library of Congress Cataloging in Publication Data

Tilly, Charles.
Trust and rule / Charles Tilly.
 p.   cm. – (Cambridge studies in comparative politics)
Includes bibliographical references and index.
ISBN 0-521-85525-X (hardback : alk. paper) – ISBN 0-521-67135-3
(pbk. : alk. paper)
1. Social networks.   2. Trust.   3. Democratization.   I. Title.   II. Series.
HM741.T55   2005
302.4–dc22   2005006329

ISBN-13   978-0-521-85525-9 hardback
ISBN-10   0-521-85525-X hardback

ISBN-13   978-0-521-67135-4 paperback
ISBN-10   0-521-67135-3 paperback

to Harrison White
a hedgehog who became a fox

Contents

Preface

Blame Doug McAdam and Sid Tarrow. It all started in 1995, before an astonished Amsterdam audience. With Ron Aminzade, Doug and Sid plotted and executed a visually vibrant parody of my work: they dressed as sansculottes and gave a rap performance. For two years before the Amsterdam spectacular, McAdam and Tarrow had been grousing together about the poor connections between studies of social movements and analyses dealing with other sorts of popular politics. They thought, for example, that my own work on revolutions, state transformations, contentious repertoires, and popular mobilization articulated badly with current analyses of social movements.

At the Amsterdam meeting, McAdam, Tarrow, and I made peace by agreeing to work together on new approaches to contentious politics, with the particular hope of coming up with ideas that would span multiple varieties of mobilization and contention. Through Bob Scott's initiative and Harriet Zuckerman's patronage, the Mellon Foundation awarded the Center for Advanced Study in the Behavioral Sciences a capacious three-year Sawyer Seminar grant for workshops, fellowships, and sojourns at the Center. The group eventually included fifteen graduate students, seven faculty members, and a great many more temporary participants.[1]

As Sid, Doug, and I were warming up for a year of intense work together at the Center, we wrote a few programmatic papers. We presented one

---

[1] In fact, the program eventually stretched over five years. In addition to Doug and Sid, I am grateful to Ron Aminzade, Jack Goldstone, Elizabeth Perry, and William H. Sewell, Jr., for their indispensable collaboration in the project. For descriptions of the program, see the prefaces to McAdam, Tarrow, and Tilly, *Dynamics of Contention* (Cambridge University Press, 2001) and to Jack A. Goldstone, ed., *States, Parties, and Social Movements* (Cambridge University Press, 2003).

of them to the 1997 meeting of the American Sociological Association as "Democracy, Undemocracy, and Contention." Still happily unpublished and forgotten, that paper pasted together disparate ideas from the three of us concerning the emergence of social movements, their relations to different sorts of regimes (especially democratic and undemocratic regimes), transformations of social movements during democratization, and how to think about contentious politics at large. Reread seven years later, it marks how far we had to go.

One road we had to travel led to clearer ideas concerning how the forms of contentious politics interacted with the character of political regimes. Although we shifted the division of labor constantly, on the whole I took more responsibility in our trio for work on regimes and democratization. It is a measure of my meager influence over Doug and Sid that almost all discussion of regimes disappeared from our major joint production, *Dynamics of Contention* (Cambridge University Press, 2001). But the book did contain a comparison of democratization in Switzerland and Mexico. That comparison stressed two processes: insulation of public politics from categorical inequality and integration of trust networks into public politics.

As I reviewed what other scholars were saying about trust, two recurrent features of the literature struck me as inadequate, at least for the purpose of explaining democratization and de-democratization. First, almost everyone portrayed trust as an attitude, an individual orientation that had somehow to include popular trust of governments and political leaders if democracy were to solidify. Second, most analysts treated the attitude as ranging from narrow to broad, with narrowness the enemy of democracy. The two features combined in the supposition that democratization depended on formation of a broadly trusting public.

I thought the analysts were on to something, but had not correctly identified the social processes involved. As I saw it:

- trust was a property of interpersonal relations in which people took risks of each other's failure or betrayal
- the same people could simultaneously maintain relations with different others ranging from deep suspicion to confident trust
- the same was likely to be true of relations to fellow citizens, political leaders, or governmental agents
- hence the problem for any explanation of democratization and de-democratization was to specify how relatively trusting relations extended into public politics.

Since far outside of democratic regimes a wide variety of risky, long-term collective activities – procreation, cohabitation, provision for children, collaboration in agriculture, long-distance trade, maintenance of ritual solidarities, and more – clearly involved extensive relations of trust, it seemed to me that the mystery concerned how nonpolitical networks of trusting relations politicized themselves, connected with political networks, or gave way to politically connected networks.

Confident that someone somewhere must have dealt with that mystery, I read widely, pestered my friends, and eventually posted a series of queries on my electronic mailing list. The posting generated an energetic, wide-ranging discussion by e-mail.[2] Responses confirmed that many people in my circle found trusting relations important but mystifying, that most considered trust to be an attitude rather than a relation, that a number of partial accounts of its causes and effects were competing for recognition, that no one in the circle had formulated a coherent account of transformations in trust networks or changes in their relations to public politics, but that a wide variety of historical studies bore indirectly on those questions.

As my search proceeded, it became more urgent. I was soon writing the book that became *Contention and Democracy in Europe, 1650–2000* (Cambridge University Press, 2004). In that book, an account of trust networks and democratization figured prominently. The account refined, corrected, and expanded my contribution to *Dynamics of Contention*. As the book took shape, however, I realized that both my story concerning exactly how connections between trust networks and public politics change and my evidence concerning those changes remained perilously thin. But I also realized that to expand the account and add new evidence would make an already complex book unwieldy. I reluctantly set aside the task for another day. The day has now come. This book is the result and for you, my readers, to judge how well it meets its challenge.

From very different angles, four scholars who were doing immediately relevant work gave me the immense favor of commenting on some or all of the manuscript as I wrote it. Alena Ledeneva helped me incorporate

---

[2] For answers to individual queries and contributions to the online discussion, I thank Ron Aminzade, Sam Bowles, Jeff Broadbent, Juan Cole, Jonathan Fox, Jack Goldstone, Thomas Heilke, Mimi Keck, David Levine, Scott McNall, Jerry Marwell, Peter Murmann, John Padgett, Eleonora Pasotti, Maritsa Poros, Eric Selbin, Jesper Sigurdsson, Marc Steinberg, Louise Tilly, Florencia Torche, Katherine Verdery, Barry Wellman, Harrison White, Richard White, Elise Wirtschafter, Bin Wong, and an electronic correspondent who signed simply Jamal.

ideas and evidence on interpersonal networks and trust in Russia. In her dual roles as expert on trust and general editor of the Cambridge Studies in Comparative Politics series, Margaret Levi made me clarify obscurity after obscurity. Reynaldo Ortega took time away from his own inquiry into Spanish and Mexican democratization to scrutinize and correct what I had to say about those two crucial experiences. Viviana Zelizer forcefully drew my attention to parallels between the political processes I was studying and the economic processes she has made her own. Jennifer Carey combed the text with perceptive care. Audiences at the Russell Sage Foundation (where a new roast by Sid Tarrow, disguised as an introduction, mercifully broke down in PowerPoint failure) and the University of Michigan taught me what was and wasn't comprehensible or credible in my arguments.

With permission, I have adapted some material from my "Political Identities in Changing Polities," *Social Research* 70 (2003), 1301–1315; "Trust and Rule," *Theory and Society* 33 (2004), 1–30; and *Contention and Democracy in Europe, 1650–2000* (Cambridge University Press, 2004).

1

Relations of Trust and Distrust

Between 1367 and 1393, Franciscan Brother François Borrel, inquisitor of the high Alpine diocese of Embrun in Dauphiné, scourged the Waldensians of his territory. From the Catholic Church's perspective, those primitive Christians qualified as heretics worthy of extermination. After all, they refused to swear oaths, opposed capital punishment, denied the existence of Purgatory, rejected papal authority including the pope's right to canonize saints, and claimed that sacraments administered by sinful priests had no efficacy. In the small, high Dauphinois valley of Vallouise, during three years for which full records exist between 1379 and 1386, the diocese prosecuted at least 300 Waldensians. When church authorities captured the accused heretics, they tried them in ecclesiastical courts, which routinely convicted them.

The church turned condemned heretics over to secular authorities for burning or hanging, then seized their property. The many Waldensians from Vallouise who fled across the border into Piedmont also lost their belongings. During those three years of inquisitorial adventures alone, Vallouise yielded about five thousand florins worth of confiscated property. That amount equaled about 40 percent of the money that the whole of Dauphiné had paid as royal taxes during the prosperous year of 1343 (Paravy 1993: II, 965).

Before the Protestant Reformation, Waldensians never called themselves Waldensians; their enemies used that name. They called themselves variously Brothers, Poor of Christ, or Poor of Lyons (Audisio 1999: 3). The pejorative label adapted the name of the sect's putative founder, a Vaudès or Valdès who belonged to a wealthy Lyonnais merchant family, underwent a religious conversion around 1170, gave up his property, and began a

1

ministry among the city's poor. Dominican Stephen of Bourbon later described Valdès' activity in these disdainful terms:

Preaching the Gospels and those things he had learned by heart in the streets and the broad ways, he drew to himself many men and women that they might do the same, and he strengthened them in the Gospels. He also sent out persons of the basest occupations to preach in the nearby villages. And these, men and women alike, unlettered and uneducated, wandering through the villages, going into homes, and preaching in the squares and even in the churches, induced others to do likewise.   (Kaelber 1998: 135)

Like the contemporaneous Cathar Perfects of Languedoc and the Pyrenees so vividly evoked by Emmanuel Le Roy Ladurie (1975) as well as the Czech Hussites of the early fifteenth century, the Poor of Lyons aspired to recover the simplicity of earliest Christianity. (Indeed, their self-descriptions eventually obscured their twelfth century origins and claimed continuity from Christianity's founding years.) The Church authorities that then governed Lyon expelled them from the city in 1182. Pope Lucius III excommunicated them from the Catholic Church in 1184. Although French, German, and Italian rulers only imposed punitive decrees on them during the thirteenth century, after their exit from Lyon Waldensians started to go underground. The Lyonnais sect fled the city and filtered up Alpine valleys, linking families across Dauphiné and Piedmont through missionaries called *barbes* for their customary beards; by that time, the preachers had become exclusively male.

From Lyon's hinterland, the Waldensians reached far into other parts of Europe. At times, the Brothers sent colonies to the Po Valley, Apulia, Calabria, Burgundy, Provence, Austria, Bohemia, and the Rhineland. Within that diaspora, separate regionally based factions such as the Poor Lombards and a distinctive brand of Bohemian asceticism emerged (Kaelber 1998: 147–151). Their relations extended far enough for Waldensians to translate some Hussite writings into Provençal (MacCulloch 2003: 38). But over four centuries of clandestine existence Waldensians congregated especially in the high Alps.

During the early Reformation, *barbe* Georges Morel wrote Protestant leaders of Basel and Strasbourg to explain the poor folks' virtuous vision of their ministry:

Our people almost always come from herding and agriculture. They are 25 to 30 years old, and have no education at all. We try them out among ourselves for three or four years during the two or three winter months . . . During that time, we

2

teach them to write and read, and to learn by heart the gospels of Matthew and John, chapters of all the canonical Epistles, and a good part of Paul . . . Those who qualify are taken to a certain place where a few women, our sisters, live as virgins. In that place they spend a year or two, actually devoting most of their time to working the earth. After that time the disciples, by the sacrament of the Eucharist and the laying on of hands, are admitted to the ministry of priesthood and preaching, and are sent out two by two to evangelize. The first one of the two admitted always leads in honor, dignity, and authority, and is the master of the second . . . None of us marries, even if to tell the truth we do not always live chastely. Our food and clothing come as alms from the people we teach.   (Paravy 1993: II, 1034)

Because of official persecution, both preachers and faithful lived under constant threat of denunciation. Just one defection to the authorities could cost them lives and property. In the face of risk, Waldensians built powerful networks of trust. The stronger those networks, the more they supported the faith, but also the more they sharpened the distinction between people Waldensians could trust and those they should distrust.

Once past their early years of activity in Lyons, the *barbes* did not preach publicly, for justified fear of persecution. Instead their proselytizing passed from household to household, from person to person, in protected secrecy. The young preacher Pierre Griot served as second man on a number of missions, but in 1532 fell into the Inquisition's hands. Brought before the Dominican inquisitor Jean of Roma in Provence, Griot gave these replies:

So why are they ashamed to preach their doctrine in public
__ he answers that he believes it is out of fear.
Questioned as to whether their doctrine is good or bad,
__ he says that they believe it is good.
Questioned, since they think it is good, why they do not preach in public
__ says in reply that it is from fear.   (Audisio 1999: 88)

As Protestantism gained public ground during the sixteenth century, most of the Brothers merged into one branch or another of the new religious movement, thus leaving behind both centuries of clandestine life and most of their distinctive practices. During the sixteenth century, for example, Calvin's Geneva sent out preachers who gradually incorporated many Waldensian congregations of the nearby Alps into the Protestant Church.

From the middle of the seventeenth century, the Dukes of Savoy asserted their anti-Protestant credentials by expulsions and massacres of the remaining Waldensians in their territories. One group of Waldensian refugees from Savoy, indeed, fled to the tolerant Dutch colony of Staten Island, New York (MacCulloch 2003: 672). Despite intermittent persecution, a formally organized (and so named) Waldensian Church became the Protestant nucleus in Piedmont. It survives today within a small but vigorous set of congregations across the Western world. But as a distinctive, clandestine, tightly knit network of trust the Poor of Lyons disintegrated during the sixteenth and seventeenth centuries.

Links among Waldensians qualify not just as an interpersonal network but as a *network of trust* because members' relations to each other put major long-term collective enterprises at risk to the malfeasance, mistakes, or failures of other network members. In the Waldensians' case, the network set lives, property, and faith at risk. A single spy, defector, or weak-kneed victim of the Inquisition could cause the Waldensian network atrocious damage. Trust networks organized around kinship, long-distance trade, or workers' mutual aid rarely face the threats of death and dispossession regularly experienced by Valdès' followers. Yet they, too, stand out from ordinary networks of communication and commerce by the high stakes of belonging and of performing well within the network.

How will we recognize a trust network when we encounter or enter one? First, we will notice a number of people who are connected, directly or indirectly, by similar ties; they form a network. Second, we will see that the sheer existence of such a tie gives one member significant claims on the attention or aid of another; the network consists of strong ties. Third, we will discover that members of the network are collectively carrying on major long-term enterprises such as procreation, long-distance trade, workers' mutual aid or practice of an underground religion. Finally, we will learn that the configuration of ties within the network sets the collective enterprise at risk to the malfeasance, mistakes, and failures of individual members.

Waldensians maintained a large trust network. They sometimes suffered persecution and dispossession for their membership in the network. Their turbulent particular history thereby dramatizes a general problem in the history of political regimes. The quality of public politics in one regime or another depends significantly on relations between people's basic trust networks and rulers' strategies of rule. *Public politics*, in this sense, includes all externally visible interactions among constituted political actors and agents of government. Without being rigid about the terminology, I will generally use the term "rulers" for national authorities as actors, "governmental agents" for those who act or speak on behalf of rulers, "governments" for the organizations those agents operate, "political actors" for nongovernmental entities having some sort of name and standing vis à vis a given government, and "regime" for regular relations among rulers, governments, and political actors. "Public politics" refers to their visible interactions.

Within public politics, *contentious politics* includes all discontinuous, collective making of claims among constituted political actors, including governmental agents and rulers (McAdam, Tarrow, and Tilly 2001). Trust networks, segments of trust networks, and members of trust networks sometimes get involved in contentious politics as makers of claims, objects of claims, and as third parties to claim making. Although sixteenth century Waldensians stayed out of public politics as much as possible, during their times of persecution they became crucial objects of ecclesiastical and governmental claims. Unwillingly and often disastrously, they entered public politics, in the confrontations of collective claims and counterclaims we call contentious politics.

Noncontentious politics still makes up the bulk of all political interaction, since it includes tax collection, census taking, military service, diffusion of political information, processing of government-mediated benefits, internal organizational activity of constituted political actors, and related processes that go on most of the time without discontinuous, public, collective claim making. Trust networks and their segments get involved in noncontentious politics more regularly – and usually more consequentially – than in contentious politics. By going underground, Waldensians managed mostly to stay out of public politics, contentious or noncontentious, for four centuries after their exit from Lyon. But their survival, therefore, depended more heavily on effective operation of their trust networks and on the networks' effective insulation from public politics.

Networks reach into every corner of social life (Watts 2003, 2004). Social networks include any set of similar connections among three or more social sites. Connections include communication, mutual recognition, shared participation in some activity, flows of goods or services, transmission of diseases, and other forms of consequential interaction. Network sites may be individuals, but they can also be organizations, localities, or social positions. A network of connections among people you don't know and who mostly don't know each other brings you your morning newspaper. Another transmits political information. Still others lend invisible structure to flows of money, disease, and linguistic innovation.

Although segments of such networks may overlap with or even constitute trust networks, taken as wholes they do not qualify as trust networks. They do not qualify because their participants do not generally place their major valued collective enterprises at risk to malfeasance, mistakes, or failures by other members of the same networks. In that precise sense, members do not trust each other. Most or all members of trust networks, in contrast, place major valued collective enterprises such as the preservation of their faith, placement of their children, provision for their old age, and protection of personal secrets at risk to fellow members' malfeasance, mistakes, or failures. Accordingly, trust networks constitute only a tiny subset of all networks.

Over thousands of years, nevertheless, ordinary people have committed their major energies and most precious resources to trust networks – not only clandestine religious sects, to be sure, but also more public religious solidarities, lineages, trade diasporas, patron-client chains, credit networks, societies of mutual aid, age grades, and some kinds of local communities. But trust networks often compete with rulers for the same resources, for example such basics as money, land, and labor power. Rulers have usually coveted the resources embedded in such networks, have often treated them as obstacles to effective rule, yet have never succeeded in annihilating them and have usually worked out accommodations producing enough resources and compliance to sustain their regimes. The Waldensians show us a trust network whose members sustained their relations under adverse conditions for centuries. But their moments of most serious persecution also show us rulers using mighty resources to break up clandestine trust networks and seize the resources embedded in them.

We participants in kinship and other trust networks usually take them for granted. But they pose important mysteries: how do they maintain cohesion, control and, yes, trust when their members spread out into worlds rich with other opportunities and commitments? Their limiting cases, isolated communes and religious communities, seem easier to explain because their very insulation from the world facilitates continuous monitoring, mutual aid, reciprocity, trust, and barriers to exit. But geographically dispersed trust networks somehow manage to produce similar effects, if not usually at the emotional intensities of isolated communities. Maintaining the boundary between "us" and "them" clearly plays an important part in trust networks' continued operation (Tilly 2004c, 2005). That fact alone helps explain why over most of history participants have avoided exposure to rulers and public politics as much as possible.

Yet from time to time regimes emerge in which many citizens actually put their lives and assets extensively at risk to bad political performance. They use legal tender, buy governmental securities, pay taxes, rely on government-backed pensions, yield their children to military service, appeal to courts, contribute to public services, and rely on publicly recognized political actors for help in communicating their grievances or aspirations. At least to that extent, they integrate their trust networks into public politics. At least to that extent, the people who currently run their governments – their rulers – gain access to precious resources that historically have stayed sequestered within trust networks, well protected from public use. Rulers gain access to previously hoarded wealth, credit, labor power, information, and sometimes even loyalty.

Integration of trust networks into public politics varies from indirect to direct. *Indirect* integration occurs when trust networks extend into politically engaged actors such as local organizations, churches, or labor unions that in turn bargain with each other and with governments over the allocation of politically mediated costs and benefits. *Direct* integration occurs when trust networks extend into government itself, for example through the incorporation of kin group members into national armed forces, establishment of state churches exercising monopolies over political participation, or government creation of social security systems tying the futures of workers to governmental performance and the reliability of government-employed providers of services. Obviously many intermediate locations open up along the continuum, for example privileged or disadvantaged communities enjoying connections with governmental agencies committed to their protection.

Enter Adam Smith

Adam Smith never used the term "trust network." Smith did, however, make a relevant argument: solidarity of the sort that appears in trust networks grows from sympathy bred by long-term familiarity, and thus forms stronger bonds within households than across kin groups or neighborhoods. Smith's *Theory of Moral Sentiments*, first published in 1759, also portrayed sheer necessity as driving members of solitary groups together in most political circumstances:

In pastoral countries, and in all countries where the authority of law is not alone sufficient to give perfect security to every member of the state, all the different branches of the same family commonly choose to live in the neighbourhood of one another. Their association is frequently necessary for their common defence. They are all, from the highest to the lowest, of more or less importance to one another.

Their concord strengthens their necessary association – their discord always weakens, and might destroy it. They have more intercourse with one another than with the members of any other tribe. The remotest members of the same tribe claim some connexion with one another; and, where all other circumstances are equal, expect to be treated with more distinguished attention than is due to those who have no such pretensions. It is not many years ago that, in the Highlands of Scotland, the chieftain used to consider the poorest man of his clan as his cousin and relation. The same extensive regard to kindred is said to take place among the Tartars, the Arabs, the Turkomans, and, I believe, among all other nations who are nearly in the same state of society in which the Scots Highlanders were about the beginning of the present century.   (Smith 2000: 326–327)

Habitual sympathy and collective self-defense, in Smith's account, converged in promoting kin-based solidarity across most political circumstances. Only those political systems guaranteeing individual security escaped that necessity.

Adam Smith's 1759 essay states a fundamental problem, but falls short of identifying the problem's solution. Under what conditions, how, and why do people rely on kin connections for their major enterprises? Institutional economists have picked up the Smithian problem, and proposed an ingenious solution: although markets and firms provide more efficient substitutes for kin-based trading in developed economies, where uncertain enforcement of contracts and high information costs prevail, naturally formed trust networks actually offer superior efficiency to reliance on impersonal economic transactions. In Janet Tai Landa's work,

Questionnaire surveys of and interviews with Chinese middlemen engaged in the marketing of smallholders' rubber in Singapore and West Malaysia in 1969 revealed that (a) the marketing of smallholders' rubber – through the various levels of the vertical marketing structure – was dominated by a middleman group with a tightly knit kinship structure from the Hokkien-Chinese ethnic group; (b) that mutual trust and mutual aid formed the basis of the particularization of exchange relations among Chinese middlemen; and (c) that within the Chinese economy transactions among middlemen were based on credit, while Chinese middlemen used cash transactions with indigenous smallholders to reduce contract uncertainty.   (Landa 1994: 101)

According to Landa, the networks activated invisible ethical codes in a "low cost clublike institutional arrangement," which economized on contract enforcement and information costs (Landa 1994: 102). In harmony with other institutional economists, Landa emphasizes the importance of social arrangements that reinforce or substitute for firms and markets by reducing transaction costs and stabilizing economic outcomes (Haber, Razo, and Maurer 2003, North 1990, 1997).

Avner Greif approaches a similar problem when he compares "individualist" Genoese merchants with "collectivist" Jewish merchants of the Maghreb. He sets up the comparison as a pair of principal-agent problems: under what conditions will principal merchants entrust precious transactions and goods to distant agents? In the individualist case, the principal will pay the agent a sufficiently high commission to forestall cheating by making the gain from cheating a single time less than the expected gain from long-term honesty; the principal will pay the agent an efficiency wage. In the collectivist case, on the contrary, the principal will rely on the network's connectedness to assure that a cheater faces shunning by all network members:

Suppose, for example, that every Maghribi expects everyone else to consider a specific behavior as "improper" and punishable in the same manner as cheating in agency relations. This punishment is self-enforcing for the same reasons as the self-enforcing collective punishment in agency relations and is feasible because there is a network for information transmission.   (Greif 1994: 936)

In the collective society, by Greif's account, customs, oral tradition, and similar informal mechanisms produce agreement about improper behavior, hence common readiness to punish infractions wherever they occur throughout the network.

So far, so good – but not good enough. First, Smith's argument and its neo-Smithian elaborations offer no explanation of the claims exercised by distant kin with whom persons have had little or no contact. How does it happen that, as Adam Smith noticed, "the remotest members of the same tribe claim some connexion with one another," and exercise rights based on that "connexion"? Is it plausible that each such kin connection belongs to a collectivist society in which custom and oral tradition have produced connectedness, shared beliefs, and a consequent readiness to punish infractions of common norms? Second, Smithian arguments do not explain how groups linked primarily not by kinship but by religion, political commitment, or trade actually acquire and maintain kinlike solidarity; both Landa and Greif, for example, assume solidarity's prior existence. Third, they underestimate the predatory approach of rulers to trust networks on which they can get their hands. Finally, they offer no account of the process by which the trust networks of what Smith calls "commercial countries" become integrated into public politics.

Smith himself argued that kin-based relations simply shrivel as civilization advances (Smith 2000: 327–328). But observers of today's rich capitalist countries repeatedly find kin relations organizing a wide range

9

Table 1.1. *Signs of Trust Networks' Integration into Public Politics*

In the contemporary world, we would be observing integration of trust networks into public politics if we saw many people in a given regime doing a number of the following things:

- creating publicly recognized associations, mutual aid societies, parties, unions, congregations, and communities, or seeking recognition for similar organizations that have existed underground
- pursuing friendship, kinship, shared belief, security, and high-risk enterprises within such organizations
- permitting family members to serve in national military and police forces
- promoting careers of family members in public service, including government office
- seeking (or at least tolerating) government registration of vital events such as births, deaths, and marriages, then using the registration to validate legal transactions
- providing private information to public organizations and authorities through censuses, surveys, and applications for services
- entrusting private contracts to governmental enforcement
- asking government agents to punish or prevent malfeasance by members of their own kin groups, religious sects, or economic networks
- using government-issued legal tender for interpersonal transactions and savings
- purchasing government securities with funds (e.g., dowry) committed to maintenance of interpersonal ties
- relying on political actors and/or government agencies for vital services and long-term security

of social activity (DiMaggio and Louch 1998, Lye 1996, Stark 1995, Yinger 1985). Clearly we must move beyond Adam Smith, while recognizing with Smith and his heirs a dual problem of explanation: 1) independence and importance of trust networks across long stretches of history and 2) transformation and possible withering of trust networks in the world's "commercial countries."

How might we recognize the political integration of trust networks? For our own time, Table 1.1 lists likely clues of that integration, ranging from indirect (creation of politically active associations containing or based on trust networks) to quite direct (promoting careers of trust network members in governmental service). Over the long historical run, such commitments of trust networks to public politics have rarely developed. Even in today's democratic countries, they have only become common during the last century or so. In addition to being consequential for individual lives and interpersonal relations, they greatly increase the stakes of network members in the proper conduct of public politics.

When and how do such things happen? Looking at the long historical interaction between trust networks and systems of rule, we face five compelling questions:

1. In the presence of political predators and greedy rulers, under what conditions and how do people maintain trust networks?
2. Given the prevalence of predation among rulers, under what conditions and how do trust networks become integrated – directly or indirectly – into systems of rule?
3. How does the connection between rulers and trust networks affect the stability of rule?
4. Under what conditions, how, and with what political consequences do trust networks and rulers benefit mutually – or, for that matter, fail to benefit mutually – from integration?
5. When it occurs, what accounts for the variety of that integration? What determines its form?

This book unpacks the five puzzles. It draws heavily on historical examples such as the Waldensians, but eventually shows that the questions have more than historical interest. The future of democracy, for example, depends on connections between trust networks and political regimes; extensive withdrawal of trust networks from public politics, when it occurs, damages democracy. Privatization of social security or health care, withdrawal of elites or minorities from public schools, and substitution of electronic communication for direct contact among political activists all have the potential of producing just such destructive withdrawal of existing trust networks from public politics in today's democracies, and therefore of damaging democracy.[1] On the way to such conclusions, however, the book explores a wide variety of connections – and disconnections – between public politics and trust networks.

Answering the five questions requires a break with customary thinking. The word "trust" commonly calls up an individual attitude toward a person or an institution. Here we must recognize, however, that certain forms of organization – trust networks – incorporate relations of trust. Political analysts, furthermore, usually think of trust as infrastructure, a phenomenon

---

[1] Anderson, Fish, Hanson, and Roeder 2001, Anheier and Thenudo 2002, Bennett 2003, Bermeo 2003, Buck 1999, Deibert 2000, Diamond 1999, Dryzek 1996, Edwards, Foley, and Diani 2001, Fishman 2004, Forment 2003, Hoffmann 2003, Ortega Ortiz 2001, Rothstein 2004, Skocpol 2003, Tilly 2004a, 2004b, Chapters 5 and 6, Warren 1999.

11

that facilitates or inhibits certain sorts of politics, but does not form part of politics as such. In order to explain change and variation in configurations of trust and rule, however, we must analyze two sites in which relations of trust and distrust play active political roles: between trust networks and other political actors, and within trust networks themselves. We have no choice but to consider trust networks as lively, changeable political actors.

Trust, Trust Networks, and Relations to Rulers

We can think of trust as an attitude or as a relationship with practices attached. For the purpose of resolving our five puzzles, it helps to concentrate on the relationship, leaving open what sorts of attitudes might motivate, complement, or result from a relationship of trust. Labels such as kinsman, fellow believer, and comember of a craft provide a first indication of a trust relationship. But we know a trust relationship more surely by the practices of its participants: if you trust me, don't just tell me so; let me take charge of your children's education, lend me your life's savings for investment, take medicines I give you, or help me paint my house on the assumption that I will help you paint yours. If you don't trust me, prove it by doing none of these things, and nothing like them.

Trust consists of placing valued outcomes at risk to others' malfeasance, mistakes, or failures. Trust relationships include those in which people regularly take such risks.[2] Although some trust relationships remain purely dyadic, for the most part they operate within larger networks of similar relationships. Trust networks, then, consist of *ramified interpersonal connections, consisting mainly of strong ties, within which people set valued, consequential, long-term resources and enterprises at risk to the malfeasance, mistakes, or failures of others*.

I have defined trust in terms of risk. People do not, however, commit weighty enterprises to trust networks because they prefer risky relationships. On the contrary, when people face serious risks to long-term enterprises they value highly, they turn preferentially to trust networks for

[2] For surveys of trust-sustaining practices, relations, and institutions, see Anthony and Horne 2003, Bates et al. 1998, Besley 1995, Biggart 2001, Biggart and Castanias 2001, Burt and Knez 1995, Castrén and Lonkila 2004, Elster 1999, Elster, Offe, and Preuss 1998, Feige 1997, Gambetta 1993, Gould 1999, 2003, Granovetter 1995, Guiso, Sapienza, and Zingales 2004, Heimer 1985, Hoffman, Postel-Vinay, and Rosenthal 2000, Landa 1994, Ledeneva 1998, 2004, Levi 1997, Lonkila 1999a, Ostrom 1990, 1998, Paxton 1999, Postel-Vinay 1998, Rotberg 1999, Shapiro 1987, Solnick 1998, Stark 1995, Weber and Carter 2003, Wuthnow 2004, Yamagishi and Yamagishi 1994.

support of those enterprises. Trust networks stand out from other sorts of social relations precisely because they build controls over malfeasance and safeguards against consequences of mistakes and failures into their routine operation. For members of trade diasporas, well-knit lineages, and clandestine religious sects, the threats of shunning, shaming, and denial of reciprocity loom much larger than in everyday social networks. Powerful figures within trust networks sometimes tyrannize their members: instill strange beliefs in them, put them through painful initiations, force youngsters into distasteful careers, require shows of respect for unworthy elders, murder young women who challenge their sexual or marital prescriptions. By no means does membership in a trust network guarantee happiness, much less freedom.

Yet members of trust networks usually receive some compensation for conformity. Faithful participants in trust networks commonly get personal attention, help with personal difficulties, long-term reciprocity, and cushioning against possible disasters or disabilities – benefits they cannot ordinarily acquire elsewhere. As neo-Smithian analysts suggest, trust networks reduce transaction costs and increase security of contracts. Conformity becomes the price of social insurance. Trust networks control their members, but they also provide their members with rewards that make exclusion costly.

Most networks support little or no trust. We will sometimes recognize *segments* of networks that qualify as trust-connected cliques. But the networks of drug use, blood distribution, and sexual contact through which HIV spreads, the networks through which routine political information flows, and the networks established by shared membership in voluntary associations mostly do not qualify. More generally, single-stranded networks containing few triads and sustaining little intimacy among their nodes rarely or never become trust networks.

Characteristic enterprises in which trust networks figure importantly include cohabitation, procreation, provision for children, transmission of property, communication with supernatural forces, joint control of agricultural resources, long-distance trade, protection from predators, maintenance of health, and collective response to disaster. With marked variation from setting to setting, trust networks often take the forms of religious sects and solidarities, lineages, trade diasporas, patron-client chains, credit networks, mutual aid societies, age grades, and local communities.

After thousands of years, trust networks continue to flourish in the twenty-first century. People often rely on such networks for such practical activities as getting jobs, migrating long distances, making major purchases, borrowing money, engaging in high-risk political activity, and finding marriage partners.[3]

At this point we should improve on Adam Smith. We should certainly avoid thinking of such trust networks as outmoded leftovers from primeval Gemeinschaft. By no means do they only appear in traditional kin groups or tradition-bound societies. People create and recreate them all the time. College classmates form lasting solidarities, firefighters bond with other members of their fire companies, immigrant women organize rotating credit associations, and new religious sects manage collective withdrawals from the secular world. Ramified interpersonal connections, consisting mainly of strong ties, within which people set valued, consequential, long-term resources and enterprises at risk to the malfeasance, mistakes, or failures of others – trust networks – may look traditional or modern, conservative or radical. But they keep reappearing.

Such new creations of trust networks sometimes have large historical impacts. Consider a remarkable analysis of credit networks in sixteenth-century England. Craig Muldrew looked closely at uses of credit in commercial transactions, which expanded rapidly after 1540 or so as England engaged more heavily in textile production and continental trade. Legal tender then consisted almost entirely of gold and silver coin. The money supply, however, expanded much more slowly than production of goods and the pace of commerce. Most likely some deflation and some acceleration in monetary circulation occurred as a consequence. But expansion of interpersonal credit – more to the point, of credit among households and the commercial enterprises embedded in those households – far outstripped changes in money supply as such. Note some crucial effects:

As credit networks became more complicated, and more obligations broken, it became important before entering into a contract to be able to make judgements about other people's honesty. The more reliable both parties in an agreement were in paying debts, delivering goods or in performing services, the more secure chains of credit became, and the greater the chance of general profit, future material

[3] Alapuro and Lonkila 2004, Auyero 2000, Bayat 1997, Bayon 1999, Clark 2004b, Cordero-Guzmán, Smith, and Grosfoguel 2001, Diani 1995, Diani and McAdam 2003, DiMaggio and Louch 1998, Fernandez and McAdam 1988, Gould 1995, Grimson 1999, Havik 1998, MacLean 2004, Meisch 2002, Morawska 1985, 1996, 2003, Ohlemacher 1993, Opp and Gern 1993, Passy 1998, 2001, Pastor, Pascua, Rodríguez-López, and Sánchez-León 2002, Piipponen 2004, Portes 1995, Singerman 1995, Tilly 1990, 2000, Tsai 2002, Wiktorowicz 2001, Zelizer 2002, 2005.

security and general ease of life for all entangled in them. The result of this was that credit in social terms – the reputation for fair and honest dealing of a household and its members – became the currency of lending and borrowing. Credit . . . referred to the amount of trust in society, and as such consisted of a system of judgements about trustworthiness; and the trustworthiness of neighbours came to be stressed as the paramount communal virtue, just as trust in God was stressed as the central religious duty. Since, by the late sixteenth century, most households relied on the market for the bulk of their income, the establishment of trustworthiness became the most crucial factor needed to generate and maintain wealth.

(Muldrew 1998: 148; see also Muldrew 1993)

As Muldrew does not quite say, the new credit networks did not simply include the worthy. More emphatically and dramatically, they excluded – and stigmatized – the unworthy. They magnified distinctions between people you could trust and people you should distrust.

In the first instance, a household's credit did not depend on its material possessions or its cash on hand. It depended on relations to other households, so much so that people commonly spoke of each other's credit-worthiness in terms of their ability to raise money from other people on short notice (Muldrew 1998: 148–172). Muldrew's analysis helps explain why ties of kinship, neighborhood, and shared religion remained crucial to risky commercial transactions as an ostensibly rationalizing and depersonalizing market expanded. It also helps explain why in a time of economic expansion members of the sixteenth century's ascendant commercial classes increasingly condemned proletarians who did not qualify for credit as improvident, bibulous, and morally unreliable.

Muldrew's analysis stands Max Weber – or at least the Max Weber of *The Protestant Ethic and the Spirit of Capitalism* – on his head. Where Weber saw the Protestant Reformation as promulgating doctrines of individual responsibility that favored capitalist achievement, Muldrew perceives a transformation of social relations that made a reputation for uprightness crucial to commercial viability. In regions and classes where heterodoxy, mayhem, debauch, and pillage had long prevailed, religious, political, familial, sexual, neighborly, and commercial irregularity all came to raise doubts about the creditability of any particular person, household, or social category (see also Wrightson and Levine 1979, 1991). Distrust became more salient and consequential.

Muldrew offers us a delightfully subversive perception; his analysis not only reverses the causal arrow between belief and practice, but also indicates that far from dissolving previously existing social ties, market expansion depended on the creation of far more extensive interpersonal relations. Instead of deriving relations of trust from general culture or contract-enforcing institutions as is currently fashionable, Muldrew derives new attitudes and contracting-enforcing institutions from alterations in social relations.

Despite some concessions to trust as attitude or belief, furthermore, Muldrew advances analyses of trust by treating it as a feature of social relations themselves; by implication, trust consists of placing valued resources and outcomes at risk to the malfeasance, mistakes, or failures of (trusted) others. Faced with a shortage of specie so severe that it blocked cash transactions, Muldrew tells us, sixteenth-century English people devised new trust networks that could absorb the risk of credit. In line with those recent economic historians and analysts of Eastern Europe who have emphasized the significance of trust-sustaining networks for markets and other forms of economic organization, Muldrew insists on the priority of social ties.

National governments eventually intervened massively in credit-connected markets by establishing central banks, issuing paper money, and regulating commercial transactions. Creation of a Bank of England (1694) and establishment of parliamentary control combined to produce major changes: a relatively secure national debt, heavy involvement of London financiers in the funding of that debt, and widespread investment of the wealthy in government securities (Armitage 1994, Muldrew 1998: 328–329). But, according to Muldrew, authorities intervened not in a void but in dynamic networks of connection among households. Indeed, Muldrew argues that credit's expansion eventually produced uncertainties that overwhelmed the capacities of person-to-person networks. That overload of credit networks favored both calls for governmental intervention à la Thomas Hobbes and the spread of a more pessimistic, individualistic view of human nature (Muldrew 1998: 315–333; see also Helleiner 2003: 42–46, McGowen 1999).

Meanwhile, local authorities and interacting households fashioned or adapted their own trust-confirming institutions: kinship, common religious affiliation, oath taking, public tokens of indebtedness, earnest payments, courts of settlement, and more. "The phrase 'to pay on the nail,'" reports Muldrew,

comes from Bristol where there were four bronze pillars erected before the Tolzey – the ancient covered colonnade where merchants conducted their business, and which was connected to the sheriff's court where most debt litigation was initiated. The 'nails' are still in existence, and have flat surfaces where downpayments, and payments in cash, would have been made, and the practice of doing so was considered to be symbolic of the trust invested in the agreements. The date of the oldest nail is not known, but the other three were erected as gifts to the city in 1594, 1625 and 1631 to meet the need of increased business. The most interesting fact about the pillars are the inscriptions around the capitals on the religious and social nature of trust, which were comments upon the bargains made over them. One repeated the classical dictum that, 'No man lives to himself', and another stated: 'The Church of the livinge God is pillar and ground of trewth'.

(Muldrew 1998: 106–107)

Thus religious beliefs and practices fortified the politics of reputation, but by no means explained the vast changes that were occurring after 1530.

Fundamental alterations of social relations brought new forms, practices, and symbols into everyday prominence. Public oaths, mutual surveillance, and representations of social ties as if they were contracts proliferated. Literature gave expanded attention to credit and contract. "Shakespeare," remarks Muldrew,

often used this language in metaphors and conceits, as in Sonnet 134 where debt, sureties, bonds, a mortgage and a law suit were all used to describe the relationship between a lover, his former mistress and her new lover. They were also a common feature in drama, with some of the most obvious examples being Shakespeare's treatment of the ethics of forgiveness and discretion versus the binding force of contract in *The Merchant of Venice*, Philip Massinger's comedy about miserliness and prodigality, *A New Way to Pay Old Debts*, and Webster's tragedy about uncharitable litigation, *The Devil's Law Case*.   (Muldrew 1998: 315)

Muldrew backs such general interpretations with systematic analyses covering thousands of sixteenth-century court cases. His evidence establishes deep, rapid increases both in uses of credit and in disputes about its abuses.

Muldrew's analysis of sixteenth-century England therefore brings two precious observations into an analysis of trust networks and political regimes. First, it shows people creating new, exclusive trust networks in response to unsatisfactory governmental performance – the failure to provide sufficient currency for expanding commercial transactions – rather than relying on old solidarities of religion, kinship, and local community. Second, it describes a process in which the trust networks thus created began to disintegrate of their own complexity, and came increasingly to rely on governmental backing. It shows us the partial integration of crucial trust networks into public politics.

Integrated Trust Networks

Despite an analytic line that at first view looks quite hostile to this book's arguments, Margaret Levi also makes an important contribution to explaining integration of trust networks into public politics. She shrewdly chooses to analyze resistance against and compliance with military conscription – a quintessential case in which individuals face the choice of bearing large costs on behalf of benefits they will share little or not at all, and to which their participation will make little difference. Conscription does not rely entirely on altruism because conscripts ordinarily belong to the citizenry on whose behalf they serve. Conscripts therefore stand to benefit, however slightly, from their own military service. Still, their service certainly exemplifies the placing of valuable enterprises – in this case, the lives and future labor of young men – at risk to political malfeasance, mistakes, or failures. Military service plays such a crucial part in the development of citizenship and patriotism that Levi's analyses bear much more generally on the problem of trust networks' integration into public politics.[4]

As she summarizes one segment of her 1997 book's argument in a later publication:

Margaret Levi investigates the institutional bases for variation in government policies and citizen responses to conscription in France, the United States, and Prussia. Levi's finding that revised norms of fairness, resulting from democratization, influence the timing and content of institutional change suggests the importance of normative considerations and the institutional bases of legitimacy in accounting for citizen compliance with governmental and regulatory agencies more generally.   (Levi 2003: 8)

Thus Levi interprets her own work as demonstrating the influence of changing institutions on citizens' political choices.

Levi self-consciously builds her analysis on game theory (Levi 1997: 7–8). She thereby commits herself to single actor explanations of social behavior: individuals make decisions that affect other individuals in response to incentives operating within constraints. She moves beyond bare rational actor formulations, however, in two significant ways. She first identifies relations with others as significant constraints on individual decision making and, second, sketches histories of the institutions that shape constraints, including relations with others. Repeatedly, as a result, she reaches beyond the

---

[4] Bradley 2002, Chambers 1987, Crépin and Boulanger 2001, Krebs 2004, Lynn 1984, Mjøset and Van Holde 2002, Tilly 1995, 1999a.

self-imposed limits of her models to examine interactive processes such as continuous bargaining. Concretely, she analyzes situations in which potential soldiers, governmental agents, and other subjects of the same government bargain out consent to military service or resistance to that consent.

Levi's model of "contingent consent" states that individual citizens are more likely to comply with costly demands from their governments, including demands for military service, to the degree that

1. citizens perceive the government to be trustworthy
2. the proportion of other citizens complying (that is, the degree of "ethical reciprocity") increases, and
3. citizens receive information confirming governmental trustworthiness and the prevalence of ethical reciprocity (Levi 1997: 21).

More loosely, Levi argues that citizens consent to onerous obligations when they see their relations to governmental agents and to other citizens as both reliable and fair. Fairness and justice matter.[5] Levi does not specify what mechanisms produce these effects; she treats them as empirical generalizations to verify or falsify. She implies, however, that the effective mechanisms are cognitive: they consist of individual-by-individual calculations concerning likely consequences of compliance or resistance. "Contingent consent requires," she declares, "that an individual believe not only that she is obliged to comply but also that others are or should be obliged to comply" (Levi 1997: 205). Like other rational action theorists, she centers her explanations on cognitive processes.

Levi means to refute several counterhypotheses. They include: 1) habitual obedience, 2) ideological consent, and 3) opportunistic obedience (Levi 1997: 19). Each of these identifies a different cognitive orientation of subjects to authorities. Habitual obedience falls away because it offers an inadequate explanation of variation and change. Ideological consent characterizes some zealots, but not the bulk of compliance with military service. Opportunism, as Levi defines it, can respond to a variety of incentives including secret satisfaction, side benefits, social security, and group pressure. In fact, argues Levi, opportunism would more often dictate draft dodging than dutiful service.

Levi's evidence from the United States, Canada, the United Kingdom, France, New Zealand, Australia, and Vietnam concerns differential

---

[5] Eliasoph 1998, Jasso 1999, Moore 1979, Shklar 1990, Vermunt and Steensma 1991, Young 1990.

compliance with demands for military service according to period, population segment, and character of war. Observed differentials challenge habit, ideology, and opportunism accounts while confirming Levi's empirical generalizations summarizing contingent consent: on the whole, compliance with conscription occurred more widely in situations of relatively high trust, and so on.

Institutions, organizations, and social relations enter Levi's explanations as background variables – not as direct causes of compliance but as shapers of the perceptions and information that themselves explain compliance. In her account, Canada's sharp division between anglophones and francophones helps explain both readiness of the Anglo majority to impose conscription on the entire country and greater resistance of the French-speaking minority to military service (Levi 1997: 163–164). Institutions, organizations, and social relations also affect available courses of action and their relative costs. Thus French history, with its long establishment of the nation in arms and its weak development of pacifist sects, made conscientious objection much less available to draft resisters in France than in Anglo-Saxon countries (Levi 1997: 191–192).

Toward the end of her analysis, Levi offers a larger opening to social processes: she argues that third party enforcement strongly affects the actual likelihood of other people's compliance, hence any particular individual's perception of fairness (Levi 1997: 213). Governmental coercion of potential defectors significantly affects not only those recalcitrants themselves but also people who become more willing to serve when they know that others will have to serve as well. At this point in Levi's analysis, networks of interpersonal commitment start playing a significant and fairly direct part in the generation of social action. Levi offers another opening to social processes by recognizing how significantly governmental performance affects compliance; poorly or erratically performing governments receive less compliance. By this point, interactive processes are doing an important part of Levi's explanatory work. Without ever saying so, she is actually analyzing the operation of interpersonal trust networks in the public politics of conscription.

Levi's two overtures to social processes deserve a whole opera. We have, for example, some evidence that in wartime workers strike more frequently and soldiers desert in larger numbers when their country's military forces show signs of losing badly (see, e.g., Lagrange 1989). Defection during wartime connects with a postwar phenomenon: a tendency of strikes, rebellions, and revolutionary situations to concentrate in immediate post-war periods (Tilly 1992a, 1993).

One Levi-style component of these phenomena seems to be the following: governments pursue major wars by imposing tightened central controls and accumulating large debts, but by doing so they also expand their commitments to all collaborating parties. During the war, signs that governments are losing capacity to meet those commitments induce collaborators in the war effort to press claims for immediate advantages and/or to withdraw their effort. After the war, few governments actually retain the capacity to meet their wartime commitments; in Levi's terms, they suffer declines in trustworthiness. The worse their losses in war, the more they lose capacity and suffer discredit (cf. Schumpeter 1947: 354). In these circumstances, disappointed political creditors respond by accelerating their demands and/or withdrawing their compliance with the government's own demands.

Parallel effects operate on the smaller scale within military units. For North Carolina's Confederate forces in the American Civil War, Peter Bearman (1991) has shown that ordinary individual-level characteristics tell us little or nothing about propensity to desert, but that collective properties of fighting units make a significant difference. Early in the war, locally recruited companies tended to stick together, while geographically heterogeneous companies suffered relatively high rates of desertion. As the war continued, however, the pattern reversed: after the summer of 1863, members of geographically homogeneous companies became more likely to desert the cause. "Ironically," notes Bearman, "companies composed of men who had the longest tenures, who were the most experienced, and who had the greatest solidarity were most likely to have the highest desertion rates after 1863" (Bearman 1991: 337).

Bearman plausibly accounts for this surprising shift as the result of a relational process: Confederate recruiters originally concentrated on forming companies locally, but deaths and tactical reorganization eventually made some companies geographically heterogeneous. Early in the war, commitment to a locality and commitment to the Confederate cause as a whole aligned neatly. In these circumstances, locally recruited companies that had kept their members stuck together with determination. As the war proceeded, however, overall losses introduced increasing discrepancies between national and local solidarity; collective connection to the same locality simultaneously activated commitments to people at home

21

and facilitated collective defection from the national military effort. Collectively, members of defecting military units withdrew their trust – their placing of their lives and home connections at risk to the malfeasance, mistakes, or failures of others – from faltering national authorities. In that concrete sense, they came to distrust a government on whose behalf they had earlier risked their lives.

Despite Levi's emphasis on cognitive orientations, shifts in compliance with governmental demands are not mere mental events; they involve genuine changes in relations among important actors within a regime. Levi gives us two structural processes to examine seriously: 1) alterations in networks of interpersonal commitment, and 2) changed relations between governmental agents and citizens. Although the terminology of trust networks remains quite alien to Levi's own analytic lexicon, her work establishes clearly that such networks sometimes do integrate partway into public politics, and thereby strongly influence public politics. It therefore makes more salient the question of how that happens.

What Must We Explain?

Comparison among Waldensians, sixteenth-century English commercial households, and conscription shows us three very different kinds of relationships between trust networks and systems of rule. Once expelled from Lyon, the Waldensians generally stayed as far from rulers as possible, and only altered that stance with their incorporation into Protestantism during the sixteenth and seventeenth centuries. English users of credit first formed their networks in uneasy relation to royal power, but eventually turned to the national government for protection. Responses to conscription varied from sustained resistance to dogged acceptance or even patriotic commitment, but generally represented a higher level of integration between trust networks and public politics. We must examine why such profound differences exist, and how such changes occur. That is this book's burden.

We can shoulder that burden more easily by following one elementary insight: both political regimes and trust networks face organizational problems whose solution simultaneously affects their internal operation and their survival. Both of them depend on a constant flow of new resources that supports their major activities and reproduces the structures making those activities possible. Regimes that fail to renew their means of coercion, for example, eventually collapse through internal dissent and/or external conquest. Similarly, trust networks that stop recruiting new, committed individuals shrivel in no more than a single generation. The book's problem arises because regimes and trust networks often depend on the same resources – labor power, money, information, loyalty, and more. Except when they ran their own trust networks or depended on allies who ran their own trust networks, most historical rulers seized resources flowing into trust networks or embedded in those networks whenever they could get hold of them. That seizure destroyed the networks, severely hampered their operation, promoted their seeking of protection from other less predatory authorities, or drove them underground.

But a few processes have promoted accommodations between trust networks and public politics: significant declines in the resources available to trust networks, decay of networks' crucial internal structures, multiplication of populations outside of existing trust networks, negotiated conquest of previously independent polities run by trust networks, seizure of power by actors organized in trust networks, and creation of effective systems of protection and/or welfare by rulers. As the progression from Waldensians to English commercial households to twentieth-century military services indicates, under some conditions citizens actually come to depend on governments for protection and welfare, accordingly connecting their trust networks with public politics.

Connections of trust networks with public politics vary enormously and consequentially. With many refinements saved for later, we can think of those connections as ranging between two extremes. At one end of the continuum, trust networks operate out of sight, in complete insulation from government surveillance and control; over most of their history, Waldensian networks followed that pattern. At the other end, trust networks form part of government, as when they take shape within regular military units. In between, we can distinguish at least two more degrees of segregation or integration. Somewhat above the Waldensians stand trust networks living under the protection of relatively autonomous intermediaries such as regional warlords. Even closer to integration we discover trust networks that either constitute or connect closely with public political actors – for example, mutual aid societies making claims on political authorities or tight-knit religious congregations joining electoral campaigns. Historically, trust networks have existed across this full range, and at times particular trust networks have shifted position within the range, becoming more or less integrated into public politics. How, why, and when that happens – and with what further consequences for public politics – will occupy the rest of this book.

If you like your books polemical, you can imagine the remainder of this book as arguing for transactional accounts of trust while challenging systemic and dispositional accounts (Tilly 2005, Chapters 1 and 2). Crudely speaking, general descriptions and explanations of social processes divide into three categories: systemic, dispositional, and transactional. *Systemic* accounts posit a coherent, self-sustaining entity such as a society, a world economy, a community, an organization, a household, or at the limit a person, explaining events inside that entity by their location within the entity as a whole. Systemic descriptions and explanations have the advantage of taking seriously a knotty problem for historians and social scientists: how to connect small-scale and large-scale social processes. They have two vexing disadvantages: the enormous difficulty of identifying and bounding relevant systems, and persistent confusion about cause and effect within such systems.

Dispositional accounts similarly posit coherent entities – in this case more often individuals than any others – but explain the actions of those entities by means of their orientations just before the point of action. Competing dispositional accounts feature motives, decision logics, emotions, and cultural templates. When cast at the level of the individual organism, dispositional descriptions and explanations have the advantage of articulating easily with the findings of neuroscience, genetics, and evolutionary analysis. They have the great disadvantage of accounting badly for emergence of new properties in the relations *among* entities, much less for the effects of aggregate properties such as population density and network structure.

Transactional accounts take interactions among social sites as their starting points, treating both events at those sites and durable characteristics of those sites as outcomes of interactions. Transactional accounts become relational – another term widely employed in this context – when they focus on recurrent features of transactions between specific social sites. Transactional or relational descriptions and explanations have the advantage of placing communication, including the use of language, at the heart of social life. They have the disadvantage of contradicting common-sense accounts of social behavior, and thus of articulating poorly with conventional moral reasoning in which entities take responsibility for dispositions and their consequences.

Systemic, dispositional, and transactional approaches qualify as metatheories rather than as directly verifiable or falsifiable theories. They take competing ontological positions, claiming that rather different sorts of phenomena constitute and cause social processes. The three therefore generate contradictory lines of explanation for social processes. In the nature of the case, however, sustained competition between social scientific explanations usually takes place *within* one of these ontological lines rather than across them; systemic explanations compete with other systemic explanations, and so on.

Systemic accounts of trust (e.g., Barber 1983) explain the extent and location of trust within a social setting by reference to the overall organization of that setting and the relations of particular sites within the setting to that overall organization. Dispositional accounts of trust (e.g., Hardin 2002), in contrast, center on individual actors' orientations, with special reference to the conditions or processes that induce individuals to trust certain others. Transactional accounts of trust, as this chapter has already illustrated, treat trust as a contingent, negotiated property of social interaction. In today's political analyses of trust, dispositional accounts predominate.[6]

My adoption of a transactional view differentiates this book from several other common approaches to trust and to networks. First comes the idea that trust is fundamentally a belief or attitude, a way of thinking about the world. Such an idea hews to the dispositional line. To the extent that social experience generates confidence that others will treat you well, goes the argument, you cooperate more readily in collaborative enterprises of all sorts, including democratic politics (e.g., Knight 2001). As the discussions of Muldrew and Levi suggest and as the next chapter says more emphatically, my own approach reverses that causal arrow, treating attitudes not as causes but as effects of social interaction.

Next – and very differently – comes the treatment of networks as homogeneous phenomena (e.g., Scott 1991). We might call this the thin version of the transactional account. Networks convey information and influence, according to this view, in pretty much the same way regardless of their content. Networks vary in being more centralized or segmented, sparser or denser, but otherwise share a large number of common properties. Chapter 2 states more clearly my paired claims that a) the organization and content of relations within trust networks differentiate them significantly from other sorts of interpersonal networks and b) along with authoritative organizations and collaborative institutions, trust networks constitute one of the three main ways that humans organize valued, long-term, high-risk enterprises.

---

[6] Barbalet 2001, Chapter 4, Cook 2001, Levi and Stoker 2000, Seligman 1997, Woolcock 1998.

Finally, we have the view that networks in general, and trust networks in particular, store or produce social capital (e.g., Pretty 2003). That view appears variously in transactional, systemic, and dispositional versions. But in all of them figures a conception of network experience as infrastructure, as support for individual or group participation in risky collective enterprises. A country rich in social capital, we often hear, takes on collective tasks that would daunt any capital-poor country. Thus social capital becomes a complement, a precondition, or even a partial replacement for financial and industrial capital. This book's analyses reject the idea of trust networks as a resource for political and economic interaction. Instead, they treat trust networks as active sites of political and economic interaction.

I have not written this book, however, either to test competing theories or to clear away conceptual debris. Instead of comparing systemic, dispositional, and transactional approaches step by step throughout the book, I simplify matters greatly by concentrating on development of a consistently transactional account of social processes that enhance and diminish trust – trust considered as a distinctive form of human relationship. I have tried to show that such a conception of trust helps explain large variations in connections between trust and rule.

If you enjoy books as fights, however, each time the following chapters call up images of trust (the placing of valued outcomes at risk to the malfeasance, mistakes, or failures of others) as a transactional phenomenon, just summon up your preferred systemic or dispositional explanation of the same phenomenon; if your alternative comes off as a more plausible and/or more economical explanation of the concrete phenomena later chapters take up, reject the metatheory within which I have located my own account. Even in that case, however, my detailed analyses should serve you in two distinctive ways. First, they state major questions about trust and rule that scholars have not sufficiently addressed, and that your superior alternative should help you answer. Second, they make the case for trust as a historical product rather than a phenomenon whose variation we can explain without reference to history. If the book makes only these two contributions, it still deserves attention.

Evidence?

We face serious problems of evidence. In our own time, states have so far extended their sway that few trust networks anywhere exist untouched by political power. Simple comparisons of contemporary trust networks differing in their current proximity to state power will not suffice to reveal how large-scale change in relations between trust networks and regimes occurs. By their very nature, however, trust networks that once existed outside the orbits of powerful states left few traces from which twenty-first-century analysts can reconstruct their internal dynamics. Although archaeological evidence from Mesopotamia confirms the existence of trade in precious metals and minerals from Neolithic times (7000 BCE onward), for example, only with the accumulation of cuneiform tablets (from about 3300 BCE) do traces of merchant networks start showing up in the record. By about 1900 BCE, however, we have evidence of far-flung networks.

Some of the most striking news comes from the merchants of Assur (now Qalat Shergat, Iraq), base of later Assyrian empires. Merchant families established in Assur typically sent out junior members to staff branches like the major center in Kaneš (Kültepe), Turkey (Roaf 1990: 113–114). In a characteristic text from a few decades after 1900 BCE, a merchant in Assur writes his counterpart in Kaneš:

As to the purchase of Akkadian textiles, about which you wrote to me, since you left the Akkadians have not entered the City (of Assur). Their country is in revolt. If they arrive before winter, and there is the possibility of a purchase which allows you profit, we will buy for you and pay the silver from our own resources. You should take care to send the silver.   (Postgate 1992: 213)

From similar sources across the ages, we can identify participants in mercantile networks and learn something about their commercial relations. But such networks always remain opaque when it comes to the give and take of personal influence and reciprocity. Even those that coexist with states or benefit directly from state patronage – as did the mercantile networks of Assur – generally shield their interior negotiations from public scrutiny. Kinship groups and religious sects likewise resist direct observation.

Yet we need not lapse into despair or careless conjecture. Properly handled, unlikely sources do yield evidence on the structure and process of trust networks. In Western Europe, the very process by which states and state-backed churches penetrated local communities often turned up information about previously existing connections among the people now being brought under central surveillance and control. As we have seen, when the Catholic Inquisition began its efforts to unmask and eradicate heretics, it often generated detailed evidence on local social relations. Even short of inquisition, ecclesiastical inspections of parish morality turned up surprising evidence on who connected with whom and how (Marsh 1998: 1–3).

27

As Protestant churches formed, they often outbid Catholics in their zeal for local surveillance. When sixteenth-century Calvinist rulers tried to impose consistories for moral control, they necessarily dug into local affairs. "When John VI of Nassau-Dillenburg introduced consistorial discipline there in 1582," comments Philip Benedict,

> he had a hard time at first finding suitable elders in many rural communities because the system was widely perceived as intrusive and unnecessary. A majority of villages inspected in 1590 could not meet the quota of one presbyter for each twenty to thirty households: many people refused the office when offered it, and those who accepted repeatedly fell short of the desired moral character. Many did not attend communion, one had fathered an illegitimate child, and another was known for urinating under the table when he drank. Those who tried to carry out their charge complained that their neighbors criticized them as traitors.   (Benedict 2002: 457)

In the very act of resisting, villagers were yielding information about local social relations, and therefore to some extent producing news about the operation of trust networks.

During the same period, Western Europe began laying down a rich record of evidence indirectly concerning trust networks in the forms of parish records and individual testaments. Inventories and bequests at death provide snapshots of the relational webs connecting older people with their social surroundings. In Whickham, near Newcastle, rich testamentary records register not only conventional pieties but also patterns of debt and credit:

> Jennet Merriman was . . . among that minority of testators who extended their consideration to embrace unrelated neighbours. She left tokens of regard in the forms of items of clothing to four female neighbours, including Elizabeth Harrison 'the mittwyfe,' who received a cap and Jennet's second-best kerchief. The neighbours, however, were much more likely to make their appearance in testamentary records either as witnesses to the making of a will, or in the lists of outstanding debts and credits appended to wills and inventories.   (Wrightson and Levine 1991: 286)

Those "lists of outstanding debts and credits" recall Craig Muldrew's analysis of expanding credit in sixteenth-century England, and its implications for alteration of trust networks. Similar sources allow historians to trace godparenthood, witnesses of marriages, and other interpersonal networks. In short, surviving evidence provides a grip, however unsteady, on the structure and process of trust networks before and outside of massive state intervention. Nevertheless, my inquiry necessarily pieces together fragmentary evidence, the occasional illuminating direct observation, and a good deal of conjecture. Therein lies the adventure: relations between trust networks and systems of rule matter so much for the quality of political life that the inquiry's stakes justify its risks.

The following chapters break the analysis of encounters between trust networks and systems of rule into several segments. Chapter 2 looks more closely at the organization and operation of trust networks in general. Chapter 3 asks how and why the internal operation and external connections of trust networks change. Chapter 4 explores interactions between trust networks and various sorts of predators, including rival trust networks. Chapter 5 focuses on processes of segregation and integration, which are crucial to our overall story. Chapter 6 applies results of the previous chapters to the place of trust networks in democratization and de-democratization. Chapter 7, finally, considers implications of the analysis and of contemporary social changes for the futures of trust networks, hence for the possible futures of politics.

2

How and Why Trust Networks Work

The vividly contrasting experiences of fourteenth-century Waldensians, sixteenth-century English mercantile families, and twentieth-century conscripts suffice to establish change and variation in relations among rulers, public politics, and trust networks. They range from energetic segregation of trust networks against intervention of ecclesiastical and political authorities (Waldensians) to contingent, consequential integration of those networks into public politics (conscription). Let us think more generally about what sorts of change and variation we have to explain. Figure 2.1 schematizes the general analytical problem: what sort of variation in connections between public politics and trust networks must we account for? The vertical axis distinguishes roughly among a) segregation of trust networks from public politics, b) negotiated connections between the two, and c) integration of trust networks directly into systems of rule. The horizontal axis distinguishes among three means of connection between rulers and ruled: coercion, capital, and commitment.

Coercion includes all concerted means of action that commonly cause loss or damage to the persons, possessions, or sustaining social relations of social actors. It features means such as weapons, armed forces, prisons, damaging information, and organized routines for imposing sanctions. Coercion's organization helps define the nature of regimes. With low accumulations of coercion, all regimes are insubstantial, while with high levels of coercive accumulation and concentration all regimes are formidable.

Capital refers to tangible, transferable resources that in combination with effort can produce increases in use value, plus enforceable claims on such resources. Regimes that command substantial capital – for example,

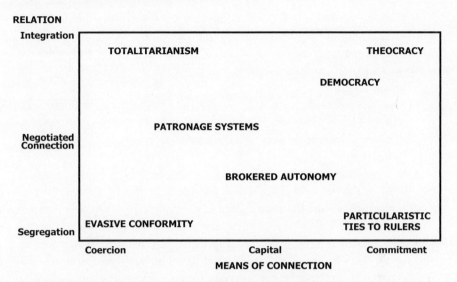

Figure 2.1 Relations of Trust Networks to Centers of Power

from rulers' direct control of natural resources, itself often undergirded by coercion – to some extent substitute purchase of other resources and compliance for direct coercion of their subject populations.

Commitment means relations among social sites (persons, groups, structures, or positions) that promote their taking account of each other. Shared language, for instance, powerfully links social sites without any necessary deployment of coercion or capital. Commitment's local organization varies as dramatically as do structures of coercion and capital. Commitments can take the form of shared religion or ethnicity, trading ties, work-generated solidarities, communities of taste, and much more. To the extent that commitments of these sorts connect rulers and ruled, they substitute partially for coercion and capital.

Following these definitions, Figure 2.1 distinguishes exemplary forms of connection between trust networks and public politics that fall into different locations within the space:

- *totalitarianism:* extensive coercive integration of trust networks into regime politics; example: incorporation of local solidarities into the Italian Fascist regime
- *theocracy:* extensive integration of trust networks organized around communities of belief; example: Iran during the 1980s

31

- *patronage systems:* combinations of coercion with capital (and at least some minimum of commitment) into patron-client chains that produce negotiated, mediated connections between rulers and ordinary people's trust networks; example: nineteenth-century Latin American cacique regimes
- *democracy:* partial (but never total) integration of trust networks into public politics emphasizing commitment, but not excluding some deployment of capital and coercion; example: contemporary Switzerland
- *brokered autonomy:* arrangements in which leaders of trust networks yield resources and compliance to rulers in return for significant autonomy within their own domains; example: the Ottoman millet system
- *evasive conformity:* arrangements in which participants in trust networks shield them from rulers to the extent possible, but yield resources and external compliance when coerced; example: Mongol empires
- *particularistic ties:* formation of religious, kinship, or other commitment-forming ties directly linking rulers differentially to distinct trust networks; example: multiple connections of Japan's Tokugawa shoguns to different constituencies

No one should take this as a rigorous or exhaustive classification. It omits, for example, interesting extreme cases such as American antigovernment militias and isolated religious communities. In their periods of successful underground activity, after all, the Waldensians kept themselves below the diagram's bottom line, in a zone of no connection whatsoever with rulers. The taxonomy serves simply to describe substantial, consequential variation in connections between public politics and trust networks. No simple yes-no, in-or-out dichotomy will serve to pose the analytic problem usefully. Nor can we settle for placing all connections on a single continuum from isolated to integrated. The mode of integration – the mix of coercion, capital, and commitment – matters fundamentally.

We can visualize the political problem thus posed from the top down or the bottom up (Tilly 1999b). Figure 2.1 provides a map of strategies as seen from the top down: rulers' choice of means – coercion, capital, and/or commitment – and of integration, negotiated connection, or segregation. From the top down, rulers face a dual challenge: how to get access to essential resources that are currently embedded in trust networks, and how to enlist cooperation and consent on the part of participants in trust networks.

Coercion, capital, and commitment provide rulers with different means of meeting the challenge; each has substantially different consequences for their own political activity and relation to their subjects. Regimes vary greatly depending on the relative weight of the three means of connection and on the extent to which they integrate trust networks directly into systems of rule. Integration of trust networks splits, furthermore, between direct incorporation into government as such and integration into political actors that play partly autonomous parts in public politics. Authoritarian and theocratic regimes stress direct incorporation, as democratic regimes offer more room for autonomous political actors and the trust networks attached to them. Top-down strategies of resource extraction and political control therefore vary accordingly.

From the bottom up, the problem looks very different. Ordinary people must worry about how to assure their own futures and those of the relations on which they rely as they defend crucial resources from expropriation. Rulers' deployment of coercion, capital, and commitment often threatens those very relations and resources, for example, by taking away young men for long-term military service. Since many vital enterprises that are either irrelevant or hostile to rulers' interests depend on the maintenance of trust networks, ordinary people or their patrons must usually preserve some insulation between their networks and public politics. Over the long run of human history, people have usually invested large efforts in segregating crucial networks from scrutiny, intervention, predation, and expropriation.

Six major exceptions, however, have sometimes occurred. Table 2.1 lists them. Bottom-up strategies for protection of trust networks vary accordingly. These varying relations of trust networks to political regimes allow us to specify what aspects of trust networks' performance we must explain, and how we might explain them. In particular, if a trust network exists, what determines the character and intensity of its relations to a) rulers or b) other major political actors? Certainly the regime's overall form – totalitarian, democratic, or otherwise – matters. So do the composition and activity of the trust network itself. But within limits set by various combinations of regime and network, we can distinguish alternative approaches of trust networks' members to creating or avoiding connections with other political actors, including rulers. With all due caution, let us call them strategies.

33

Table 2.1. *Major Exceptions to the Segregation of Trust Networks from Public Politics*

1. Trust networks in the form of religious sects, kinship groups, or mercantile networks have occasionally established their own autonomous systems of rule.
2. Regimes have sometimes conquered other regimes that were already run by trust networks.
3. Political actors organized as trust networks (e.g., religious cults) have sometimes seized power in already constituted regimes.
4. Once in power, rulers have often created their own trust networks in the forms of dynastic marriage alliances and internal patronage systems.
5. At least temporarily, totalitarian and theocratic regimes have managed extensive incorporation of existing trust networks into authoritarian systems of rule.
6. Democracies accomplish partial integration of trust networks into public politics.

Bottom-up strategies include:

concealment: avoiding detection and manipulation by authorities

dissimulation: feigning conformity by adopting some available public identity, but minimizing both compliance and visibility of internal operations and resources

clientage: acquiring protection by intermediate authorities, thus reducing compliance and visibility, but usually at a price

predation: organizing enough externally effective force both to acquire resources and to defend against predation by others

enlistment: active integration into an existing regime's available niches

bargaining: establishing relations with major political actors on the basis of mutual contingent consent

dissolution: destruction of an existing network through either incremental departures or collective dismantling

As we will soon see, imputing deliberate, unitary strategies to whole trust networks radically simplifies processes of segregation and integration. Few trust networks create central decision mechanisms capable of producing rapid collective decisions. Such "strategies" as enlistment and dissolution often occur incrementally and against many members' wills. Yet it sets our problem more clearly to treat these alternative forms of bottom-up interaction with public politics as implicit strategies.

Top-down and bottom-up strategies interact to produce different systems of rule. Relatively effective totalitarian regimes succeed in weakening most trust networks they do not incorporate, but they always drive some underground. One plausible line of argument claims, indeed, that highly centralized regimes always depend in part on illicit networks for the actual execution of top-down plans, because central planners can never anticipate variation in local conditions and because subordinates cope by working out their own accommodations.[1] Something similar seems to happen in concentration camps, in which clandestine networks that prisoners form in the effort to survive reproduce and even sustain the camps' structure (Narotzky and Moreno 2002). Thus we might expect a three-way split in such regimes: privileged trust networks extensively integrated into public politics, illicit trust networks operating in uneasy symbiosis with the regime, and underground networks practicing dissimulation or concealment.

Although some patronage obviously occurs in highly centralized regimes, full-fledged patronage systems operate rather differently. Where warlords, landlords, lineage heads, ethnic leaders, or religious magnates control extensive followings through their own applications of coercion, capital, and/or commitment, from the top down rulers must choose among co-opting those intermediaries, bypassing them, destroying them, or granting them significant power within their own domains. Historically, most durable large-scale systems of rule have incorporated substantial elements of patronage. But they generate their own bottom-up strategies, since patron-client relations remain contingent on continued distribution of benefits and provide strong incentives for new patrons to vie for their own clienteles.

Despite the existence of some patronage within democratic regimes, democracy operates in yet another manner from systems relying heavily on patronage. In this schematization, it combines extensive (but by no means total) integration of trust networks into public politics with heavy reliance of rulers on commitment rather than coercion and capital as means of assuring political compliance. If trust network integration became total, goes the reasoning, citizens would lack the means of contingent consent so acutely analyzed by Margaret Levi; super-integration of trust networks de-democratizes. In democracies, partial integration of trust networks into public politics ranges from indirect to direct. It may mean reliance on government guarantees, subventions, and services for sustenance of valued long-term resources and enterprises. But it also commonly takes the form of involvement in labor unions, political parties, and other partly independent organizations that retain some autonomy from governmental control.

---

[1] Feige 1997, Fox 1996, Humphrey 1999, 2001, Ledeneva 1998, 2004, Lonkila 1999a, 1999b, Scott 1998. ·

Hence the question: given the usual antagonism of trust networks to public politics across history, how does such a junction ever form?

In general, the junction forms dialectically: on one side, trust networks disintegrate and/or lose their capacity to guarantee risky enterprises; on the other, ordinary people, their patrons, and those who run their institutions bargain out contingent agreements with public authorities. Those agreements may emerge incrementally and need not belong to explicitly democratic programs. But they provide crucial support for democratic practices and relations.

Compatibility Between Trust Networks and Regimes

Let us avoid the illusion that all trust networks look and work exactly the same. No one should confuse trade diasporas with clandestine religious networks. Trust networks have in common valued, high-risk, long-term activities, exposure of those activities to malfeasance, mistakes, or failures on the part of network members, exclusive and competitive operation, high costs of entry and exit, and reliance on commitment in addition to whatever coercion and capital they deploy. But beyond those common properties they vary enormously in the sorts of high-risk, long-term activities they coordinate; consider the difference between procreation and long-distance trade in precious commodities. They vary in size, in durability, in geographic scope, extent of hierarchy, and mode of control over pooled resources. Most important for present purposes, they vary in the stakes of individuals' relations to the network and in the quality of interpersonal relations within the network.

Compatibility of different kinds of trust networks with top-down systems of rule varies accordingly. It varies with the stakes and quality of relations within trust networks. *Stakes of relations* means the extent to which termination of membership in a network damages a participant's long-term welfare; exclusion from low-stakes relations costs participants relatively little over the long run. *Quality of relations* means location on a continuum from relatively impersonal (as in credit) to quite intimate (as in cohabitation). Intimacy, more precisely, refers to the extent that interactions within relations depend on particularized knowledge and attention provided by at least one person, knowledge and attention that are not widely available to third parties; if little particularized knowledge or attention arises in the relationship, we call it impersonal (Zelizer 2000).

Broadly speaking, the higher the stakes and the more intimate the relations, the higher the level of trust involved – that is, the larger the knowing exposure of valued endeavors to the malfeasance, mistakes, or failures of others. Here we are not dealing with a definition, but with a fundamental proposition: where valued endeavors run the risk of other people's malfeasance, mistakes, or failures, the people involved turn preferentially to intimate, high-stakes social relations for the pursuit of those endeavors.

According to this argument, relatively low-stakes, impersonal trust networks such as those constituted by credit circles integrate more easily into top-down systems of rule than do relatively high-stakes, intimate networks such as kinship. Both networks through which criminal capital flows and those linking prostitutes to their customers, the argument continues, fall between those extremes, but for opposite reasons: because of high stakes in the case of criminal capital, and because of temporary but risky intimacy in the case of the sex trade. The distinctions help explain why financiers more often make deals with governments than do lineage heads. When Adam Smith argued that kinship loses its connective power in "commercial countries," he got the historical facts and causal mechanisms wrong, but as usual he was on to something. Except for families of ruling classes, extensive kinship networks integrate badly into the politics of centralized regimes.

An unexpected illustration of compatibility comes from Russian computer hackers – electronic whizzes who compete and conspire to break into other people's computers as a sort of high-risk game. Alena Ledeneva reports that hackers of the post-Soviet era adopt the economy of mutual favors known under the Soviet regime as *blat*. In Soviet *blat*, people routinely exchanged access to goods and services in ways that were technically illegal but absolutely essential to survival under inefficient centralized planning. "*Blat* practices," remarks Ledeneva,

are at the core of the computer underground in Russia today. Not simply because computer software and other items are obtained through friends and connections or in a black market. In a much wider sense, the networks that make up Russian cyberspace serve to circumvent the formal institutional rules and hierarchies. Rafal Rohozinski argues that while Russia's virtual community is small, probably numbering less than one million individuals, this virtual world binds its adherents into a conspiracy of sorts where formal rules and laws are replaced by an unwritten code of practice. Moreover, the informal codes inherent in Russian cyberspace follow the pattern and reproduce the logic of informal practices in social life. So far, Russian cyberspace is a domain where, according to experts, the informal spirit of the Soviet era is still alive. Rohozinski describes it as '*cyberblat*,' as the codes and ethics are similar to those of Soviet *blat* where both demands and damages were quite moderate. (Ledeneva 2000: 164)

So far, Russian hackers' networks operate in a relatively impersonal way for low stakes: the prestige of breaking into security-protected computer systems. They should integrate into Russia's top-down systems of rule more easily than, say, kinship groups and sworn bands of criminals. Take the analogy of security specialists, who proliferated during the early post-Soviet years but then started moving into accommodations with Russian tycoons and officials. On that analogy, it seems likely that hackers will split into those that legitimize themselves and those that take up fully criminal enterprises (Volkov 2002). Relatively impersonal, low-stakes trust networks will integrate into systems of rule more easily than intimate, high-stakes networks.

The usual exceptions apply: trust networks including high stakes and intimacy sometimes create independent top-down systems of rule, rulers in power often establish dynasties and other intimately organized high-stakes networks, and so on. On the average, nevertheless, the argument predicts greater overall resistance to top-down integration on the part of kinship and similar trust networks than on the part of credit circles and mercantile networks. Since historically the bulk of durable trust networks have involved both intimacy and relatively high risk, it also helps explain the long insulation of most trust networks from top-down systems of rule.

Trust Networks Revisited

Social life has always posed a fundamental problem for any group: in the face of strong incentives for individuals to serve themselves first and to avoid calls for cooperation in collective efforts, how nevertheless to produce collective benefits such as protection from predators, maintenance of the environment, and guarantee of future food supplies. In response to the problem, humans have repeatedly devised three different ways of creating collective benefits: authoritative organizations, collaborative institutions, and trust networks. Although the distinctions have not gained wide recognition in political analysis, students of economic processes have often made a parallel distinction among hierarchies, markets, and networks as alternative ways of organizing production, distribution, and even consumption:[2]

[2] Biggart and Beamish 2003, DiMaggio 2001, Powell 1990, Tilly and Tilly 1998, Williamson 1996, Zelizer 2004, 2005.

Economic	Political
hierarchies	authoritative organizations
markets	collaborative institutions
networks	trust networks

Institutionally inclined economists and sociologists, to be sure, make the parallel stronger than do conventional economists, who tend to ignore or deny the institutional infrastructure on which markets depend. Indeed, neo-classical economists often suppose that in business network connections of kinship and friendship *corrupt* markets by substituting personal considerations for the efficient effects of impersonal competition. In the institutional view, however, markets (like collaborative institutions) rest on an often invisible infrastructure of shared meanings, rules, practices, and social relations without which ostensibly impersonal markets would, in fact, collapse (Landa 1994, North 1997, White 2002). Extended from the economic to the political arena, the three-way division greatly clarifies processes of political change.

Let us be clear: the three types describe ideal organizational principles rather than neatly separating concrete structures from each other. Economic sociologists delight, for example, in showing how and with what effects trust networks form within firms or other authoritative organizations and cross-cut their boundaries.[3] Authoritative organizations can incorporate more or less collaborative structure, and collaborative institutions obviously include networks around which participants can sometimes build extensive trust. Chapters to come will often show us trust networks of kinship, migration, or trade forming authoritative organizations at their intersections with public life.

We should treat the three models, then, as matters of degree. We should therefore translate every statement in the form "Authoritative organizations do X" into other statements such as "*In so far* as a concrete structure has features of an authoritative organization, it does X" and "*To the extent that* a concrete structure combines principles of authoritative organization and collaborative institutions, it does Y." But it will save a great many words to take those translations for granted from now on.

---

[3] e.g., Bandelj 2002, Darr 2003, Knorr-Cetina and Bruegger 2002, Morrill 1991, Saxenian 1994.

Authoritative organizations vest top-down control over coercion, capital, and commitment in concentrated authorities whose efforts create the benefits. At least until the time when some multinational corporations began to loom larger than the average state, states long predominated among authoritative organizations. They exercised more extensive control over coercion, capital, and commitment than any of their rivals, and coordinated activities over far larger ranges of activity, population, and resources. But at times business firms, churches, smaller-scale governments, and even households also operate as authoritative organizations.

As producers of collective benefits, authoritative organizations have obvious weaknesses: authorities often produce few collective benefits, impose large collective costs, use their control over resources chiefly to benefit themselves, and use those same means to perpetuate themselves in office regardless of popular suffering or discontent (Rotberg 2004). But when they work well, authoritative organizations create collective benefits through top-down application of incentives: coercion, capital, and commitment.

Collaborative institutions overlap with authoritative organizations to the extent that their members vest authority for coordination, however temporarily, in small numbers of individuals or even a single person. They differ from authoritative organizations, however, in resting on mutual consent with a right of exit. Use of common pooled resources sometimes generates such institutions. Considering situations in which connected people jointly draw sustenance from a pooled resource such as a fishing area or pasturage, Elinor Ostrom makes an illuminating argument. The following conditions, Ostrom indicates, increase the likelihood that the people involved will incrementally adopt rules – institutions – improving joint welfare:

1. Most appropriators share a common judgment that they will be harmed if they do not adopt an alternative rule.
2. Most appropriators will be affected in similar ways by the proposed rule changes.
3. Most appropriators highly value the continuation of activities from this CPR [common pooled resource]; in other words, they have low discount rates.
4. Appropriators face relatively low information, transformation, and enforcement costs.

5. Most appropriators share generalized norms of reciprocity and trust that can be used as initial social capital.

6. The group appropriating from the CPR is relatively small and stable.[4]

Under such conditions, participants are more likely to recognize the benefits they will gain from cooperation, and have more effective means of controlling free riders. More generally, Ostrom argues cogently that sustained collective cooperation in the face of contrary individual self-interest depends on the mutual reinforcement of three elements: trust that individuals have in others, investments they make in reputations for trustworthiness, and adoption of reciprocity norms (Ostrom 1998: 12). Institutions that sustain CPRs combine those three elements.

Trust networks consist of ramified interpersonal connections, consisting mainly of strong ties, within which people set valued, consequential, long-term resources and enterprises at risk to the malfeasance, mistakes, or failures of others. They differ from Ostrom's pooling institutions in five crucial respects. First, to a larger degree than the specialized scope of collaborative institutions, they place their members' valued activities at serious risk to other people's malfeasance, mistakes, or failures. Second, they operate exclusively and competitively: members of any particular network form a minority of the populations within which they live, exclude most others rigorously from membership, and compete with other networks for control of resources. Third, they make exit difficult or even impossible; lineages and clandestine sects do not easily release their members. Fourth, although they often deploy coercion and capital as internal incentives, they always rely on some minimum of commitment – relations among social sites that promote their taking account of each other. Fifth, as a consequence of these first four conditions, the costs of exclusion from trust networks typically run high: loss of membership strikes a hard blow to well being.

On the average, authoritative organizations, collaborative institutions, and trust networks differ according to the pattern of Table 2.2. Authoritative organizations, that is, combine variable ease of exit (you don't get out of prison easily, but you can quit most jobs) with concentrated control over pooled resources, medium vulnerability to malfeasance, mistakes, or failures on the part of their members, medium stakes of exclusion from the

---

[4] Ostrom 1990: 211; see also Adams, Brockington, Dyson, and Vira 2003, Dietz, Ostrom, and Stern 2003, Dolšak and Ostrom 2003, Ostrom, Dietz, Dolšak, Stern, Stonich, and Weber 2002, Pretty 2003.

Table 2.2. *Differences Among Major Types of Coordinating Structures*

Feature	Authoritative organizations	Collaborative institutions	Trust networks
ease of exit	variable	voluntary and easy	rare and costly
control over pooled resources	concentrated	shared and collective	variable
vulnerability to mistakes, malfeasance, or failures	medium	low	high
stakes of exclusion	medium	medium to high	high
ratio of vertical to horizontal ties	high	low	variable

organization, and a high ratio of vertical (hierarchical) to horizontal (relatively equal) ties. That contrasts them sharply with most trust networks, in which exit is rare and costly, control over pooled resources variable, vulnerability to malfeasance, mistakes, or failures high, stakes of exclusion high, and the ratio of vertical to horizontal ties quite variable: in some trust networks, elders wield extensive authority, while in others equality prevails. The differences fit with very different operating procedures and dominant activities.

Rare and costly exit from trust networks does not mean either that no one ever wants to leave or that no one ever gets expelled. It means that high barriers to voluntary exit prevail, and that shunning or expulsion imposes great costs on their victims. For voluntary exit, leaving requires sacrificing old forms of support and finding new ones (Ebaugh 1988). The same applies to involuntary separation. Take the case of the Chippewa reservation in Grand Portage, Minnesota. In 2003, the reservation council expelled a family for a night of drunkenness, vandalism, and fighting. The mother suffered:

The woman, Jacquelyn Jackson, now lives wherever she can. She sometimes sleeps on a cot in an elderly friend's shabby apartment near downtown Duluth. Other times, she stays in a pile of blankets inside a tent in a dark basement of a relative's girlfriend's house. Mrs. Jackson, 43, acknowledged that she behaved terribly that summer night. She was drunk and violent and wrong, she said on a bitterly cold recent morning in Duluth. But she said the punishment was too severe: losing her subsidized duplex on the reservation, losing her friends, losing her way of life in an isolated, quiet place. 'That's my land, too,' Mrs. Jackson said. 'I've never been homeless in my life. I'm never homeless. But I guess I am.' In her furious moments, she said tribal politics left her banished while others – those with friends or family members on the tribal council – did wrong but were not sent away. In sadder moments, she wondered aloud about what was happening back in Grand Portage. What were her friends doing? What had become of the grill, microwave and fans she left in her house and was too afraid and embarrassed to go back for? 'I cry every night because I want to go home,' she said. 'I miss that place so bad.' (Kershaw and Davey 2004: 4)

Losing a job in an authoritative organization or being expelled from a collaborative institution also imposes costs. But forced exit from a trust network, on the average, costs much more. It costs more because expulsion threatens the survival of highly valued enterprises, or the expelled individual's access to those enterprises.

Over the long historical run, typical enterprises involving trust networks have included: cohabitation; procreation; placement of children; stigmatized pleasures; sharing of esoteric knowledge, including heretical beliefs; barter; credit; private warfare; long-distance trade in goods with high value for weight and bulk; pooled water control; and finally, provision for illness, madness, and old age. Some of these enterprises, as we have seen, can also proceed under the top-down authority of rulers; governments have repeatedly taken control of credit, long-distance trade, water control, and private warfare, converting them into public enterprises.

As Ostrom's analysis indicates, under favorable conditions such collective activities as water control generate collaborative institutions. Others such as procreation and stigmatized pleasures ordinarily resist both top-down control and collaborative institutionalization (Zablocki 1980: Chapter 8). But all of these high-risk activities and others like them have often become the business of interpersonal networks in partial or complete independence from governmental control. Over the last five thousand years, most people across the world have relied on trust networks for these enterprises, and have guarded the responsible networks as much as possible from governmental intervention.

Networks and Trust Networks

Among the vast majority of networks that do *not* bear significant amounts of trust, how can we recognize relevant networks as genuine trust networks? Certainly not all interpersonal connections qualify. In addition to strong ties and coordination of weighty collective enterprises that are vulnerable to malfeasance, mistakes, or failures by their participants, we look for relations among at least three persons such that:

a. the relation has a name mutually known to its participants
b. involvement in that relation gives all participants some minimum of shared rights and obligations
c. participants have means of communicating and representing their shared membership
d. participants mark and maintain boundaries separating all members from outsiders

Relevant networks are named, bounded, internally communicating sets of relations entailing mutual obligations. Together, the four criteria exclude most networks defined by personal acquaintance, political influence, engagement in similar work, transmission of economic media, goods, services, information, or diseases, common membership in associations, and use of common facilities such as public transportation or the internet. When sets of durable connections among persons meeting the four criteria coordinate consequential enterprises, however, we recognize them as trust networks.

In general, trust networks differ from other networks in several interesting ways. Although they differ in their degree of intimacy, on the average they involve more intimacy than other networks; relations depend more heavily on particularized knowledge and attention that are not widely available to third parties. Ties within trust networks tend to last longer than other ties. Ties also more frequently form parts of triads: A connects with B and C, who are also connected. Loosely speaking, we can think of trust network ties as thicker, on the average, than other interpersonal ties.

These characteristics impose certain rigidities on trust networks' activities. As compared with authoritative organizations and collaborative institutions, trust networks do not adjust their sizes, memberships, major activities, or organizational strategies flexibly or rapidly. Nor do they readily shift members from position to position within the network or socialize new recruits to their shared understandings and practices.

In compensation, they often prove capable of feats that only occur extraordinarily in collaborative institutions and authoritative organizations: carrying on complex activities over great expanses of time and space without continuous monitoring, entrusting individuals with extensive resources likewise in the absence of continuous monitoring, eliciting dramatic sacrifices from individual members, and surviving large inequalities of rights,

privileges, obligations, and power among nominally full-fledged participants. To a larger degree than authoritative organizations and collaborative institutions, furthermore, trust networks offer mutual aid and social
security to their faithful members. Precisely those characteristics make the
confrontation – and occasional integration – of trust networks with governments dramatic, conflict-filled, and consequential.

As a practical matter, identifying trust networks amid the much wider
array of interpersonal connections poses serious difficulties. It is hard
enough to establish the full set of connections within a population of persons
and social sites (Wasserman and Faust 1994). A generation of researchers
has tracked down such connections, and shown that their configurations
significantly affect the operations of authoritative organizations, including
governments.[5]

To identify which of these networks actually contain high proportions of
trust-bearing relationships, however, we must go beyond the simple tracing
of connections and their absence. A first set of clues comes from the networks' internal structure, especially the extent to which they include triads
and tightly connected cliques. But in the long run we have no choice but to
gather evidence on how they actually work: whether a similar relation links
all participants, whether that relation has a name, whether rights, obligations, and standardized means of communication come with the relation,
whether participants maintain and mark a network boundary, and whether
they do, indeed, place consequential enterprises at risk to malfeasance, mistakes, or failures on the part of other network members.

Over the long historical run, kinship – the establishment of publicly recognized ties through combinations of cohabitation and procreation – has
no doubt provided the most frequent matrix for the formation of trust networks. Not all kinship networks, by any means, constitute trust networks.
Indeed, bilateral lineage systems like those prevailing in most Western
countries practically forbid that any person's full kinship network could
constitute a trust network, if only because it differs in membership from
those of the person's father, mother, children, or cousins.

We must distinguish, furthermore, between the formal reckoning of
genealogies and the creation of active social relations within the broad

---

[5] Bearman 1993, Braddick 2000, Broadbent 1998, Buck 1999, Diani 2003, Glete 2002, Ingram
and Roberts 2000, Keck and Sikkink 1998, Knoke 1990, Laumann and Knoke 1987, Podolny
and Page 1998, Powell and Smith-Doerr 1994, Riles 2000, Skocpol and Oser 2004, Uzzi
1997, Vertovec 2003, Watts 2003.

framework provided by genealogy. In many kinship systems, for example, adoption and fictive kinship establish binding social ties. In order to qualify as trust networks, kinship connections also require the actual performance of kinship, not the mere establishment of shared ancestry. Katherine Verdery's remarkable ethnography of postsocialist privatization in a Romanian agricultural village traces the judicial and administrative assignment to individuals and families of agricultural plots that had passed through many hands and forms of cultivation since the regime of relatively private property existing before World War II.

Verdery argues that in figuring rights to collectivized property the Romanian government adopted a formal, genealogical conception of rights in land, ignoring for instance who had actually worked various plots under socialism, who had invested care in older former proprietors, and so on. From the government's perspective, any individuals who occupied similar positions within the genealogy – two brothers, two cousins, two aunts – had equal rights to shares in privatizing property over which a household or kin group had a legal claim. That formalistic reasoning clashed with local moral codes. According to Verdery:

Villagers, however, had not understood kinship that way; for them, it was performative. To be kin meant *behaving* like kin. It meant cooperating to create marriage, baptismal, and death rituals; putting flowers on relatives' graves; helping out with money or other favors; and caring for the elderly (who might not even be one's parents) in exchange for inheriting their land.   （Verdery 2003: 165)

To put it in terms Verdery does not use and might well reject, relations to kin qualified as genuine kinship to the extent that they conformed to the model of trust networks.

Even if whole kinship networks, formally computed, rarely qualify as trust networks, by virtue of cohabitation and procreation, some *segments* of kinship networks often undertake consequential collective enterprises such as placement of children, and lend themselves to other enterprises such as trade and provision for incompetent persons. In the course of doing so they accumulate resources that remain under their collective control. As age-old struggles over land, cattle, money, and labor power indicate, a kinship network's accumulation of resources then frequently becomes the object of competition between segments of the network, between rival kinship networks, and between network members and authoritative organizations seeking to seize resources for support of their own activities.

For villages west of Genoa during the century from 1550 to 1650, Osvaldo Raggio gives us a privileged picture of the interplay between local trust networks and higher-level authorities. Influential families – more exactly, patrilineages – organized their lives in three circles: those of individual households, people who combined a shared family name with recognized kinship, and larger circles of related kin groups. In economic activity, property transfers, political life, and marital strategies, the more extended *parentele* dominated village affairs. With incessant competition for advantage among extended kinship groups and avoidance of higher authorities (including those of the then independent Genovese state), kin groups frequently engaged in feuds, attacking each other's persons and property in round after round of retaliation.

Within the region, feuds ran from small scale to large, building on the fissiparous structure that created kin groups out of households sharing common names and ancestors, but aggregating up the scale to "leagues" and factions incorporating multiple leagues. In the mid-sixteenth century, a noble Genovese "captain" bore responsibility for the top-down administration of the town of Chiavari and its dependent political territories. Local people paid his salary. In 1549, captain Ambrosio Rivarola enumerated two major factions that set seventy-one kin groups in five leagues, on one side, against twenty kin groups in four leagues (Raggio 1990: 163–168). Although the factions, leagues, and smaller scale kin-based organizations constituted the region's de facto government below the highest levels, they also provided the basis for blood feuds.

Feuds, however, rarely ended without external intervention, either of authoritative kinsmen or of Genovese officials. Often Genovese officials supervised the formation of peacemaking deputations elected from heads of kin groups outside the feud, and backed the deputations' authority to craft peace settlements. In the process of feud and settlement, argues Raggio, kin groups consolidated their boundaries but also found themselves connecting unintentionally yet firmly to state authorities. As Raggio puts it:

Like the feud, pacification assumes strong coherence of all relatives with regard to their 'principals.' Through the negotiations Genovese officials 'gave voice' to all parties and legitimized state intervention along with the Prince's authority; but in the same process they legitimized the role of notables and reinforced local forms of social-political organization: *parentele*. (Raggio 1990: 247)

Thus Genovese trust networks, for all their resort to dissimulation and clientage, depended on backing from the state, and yielded a share of their resources in return for state intervention in otherwise murderous conflicts.

In fact, precisely because of their structure trust networks often become vulnerable either to external predation or to externally initiated divide-and-conquer tactics. To the extent that they control visible, desirable resources such as land, labor power, or commercial wealth, they become objects of envy and greed. As a consequence, leaders of trust networks often engage in countertactics of divide-and-defend with regard to would-be exploiters: playing one ruler off of another.

Of all places, thirteenth-century Galicia, on Spain's west coast, provides surprising documentation. There, the nominal authority of León's king lay thin on the ground, and well-armed local nobles did what they could to gain control over peasant communities, which typically organized around extended kinship systems. Communities themselves had only weak means of military self-defense. Instead of armed resistance, a peasant countertactic consisted of bargaining with powerful monasteries for transfer from royal to ecclesiastical feudal control:

To offer *amorem y defensa* [love and protection] thus seems to have been a general framework for reciprocity, which in some instances was expressed through additional offers of 'help and protection' or 'refuge and protection.'

Peasants therefore received some sort of guarantee that monastic 'defence,' 'protection,' and 'love' would offer them support against other social elements that they either objected to or felt threatened by. Such guarantees stabilized the local social system and, as mutual sociability was an objective common to both peasants and their lords, were recognized by both as an indispensable mechanism of reciprocity.   (Pastor, Pascua, Rodríguez-López, and Sánchez-León 2002: 287)

Thus emerged either particularistic ties to rulers, brokered autonomy, or patronage systems, depending on the relative prevalence of commitment, capital, and coercion in the negotiations between protectors and protected.

Far outside the central concerns of governments, kinship networks have often coordinated weighty collective enterprises. Take the case of long-distance migration: the mediation of kinfolk repeatedly produces chains in which migrant A facilitates migrant B, migrant B facilitates migrant C, and so on until close ties exist between kin-connected localities at one end of the chain and the other (Tilly 1990, 2000). Marcelo Borges has reconstructed chain migration from a small, kin-connected cluster of villages in Portugal's southernmost region, Algarve, to the agricultural region of Villa Elisa, Argentina, between La Plata and Buenos Aires. In Villa Elisa, Portuguese immigrants started arriving as agricultural laborers during the 1920s, bought land of their own, and created a viable economic niche as commercial flower gardeners. They married largely within their own population. As is often the case, kinship networks promoted ethnic endogamy.

Borges reports an interview with Francisco M., who arrived from Portugal in the early 1930s. Within six years, Francisco had bought land and set himself up as an independent flower grower. At that point, he brought his wife and child to Villa Elisa and started helping other members of his kin group to migrate. Part of his story ran like this:

First, I asked my sister to come. She came here single. Her husband was my friend. He was single. And I told him – since I had two or three single sisters over there [in Portugal] – that if he wanted one, I would ask her to come. And that's the way it was. So he agreed and I asked . . . her to send him her picture so he could get to know her, and I also asked him to send her his picture. And that's the way it was. So he liked her and asked her to come . . . He was also Portuguese. He was Algarvian, but from another sitio [hamlet].   (Borges 2003: 468–469)

Hundreds of transactions on this model formed a Portuguese ethnic community based on Villa Elisa's flower trade. Through just such humble, incremental transactions, trust networks accomplish consequential enterprises – in this case the transplantation and transformation of migrant communities and their economic specialties.

Nonkinship networks sometimes perform similar feats. With the Waldensians, we saw clandestine religious ties producing momentous effects with no more than incidental support from kinship. In sixteenth-century England, we saw trading households creating their own credit networks with little assistance from kinship. Elsewhere we could find age grades, religious fraternities, school alumni, military orders, and rotating credit circles forming similar named, bounded, internally communicating sets of relations entailing mutual obligations. But the employment of kinship networks in migration, trade, credit, religion, and children's social mobility nicely illustrates the significance of trust networks to consequential collective enterprises not coordinated by authoritative organizations or collaborative institutions.

Let us not suppose for a moment that trust networks usually operate pleasantly and benignly. They often tyrannize and exploit their recalcitrant members. Formation of sharply bounded trust networks generally increases external distrust as it augments internal trust, and therefore establishes barriers to cross-network collaboration. We are examining the encounter of very different coordinating structures, the encounter of trust networks with top-down systems of rule.

Back to the Big Questions

That encounter brings us back to the big questions with which we began. This chapter's preliminary survey suggests some tentative answers for the rest of the book to pursue:

1. *In the presence of political predators and greedy rulers, under what conditions and how do people maintain trust networks?* Trust networks survive and hold off predators when they generate enough resources to reproduce themselves, solve problems for their more powerful members, give others strong incentives to maintain the boundary, and erect strong defenses at the boundary.

2. *Given the prevalence of predation among rulers, under what conditions and how do trust networks become integrated into systems of rule?* When existing autonomous trust networks disintegrate or cease to provide substantial benefits, when leaders of trust networks negotiate accommodations with rulers, when the population excluded from existing trust networks grows substantially, when trust networks create regimes of their own, and when major political actors including rulers form their own benefit-producing networks, in different ways those processes integrate trust networks into systems of rule.

3. *How does the connection between rulers and trust networks affect the stability of rule?* To the extent that rulers become indispensable to the operation and reproduction of trust networks and guarantee the means of maintaining them, rule becomes more stable. Conversely, increasing alternatives to rulers' intervention and decreasing reliability of that intervention promote instability. (Of course, many other factors – for example, the accumulation of military means by competitors for regional or central power – also affect political stability.)

4. *Under what conditions, how, and with what political consequences do trust networks and rulers benefit mutually – or, for that matter, fail to benefit mutually – from integration?* The question requires a much more serious specification of costs and benefits than this chapter has carried on, but in general benefits become mutual to the extent that members of trust networks offer contingent consent to their yielding of resources, that rulers rotate, and that rulers overlap with members of trust

networks – in short, to the extent that democracy prevails. Decline of any of these conditions undermines mutual benefits.

5. *When it occurs, what accounts for the variety of that integration? What determines its form?* We are trying to explain variation among such different systems of rule as totalitarianism, theocracy, patronage, democracy, and brokered autonomy. Major factors include a) internal organization of trust networks prior to integration, b) the mix of coercion, capital, and commitment employed by rulers in promoting integration, and c) the extent and character of mediation by patrons, leaders, and such secondary rulers as regional warlords.

These principles apply at many different scales, within local communities as well as in worldwide systems of power. To discipline the inquiry, however, the following chapters focus on states: relatively centralized organizations that control the principal concentrated means of coercion within bounded territories, and exercise priority in some regards over all other organizations operating within those territories. That simplification will make it easier to recognize that "rulers" sometimes mean just one person or a few, but sometimes include a wide variety of persons, offices, and affiliated organizations. Democracy, when it works well, incorporates a significant portion of the subject population into its ruling class by means of elections, representative government, social movements, public opinion, and other forms of voice. That fact gives us yet another reason to give democratization and de-democratization special attention.

3

Transformations of Trust Networks

migration

"Dear Mother," wrote sisters Edith and Sara Pilap from their New York home to their native Polish village of Rypin in 1891,

> do not think that the country here is like a village at home. Many people from Rypin live here and that is why Sarah [sister] wants to be here ... With God's help, we shall send a steamship ticket for father even before Passover. And I hope that after our dear father will arrive here, we shall be able to send for our dear mother and our little brother, even before the summer. (Morawska 1996: 29)

Yet another migration chain was drawing people linked by kinship, ethnicity, and religion across the Atlantic to America. Polish villagers vigorously fashioned new social lives in teeming New York City.

Chain-linked, long-distance migration provides a privileged laboratory for study of transformations in trust networks.[1] Long-distance migration poses serious risks. Those risks dispose potential migrants who do not have extensive professional connections to rely on members of their trust networks for information and advice. The same risks inhibit potential migrants who lack the mediation of trust networks from migrating at all. Instead of a broad distribution across destinations as a function of economic opportunities at those destinations, chain migration channels long-distance moves into a few origin-destination streams; large numbers of people from the same village end up in the same towns or urban neighborhoods thousands of miles away. Networks persist in the process, but change structure and

---

[1] Bodnar 1985, Borges 2003, Cordero-Guzmán, Smith, and Grosfoguel 2001, Fussell and Massey 2004, Green 2002, Grimson 1999, Hagan and Ebaugh 2003, Hoerder and Moch 1996, Kamphoefner 1987, Massey et al. 1998, Moch 2003, Poros 2001, Portes and Rumbaut 2001, Roberts and Morris 2003, Sanders 2002, Smith 2000, 2005, Tilly 1990, 2000, VanWey 2004.

geographic distribution. Since participants generally rely on strong ties to others with whom they are carrying on consequential long-term enterprises and placing those enterprises at risk to the malfeasance, mistakes, or failures of others, the networks in question commonly qualify as trust networks.

The migration process inevitably transforms trust networks, at least to the extent of changing the relative salience of different previously existing social ties. It affects jobs, marriages, household structures, and patterns of solidarity within the network. I remember wondering as a child why my mother urged me to treat certain dull older relatives of hers with special consideration. My puzzlement continued until I learned about the heroic parts they had played in the migration of my mother's family from the depressed mine fields of South Wales to Chicago.

Although external conditions over which migrants exercise little or no control significantly affect the fates of different migration streams, chain migration exposes to view a set of internal processes that other trust networks often keep hidden. Migrants experience alterations in their networks close up, and tend to remember them. After the fact, participants in chain migration consequently report the details of mutual aid or its failures more readily than do members of most other sorts of trust networks. Whereas we must usually squeeze evidence of internal operation and alteration in trust networks from recalcitrant sources, stories of chain migration often overflow with relevant information.

By no means, furthermore, does the influence of trust networks end with the arrival of newcomers at migration's destination. The channeling of migration by trust networks forms new configurations of rights, obligations, and mutual aid at the destination. Ewa Morawska's rich study of Jews in Johnstown, Pennsylvania shows us how regularly kin, earlier migrants within the same stream, and fellow members of religious congregations shaped the careers of new arrivals. Most of Johnstown's Jews arrived through migration chains from the Russian Empire's Pale of Settlement – regions we now call Poland, Lithuania, Belarus, and Ukraine. After the assassination of Russian Tsar Alexander II in 1881, the Russian government began systematic persecution of religious minorities, especially of Jews. Laws of May 1882, for example, banned Jews from any new settlement even within the Pale. Government-backed massacres and dispossessions – pogroms – became common. Jewish migration from the Russian Empire to the United States accelerated after 1890, with Johnstown only one of many destinations in the Eastern United States.

Unlike the Jews of New York City garment manufacturing, Johnstown's Jews concentrated heavily in retail trade; entering business required initial capital and connections, which came overwhelmingly from within the trust network. Morawska illustrates how it worked:

Abe F. opened a shoe store in Johnstown with his own savings of $340 and an additional $1,000 borrowed from his brother and from two local Jewish friends already established as merchants, both active leaders of the Rodef Sholom Congregation. Jacob C. first worked for his cousin as a salesman, part-time in his store and part-time on the road as a peddler, and then, having saved some money, 'let a *landsman* [of his] from a nearby town persuade him to open a men's clothing store in Ebensburg . . . since there was no [such establishment] there.' The same wholesalers who 'took care of the peddlers' later helped them to start their own businesses by giving advice on location and advancing the first merchandise. Abraham K., for example, was told 'to go here rather than there [as he originally intended]' because – in the opinion of the jobber who had befriended him and who was also a leader in the local synagogue – 'it was a better place.' (Morawska 1996: 55)

As they expanded their own businesses, Johnstown's jobbers were thus altering the territorial distributions of Eastern European Jews' trust networks across the Johnstown region. In the course of that alteration, members of those trust networks continued to place consequential enterprises – not only their precarious businesses, but also their children's futures – at risk to malfeasance, mistakes, or failures by other members.

Internal transformations of Jewish trust networks also occurred over the longer run. Successful immigrant merchants, for example, commonly sent their children to college. As a result, few children entered the family business, and many moved away from Johnstown when they left school. Combined with external factors – notably the decline of Johnstown's pace-making steel industry from the 1960s onward – that postwar exodus simultaneously shrank and aged the local Jewish population. Only the establishment of new high-tech industries during the 1990s, which brought in Jewish professionals from elsewhere, kept Johnstown's Jewish community from disintegrating (Morawska 1996: 247–251). We learn again that the process by which a trust network reproduces itself matters as much for its longer-term operation as the initial process by which it forms.

How Networks Change

Transformations of trust networks range from arrivals or departures of particular members to utter changes of form. Both sorts of changes occurred

members or expel old members? In the case of Johnstown's Jews, for example, despite multiple native languages and religious traditions, the earliest phases of immigration created a well-marked boundary between foreign born multilingual Jews and their predominantly Christian and often monolingual neighbors. Later, acquisition of English, loss of European languages, near-extinction of Orthodoxy, coalescence of Conservative and Reform congregations, and intermarriage of later generations all blurred the boundaries between Jews and others in Johnstown.

Speaking more generally, trust networks that mark, maintain, and monitor sharp boundaries between insiders and outsiders generally operate more effectively than others (Tilly 2004c). Trust networks that *fail* to mark, maintain, and monitor sharp boundaries between insiders and outsiders shrivel or disappear. Blurring of boundaries facilitates exit or straddling and increases the difficulty of monitoring and of enforcing obligations while increasing opportunities and incentives of members to pursue agendas that undermine the network's dominant activities.

External Connections: How does the network interact with other structures whose actions significantly affect its boundaries, sustenance, and internal relations? In Morawska's account, Johnstown's Jewish merchants came disproportionately from East European families of small merchants, large numbers of Christian peasants and workers from the same regions migrated to Johnstown for employment in its heavy industries, and Jews established relations with their Christian neighbors similar to those that had prevailed in Eastern Europe, except that Jews now had less to fear from pogroms and governmental persecution than had been the case in Eastern Europe. Over time, implies Morawska, Jews became just another variably observant religious minority whose more committed members participated only intermittently in Johnstown's public life as representatives of their faith. More generally, external connections strongly affect both a trust network's boundaries and its access to sustaining resources; as network leaders often fear, strong ties of some members to a relatively small and powerful set of outsiders tend to undermine a trust network's viability.

Sustenance: Where, how, and with what consequences does the network acquire the resources to maintain its collective activities? Early on, retail business provided the context and wherewithal for daily operation of Johnstown's Jewish trust networks. Jobs, housing, loans, religious activity, and sponsorship of migration itself all depended heavily on the viability of Jewish retail trade. With the arrival of Jewish professionals from elsewhere during the 1990s, a considerable shift toward voluntary contributions supporting religiously identified organizations occurred.

More broadly, trust networks that sequester their own supplies of sustaining resources usually operate more effectively, other things equal, than networks that rely on contingent external sources of supply. Trust networks that lose their connections with supplies of sustaining resources, including new members to replace departures, shrivel or disappear. (Of course, resources often disappear because of processes first affecting the source, as when Johnstown's steel mills began closing after 1960.) Trust networks can also outrun their sources of supply: networks that expand more rapidly than their sustaining resources shrivel, disappear, lose members, or split.

Internal Relations: What rights, obligations, transfers of resources, shared activities, collective controls, and divisions of labor do members of the trust network establish? Morawska's generally upbeat account does not offer us much information on conflict and coercion, but the stories she tells about the initial toeholds of new arrivals make clear that in the early phases of Jewish immigration a small number of established merchants exercised great control over who occupied what economic niche, and therefore whose households eventually joined the local Jewish power structure. As time went on, it looks as though multiple centers of power and some factions formed, but never enough to blow Jewish trust networks entirely apart.

What might we say more generally about internal relations in trust networks? Some features of interpersonal connections significantly affect network viability. Strong overall attractions among members of trust networks sustain network solidarity. Declining mutual attractions weaken networks. However, formation of strongly bonded and exclusive pairs or cliques within trust networks threatens networks with fragmentation. Effective trust networks build in mechanisms that either inhibit formation of strongly bonded and exclusive cliques or insulate such cliques from overall network operations.

Uses of resources for internal coordination also matter. Below some threshold for each sort of incentive, decline of collectively available coercion, capital, and/or commitment causes trust networks to shrink or disintegrate. Above those thresholds, a trust network's relative reliance on coercion, capital, and commitment as internal incentives strongly affects the conditions for disintegration or schism; heavy reliance on coercion breeds vulnerability to competing coercion from inside or outside the network, extensive use of capital fosters vulnerability to competing opportunities and/or dwindling external supplies of capital, and strong emphasis on commitment encourages fragmentation along ideological lines, including defection to competing cultural groups. Combined with increasing inequality and formalization of interpersonal relations, a shift from commitment toward coercion and capital converts a trust network into an authoritative organization.

The extreme case of reliance on commitment, in contrast, occurs with charismatic leadership. Charismatic leaders usually produce more effective trust networks, but at the double cost of a) losing resistant members and b) increasing the likelihood of disintegration or schism at times of succession. Like intense pairing and clique formation, charisma threatens trust networks' stability. A durable, effective trust network, it follows, builds in means of sustaining commitment among members at large while insulating its collective activities from islands of charisma and/or intensive bonding.

Table 3.1 sums up the major internal changes just inventoried and their likely effects on overall network operation. The table suggests an important conclusion: despite all the importance of external connections to sources of protection and sustaining resources, internal alterations of relations within a trust network play a significant part in increasing or decreasing the network's viability. Independent of their connections with rulers and regimes, trust networks' internal dynamics and relations to their immediate environments produce changes in their structures, activities, and viability. Trust networks sometimes thrive or collapse without strong intervention from rulers and regimes.

Today's transnational migration streams, for example, certainly interact with governments. But they display remarkable changes resulting chiefly from interactions of their members with each other and with their environments at origin and destination. Johnstown's Jews mostly pulled up their stakes from Eastern Europe, rarely returned to their places of origin, and maintained contact with the old country chiefly through the recruitment of new migrants. Many international migration streams, however, feature mass movement in both directions between origin and destination. When they do so, internal transformations of trust networks inevitably occur.

59

Table 3.1. *Major Internal Changes in Trust Networks*

Aspect of network	Type of change	Effects of change
boundary	sharpening	increasing viability (blurring: decreasing viability)
external connections	increasing ties to powerful outsiders	weakening boundary, increasing vulnerability to resource shifts (mitigated by collective internal control over ties)
sustenance	sequestering of resources	increasing viability (weakened control: decreasing viability)
sustenance	enhanced connections with supply sources	increasing viability (diminishing connections: decreased viability)
sustenance	increase of available resources	increasing viability (decrease: declining viability)
internal relations	heightening of mutual attraction	increasing viability (diminution: decreasing viability)
internal relations	equalization of mutual attraction	increasing viability (rising inequality: decreasing viability)
internal relations	formation of dyads and cliques	decreasing viability, except where insulated from overall operation
internal relations	creation of charismatic center	increase in short-term viability, rise in longer-term instability
internal relations	shift in emphasis on a) coercion, b) capital, and c) commitment as incentives	affects relative vulnerability to a) competing coercion, b) competing opportunities or dwindling external capital supplies, and c) ideological fragmentation

The rest of this chapter illustrates the main points of Table 3.1 without by any means proving them. First, it sets out to establish that different varieties of trust networks do, indeed, change significantly in partial or total independence of governmental intervention. Second, it undertakes to show that the simple device of partitioning external connections, boundary, sustenance, and internal relations provides a useful grasp of the relevant changes. Third, it suggests that the causal connections of Table 3.1 hold widely: that sharpening of boundaries increases the viability of trust networks, that loss of control over sequestered resources decreases their viability, and so on.

Further studies of chain migration, trade diasporas, and intentional communities provide backing for these claims.

Tales of Migration and Trust

I still remember vividly the tumultuous day when Louise Tilly, our children, and I first visited the Piedmontese hill village from which Louise's father Hector Audino had emigrated for New York restaurant work half a century earlier. Despite our non-Piedmontese names, faulty Italian, and utter lack of the regional language *Piemontese*, local relatives and the parish priest greeted us as rediscovered kin. They first took us to the village *campo santo* (burial ground) for a meeting with deceased ancestors, each tomb marked with a headstone bearing name and an inset oval photograph. We heard what each person had done in life, and how each had died. Only much later did I realize that the ceremony inducted us into a trust network based on kin and locality.

Soon we met the local *Americani* who had left for America poor but made enough money working in New York restaurants to buy local properties and retire comfortably in their village of origin. Meeting them called up my father-in-law's indignant stories about returning migrants who had betrayed the trust by absconding with the money given them by New Yorkers to support local enterprises, including the radical politics my father-in-law had once championed. A chain of connections between a Piedmontese village and New York City Italian neighborhoods transformed communities at both ends as well as the ties between them.

Even when most emigrants belonging to a given chain stayed in the United States or Canada, North America's history resounds with similar stories.[2] Existing trust networks at the origins of a migration chain selected individuals and households for particular distant destinations, provided information and funds to migrants en route, guaranteed connections at the destination, but then altered in structure as a result of their use in the very process of migration.

Take the case of Lutheran migrants from Pomerania to Milwaukee when Wisconsin still lay on the American frontier during the early nineteenth century. After 1817, when Prussia's King Friedrich Wilhelm III

---

[2] Anderson 1974, Bodnar 1985, Light and Bonacich 1988, Portes 1995, 1996, Portes and Rumbaut 1990, 2001, Reitz and Sklar 1997, Waldinger 1996, Waldinger and Bozorgmehr 1996.

united his kingdom's Lutheran and Reformed Churches into a single United Evangelical Church, diehard Lutherans began the dissent that eventually earned them the name Old Lutheran. Some Old Lutherans advocated emigration as the proper response to religious tyranny. In 1839, the first organized group of emigrants left Hamburg for North America. Between then and 1854 about 5,000 Old Lutheran emigrants went to America (Kamphoefner, Helbich, and Sommer 1991: 301). One of 1839's emigrants was the shepherd Johan Carl Wilhelm Pritzlaff, known back home as Carl, who ended up in Milwaukee transmuted into the prosperous merchant John Pritzlaff. By 1842, Pritzlaff had worked on the Erie Canal, labored in Pennsylvania, and finally earned enough for the boat trip up the Erie Canal to Buffalo, then through the Great Lakes to Milwaukee.

From a base in Milwaukee, Pritzlaff worked on a farm, cooked on a steamboat, and hired on as a lumberjack. In 1843, however, he began clerking in a Milwaukee hardware store. Pritzlaff's job as clerk started him in the business he pursued the rest of his life. That year Pritzlaff wrote his family in Pomerania:

How happy I would be if [his brother and sister] Heinrich and Elisabeth came here. Even if emigrating is not a matter of conscience for them, it could still do them good in the future. No one should fear that he is committing a sin if he emigrates in order to make a better living here than over there. For the earth is the Lord's and given by God to mankind, and he can go wherever he will. Also wish with all my heart that my dear mother would come, if it were possible. I would not be afraid of taking care of her here, for it is my duty as a child, and the dear Lord will grant me His grace to do it. If some others emigrate next summer from your area and mother or Heinrich and Elisabeth want to come over here, then I ask someone to advance them the money, especially if C. Heidke or master shepherd Wangerin is along, since I will gladly commit myself that they will get their own back again. If mother does not come, then I ask her not to keep her children back and to consider what a yoke they have to bear over there and what glorious freedom they could enjoy over here.   (Kamphoefner, Helbich, and Sommer 1991: 307)

In those days, Pritzlaff dared not risk sending cash all the way back to Pomerania. Instead, he asked relations at home to advance the necessary funds against his good faith. Here, as in Argentina and Johnstown, we see chain migration in action. But we also see it operating within trust networks, changing their structure as the process continued. In particular, we see how the very structure of successful migration chains facilitates their attachment to new sources of sustaining supply at the destination. Money made in Milwaukee promoted departures from Pomerania. In this and many other similar cases, wages and profits at the destination paid for the maintenance of ties with the place of origin as well as promoting further migration via the same set of social relations. External connections, group boundaries, sustenance, and internal relations changed in tandem.

Religiously tinged trust networks exerted influence in both directions across the Atlantic, sometimes deeply altering religious beliefs and practices in the European place of origin. Robert Ostergren's meticulous tracing of migration and communication between Rättvik parish, central Sweden, and a rural area of Minnesota reveals the bidirectional influence. Chain migration from Rättvik to the St. Croix and Rum River Valley districts of central Minnesota concentrated between 1865 and 1885. It eventually brought about 1,600 Swedish natives to Minnesota. As we might now expect from the mechanisms of chain migration, within Rättvik emigration not only frequently involved whole nuclear families, but also drew disproportionately from a minority of local kinship networks (Ostergren 1988: 138–146).

To a remarkable degree, furthermore, emigrant households maintained their kinship relations as well as reproduced their Swedish geography of neighborhood in Minnesota (Ostergren 1988: 184–185). Although emigration slowed dramatically after 1885, travel and communication continued between Rättvik and its Minnesota offshoots. Because both communities stuck to similar forms of agriculture for decades, they maintained similar external connections, boundaries, sustenance, and internal relations.

Popular religion showed the impact of transatlantic networks. The Minnesota Swedes remained mostly Lutheran or Baptist despite many denominational splits. But during the 1880s Seventh Day Adventist preachers began gaining substantial numbers of converts in the areas of Rättvik immigrant settlement. Rättvik itself established a Seventh Day Adventist congregation in response to a tract sent back by a woman who had emigrated to America (Ostergren 1988: 306). Other evangelical sects likewise influenced the home country:

There was an exceptionally strong link between the mission congregation in Övre Gärdsjö village and the Athens settlement in Isanti County. One of the most fascinating indications of the linkage is the fact that, in the 1910s, the mission church in Övre Gärdsjö and the Lutheran church in Athens township contained nearly identical altar paintings. The duplication apparently was the result of influences moving across the Atlantic from daughter to mother community. Around 1909, the Athens church acquired an altar painting by the Norwegian-American artist, designer, and dealer in church furnishings August Klagstad, whose work appeared in a number of Scandinavian churches across the American Middle West. Someone was sufficiently impressed to take the image home to Sweden, for within a few years, the Mission Church in Övre Gärdsjö produced a nearly identical altar painting, although done by a local artist. The incident is remarkable and is as clear an indication as any that there was a steady trans-Atlantic trade of ideas and cultural influences between migration-linked kinship groups that persisted well into the twentieth century. (Ostergren 1988: 306–307)

Ostergren's superb analysis does not reveal all the interchanges that constituted mutual influence between Rättvik and its central Minnesota emigrant settlements. But it establishes without doubt that influence ran in both directions, passed through durable if changing ties of kinship and neighborhood, persisted after migration slowed, and influenced daily practices on both sides of the Atlantic. Once again we observe how trust networks reproduce themselves, but change form as they do so.

Chains Today

Robert Smith's close, long-term study of the migration stream between a Mexican village and New York City reveals how such changes work. Migration from Ticuani, Puebla to New York started during the 1940s, but only accelerated during the 1970s. By 2000, native-born Ticuanenses numbered about 1,800 in the village and 2,700 in New York. But many New York-based Ticuanenses, including those born in New York, actually returned frequently to Mexico and spent significant portions of their time in Ticuani. Modest incomes in New York made it possible to cut fine figures in Mexico.

Since the 1970s, for example, many Ticuanense New Yorkers fulfill their village work obligations, or *faenas*, by means of financial contributions channeled to Mexico through a powerful New York based-committee of emigrants:

More than $100,000 of the $150,000 needed for the town's potable water project was raised in New York among Ticuanenses residing there, by the New York Ticuanense Committee, outstripping the donations of the local, state, and federal governments in Mexico. Each household judged by the New York Committee to be able to pay was assessed a $300 'cooperation' – read 'tax' – toward this project. Those households that did not pay were threatened with having their water not turned on in Ticuani. Almost all households in New York and Ticuani paid, including people who had not been back to the town in more than thirty years or who had been born there but raised in other parts of Mexico. Out of the entire Ticuani population, only twenty-eight households judged capable of paying did not. These non-payers were the local elite, led by the *cacique* or 'political boss' who contested the Committee's authority to make them pay. (Smith 2000: 212)

Thus the New York Committee's activity was undermining the old structure of local power. It was also converting a segment of the migration-formed trust network into a collaborative institution.

At the same time, remittances from New York money earners to Ticuanense relatives, building of vacation houses in Ticuani, participation of returning emigrants in public ceremonies, direct intervention of emigrants (whether returned or not) in Ticuani politics, establishment of New York-style youth gangs in Ticuani, and entrusting of New York-born children to their grandmothers in Mexico all help transform social structures connecting New York with Puebla. These changes have triple effects:

- deeply altering the organization of power and wealth in Ticuani
- reshaping the lives of Ticuanenses in both locales
- creating a new transnational set of trust networks

Without a continuous flow of earnings from mostly modest occupations in New York, the continuously changing system would collapse. But fed by those resources and by new generations of migrants in both directions, the process sustains boundaries between Ticuanenses and others, shapes relations across those boundaries in both Mexico and the United States, and increases the relative prominence of network segments closely connected to the Ticuanense population in New York. In the medium run, then, the partial success of chain migration has reinforced the viability of trust networks at its core.

In the longer run, we can speculate that further New York success of Mexican emigrants will increase differentiation within the network, enhance involvement of New York emigrants in competing projects, reduce the average commitment of emigrants and their offspring to enterprises operating in Ticuani, and thereby undermine the system. They will probably multiply external connections with different segments of the migrant population, erode the group boundary, reduce collective control over means of sustenance, and fragment internal relations. So far, however, Ticuanense transnational trust networks remain viable.

Trade Diasporas

Trading diasporas likewise produce their own internal transformations of the trust networks that regularly arise in their midst. The word *diaspora* itself comes from the Greek for scattering, as in the sowing of grain. The metaphor, however, misleads us to the extent that it suggests individual seeds flourishing or shriveling as a function of the soil they reach. Long-distance trading networks identified by religion, language, kinship, and/or place of origin have played remarkably prominent parts in the transmission of precious goods for millennia. They prosper precisely because their members maintain connections with each other over great distances. Members use their previously existing contacts (or relations to third parties) preferentially as they offer credit, make agreements on a handshake, acquire or transmit valuable goods, and collaborate in complex enterprises with little or no formal organization. Without extensive trust networks, they would fail.

Although trade diasporas often lay down emigrant enclaves and sometimes initiate systems of chain migration, overall they maintain a much greater multiplicity of connections than chain migration networks, shift more rapidly among connections, alter their supplies of sustaining resources more easily, and thus experience much more frequent short-term alterations of internal structure. More so than migration chains, furthermore, they generally make their peace with governments en route and at their destinations; relations between diasporas and regimes typically range from evasive conformity with existing governments through patronage by regional power holders to direct licensing or sponsorship by governments. Nevertheless, trade diasporas produce enough internally initiated change in structure to deserve comparison with migration systems.

Ethnically or religiously organized trade diasporas date at least as far back as the earliest archaeological evidence of cities and states. What archaeologists call Phase B2 at Hacinebi Tepe, Turkey, extended from 3700 to 3300 BCE. Hacinebi lies in the Piedmont of the Taurus Mountains of southern Anatolia, near the northernmost navigable stretch of the Euphrates River. Hacinebi therefore had a waterborne connection with the great city of Uruk, some 700 miles downstream. During Phase B2, unmistakable evidence of a minority trading colony from Uruk appears in Hacinebi's archaeological record: ceramics, architecture, stamp seals, jewelry, tools, and tar (bitumen) of Mesopotamian origin (Stein 1999: 139–145).

Uruk traders received sealed goods from southern Mesopotamia, and moved those goods into southern Anatolia's copper-exchange network; very likely they were also shipping lumber, gold, and semiprecious minerals back to Mesopotamia (Stein 1999: 157). Since transporting goods upstream cost far more than floating them downstream, the Mesopotamian traders based in Anatolia were almost certainly purveying homeland goods of high value for bulk. The majority Anatolian and minority Mesopotamian populations of Hacinebi maintained distinct adjacent settlements and cultural styles for at least two centuries (Stein 1999: 166). In short, we have convincing evidence of a trading diaspora that maintained a solid us-them boundary almost six millennia ago.

Consisting entirely of material remains, the evidence for the trade-based trust network reaching Hacinebi tells us little about interpersonal dynamics within that network. But since that time, long-distance traders who could not rely on well armed states to back them have repeatedly created diasporas of merchants identified with the same religion, ethnicity, or place of origin. Jews, Armenians, Hainanese, Fukienese, Swatowese, Cantonese, Gujaratis, Tamils, Arabs, Venetians, Genoese, and Lebanese eventually formed vast trade-based trust networks that lasted for centuries and spanned much of their known worlds (Chaliand and Rageau 1997, Mauro 1990). As Philip Curtin puts it:

Trade communities of merchants living among aliens in associated networks are to be found on every continent and back through time to the very beginning of urban life. They are . . . one of the most widespread of all human institutions over a very long run of time, yet limited to the long period of human history that began with the invention of agriculture and ended with the coming of the industrial revolution. Some of the best evidence of how they worked comes from Africa between the seventeenth century and the nineteenth, but other examples are as various and familiar as the chains of Phoenician and Greek trading towns that spread westward from the Levant or the Aegean coasts. Or, some two thousand years later, merchants from Cologne on the Rhine settled along the trade routes leading down the Rhine and then eastward along the coast of the North Sea and the Baltic, laying the foundations for what was to become the Hanseatic League of independent trading towns. (Curtin 1984: 3)

In general, trade diasporas established their advantages by combining controls over dedicated systems of transportation, communication, and credit with access to valuable goods. Unlike chain migration systems, however, they necessarily sought profitable contact with non-members of their social categories, especially at the sites where they sold their goods. Like the Jewish merchants of Johnstown who initially transplanted relations with East European Christians to industrial America, diaspora traders gained from being multilingual, knowledgeable in the ways of other cultures, and connected with the rest of the world by channels their customers did not enjoy. As a consequence, their internal structures and geographic distributions shifted in response to new commercial opportunities.

Curtin provides the telling example of *asali* in the Hausa regions of what is now Ghana. Asali are bounded, endogamous populations reputed to come from the same (usually distant) origin. Hausaland asalis nicely illustrate the adaptability and durability of trade-based trust networks:

Asali in Hausaland are not necessarily commercial, but three commercially oriented asali came to dominate movement along the trade routes to and from the kola groves of the Volta basin. These three asali had become Hausa by assimilating Hausa culture, but all three trace their origin to the desert edge farther north, underlining once again the importance of the sahel in the origin of African commercial undertakings. Their very names are indicative. One was called Kambarin Beriberi; the name in Hausa means 'Borno merchants,' and they were in fact originally from Borno. A second group was called Tokarawa, a collective term used to describe people of servile origin who had immigrated from the desert-edge society of the Tuareg directly to the north. The third, the Agalawa, were also servile Tuareg to begin with, but their name meant 'people of the south,' probably because they lived at the southern end of the Tuareg commercial network. Their home villages were initially part of the Tuareg trade diaspora that led south from the desert into Hausaland. The significant point is that all three were offshoots of trade diasporas *into* Hausaland. After a time as settlers, at a distant node in one trade diaspora, all joined a new trade diaspora *out of* Hausaland. Their advantage over other Hausa who might have responded to the same opportunity was that they had family experience in long-distance trade   (Curtin 1984: 54)

Trade diasporas almost always create extensive systems of credit. Unlike small-scale retail credit, the credit of trade diasporas typically takes a multilateral form, allowing merchant A to buy from merchant B with a promise of reimbursement – or settlement of accounts – from merchant C. Multilateral credit relieves merchants of the risk and burden imposed by carrying ready cash. It also makes possible exchange over great distances and long periods of time. The Muslim-based system of *hawala* not only links merchants all over Asia and the Middle East, but also mediates a large share of homebound remittances by emigrant workers from those regions. The terrorist network al-Qaeda used hawalas extensively in financing its activities of the later 1990s and early twenty-first century (Farah 2004: 6, 113–120). Well outside circuits of terror, similar Muslim credit networks have facilitated Asian, Middle Eastern, and African trade for centuries.

Although the rise of joint-stock commercial companies with statesponsored armed force to back them eventually reduced the worldwide dominance of diasporas in long-distance trade, they continue to form in our own time. Enterprising women from Cape Verde, for example, build on centuries of commercial interchange between that African archipelago and its former colonial master, Portugal. Many Cape Verdean women travel constantly, buying goods overseas for resale in the islands; the petty traders have acquired their own Creole name: *rebidantes*. Some of them run regular businesses in Cape Verde, but bolster those businesses by means of their foreign contacts:

This was the situation of a sixty-year-old woman who also has relatives living in Portugal, and prefers to stay in a boarding house in Lisbon's historic centre. Cape Verdean *rebidantes* engaging in grassroots business in Portugal and elsewhere are major clients of the boarding house, enjoying a special status. Furthermore, as frequent flyers they also get free aeroplane tickets. This woman, who had never migrated herself, although her husband had migrated to Holland, invested their savings in a drugstore on the island of São Vicente in Cape Verde. There they enjoy a reputation of seriousness and some wealth. Responding to the increase in young people's demand for costume jewellery and other fashionable items, the woman started to engage in transnational commerce. In Senegal and Guinea, she buys African cloth and clothes; in Portugal, clothes and jewellery; in Brazil, lingerie; and on her rare trips to Holland, where her sister lives, she buys cosmetics. Although she has obtained a visa for the USA, she is still waiting for the right opportunity to go there. In every country where she goes, she has kin and acquaintances among the Cape Verdean community. She still prefers, whenever possible, to maintain a very independent course of action; it is only when she does not feel at ease (because she does not speak the local or commercial language) that she relies heavily on her close relations. Not being able to secure such a contact in the USA so far has been the single obstacle to her trip there.   (Marques, Santos, and Araújo 2001: 286)

In a set of practices running back five millennia or more, this woman and her counterparts are simultaneously creating, using, and transforming trust networks organized around risky but profitable long-distance trade. Since some ethnic diasporas – for example, Chinese, Jewish, Armenian, and Arab – maintain themselves for centuries despite ceaseless shifts in merchandise and geographic scope, we have no reason to think of trade-based trust networks as more fleeting or ad hoc than their migration-centered counterparts. Like systems of chain migration, they can survive so long as they exercise some collective channeling of members' external connections, maintain control over an us-them boundary, assure means for sustenance of collective activities, and resist extensive differentiation of internal relations. Their conversion into authoritative organizations or collaborative institutions would sap their creative flexibility.

Intentional Communities

While chain migration systems and trading diasporas clearly constitute or contain trust networks, intentionally formed separatist communities offer a limiting case: geographically segregated, avoiding far-flung enterprises, and often regimented from day to day in ways that Swedish emigrants and Hausa traders could never have managed. Even Waldensian communities, after all, relied heavily on the training and commitment of itinerant preachers for periodic reinforcement in the faith; they did not quite qualify as intentional communities. Intentionally formed communities of like-minded individuals face extreme versions of the problems involving external connections, boundary, sustenance, and internal relations that confront all trust networks (Hechter 1987, Chapter 8).

Intentional communities sometimes form with purely secular programs of political reform or with commitment to a distinctive style of life, but over the long historical run separatist religious ideals have surely inspired the bulk of such communities. The Quaker-inspired Fellowship of Intentional Communities defined their form of organization in this way:

An intentional community is a group of persons associated together [voluntarily] for the purpose of establishing a whole way of life. As such, it shall display to some degree, each of the following characteristics: common geographical location; economic interdependence; social, cultural, educational, and spiritual inter-exchange of uplift and development. A minimum of three families or five adult members is required to constitute an intentional community. (Zablocki 1971: 19)

Such communities have in common a commitment to an explicitly formulated "whole way of life." As with chain migration systems, the distinctiveness of their members' experiences increases the likelihood that some members – or renegade former members – will record their histories.

We secular outsiders often wonder how members can endure the hothouse atmospheres of intentional communities, and therefore how such communities can possibly survive. Under what conditions and through what processes do they reproduce themselves from year to year? Rosabeth Kanter took up the challenge by examining thirty "communes" that formed in the United States at some time between 1787 and 1853. By commune, Kanter meant a geographically separate, voluntary settlement with the following characteristics:

- identifiable as an entity, with physical and social boundaries
- intentional implementation of announced values
- membership based on commitment rather than coercion
- collective controls over members
- claims to self-determination
- sharing of resources and finances (Kanter 1972: 2)

These characteristics distinguish communes, thus defined, from authoritative organizations and (a bit less clearly) from collaborative institutions. We can reasonably treat them as extreme forms of trust networks, distinguished from most other trust networks by geographic segregation and daily mutual monitoring.

Of the eighteenth- and nineteenth-century communes Kanter studied, nine succeeded in the sense that they survived twenty-five years or more; the Shakers, for example, formed in 1787 and still exist with communal discipline today. The remaining communes, twenty-one in all, broke apart or ceased meeting the criteria above in fewer than twenty-five years; Brook Farm, for instance, survived as a commune from 1841 to 1847, but then converted itself into a Fourierist phalanx, a variety of collaborative institution without the extensive controls of a commune. By Kanter's criteria of communalism, the Shakers count as a success, Brook Farm as a failure.

Consistently with this chapter's arguments, Kanter emphasizes the importance of commitment mechanisms: organizational arrangements that promote unity, distinctness, and a sense of shared membership. Each commune put together its own ensemble of commitment mechanisms, but strong relationships existed between the array of mechanisms and the chances of survival. Kanter frames the problem in terms of individual commitment to the collective enterprise. She identifies six commitment processes as essential to collective survival: 1) sacrifice of outside activities, 2) renunciation of outside relations, 3) investment in inside attachments, 4) communion with the collective whole, 5) mortification (i.e., rejection of old identities for new collectively imposed identities), and 6) transcendence: delegation of individual decision making to a higher power. Commitment mechanisms forward those six processes.

From histories of the thirty communes, Kanter drew a list of about forty different commitment mechanisms, grouped into clusters, which in turn group into the six major processes. The process of mortification, to take a case in point, includes clusters called confession and mutual criticism, sanctions, spiritual differentiation, and deindividuation. Some mechanisms, in Kanter's analysis, forwarded more than one of the fundamental processes; Kanter counts wearing a communal uniform, for example, as a mechanism of renunciation as well as of mortification (Kanter 1972: 92, 112). According to her general argument, the fit among mechanisms significantly affected the quality of life within a commune, hence the likelihood that it would shrivel, explode, or divide.

Quantitatively, a curvilinear relationship prevailed: up to a point, the more commitment mechanisms a commune established, the more likely it was to survive; beyond a high point, however, too many mechanisms could destroy the commune. "Successful nineteenth-century groups," reports Kanter,

> used most but not all of the commitment mechanisms outlined. Each group made its own selection and put together a 'commitment package' out of all the possible ways to build commitment. There were always some commitment mechanisms that certain groups did not utilize. Amana, for example, retained the family, while Zoar did not have a particularly elaborate ideology.
>
> Moreover, most of the successful nineteenth-century groups retained some private space. All of them had enough land and buildings to provide a sense of movement around community territories; members were not tightly enclosed in a small space. There were many options about places to be within the community, even if these places were not always totally private. In fact, it was the unsuccessful rather than the successful groups that more frequently developed communal households in which all members lived together in one space, this being the only instance in which a higher proportion of unsuccessful groups utilized a commitment mechanism.
>
> (Kanter 1972: 132–133)

Kanter also points out an important paradox: communes that managed to foster a belief in their transcendent, charismatic properties did better, on the whole, than those that permitted more utilitarian approaches. The presence of a hierarchical authority structure and/or founding by a charismatic figure reinforced such a belief. Yet the most successful communes both institutionalized a measure of participatory democracy and insulated day-to-day operations from any charismatic leader's micromanagement (Kanter 1972: 116–118). Charisma seems to have promoted survival, but only if contained. We can most likely resolve the paradox by distinguishing between processes that brought committed members into a commune (where charisma mattered critically) and other processes that assured its continuity from day to day (where participation, responsibility, and individual efficacy mattered crucially). Day to day, communes that insulated collective activities from intrusive charisma did better.

Table 3.2 provides an opportunity to check the claims of my Table 3.1. The earlier table argued that the following changes increased viability of trust networks:

- sharpening of boundary
- sequestering of resources

Table 3.2. *Commitment Mechanisms Distinguishing Successful and Unsuccessful Communes Forming in the United States Between 1787 and 1853*

Included: all mechanisms in which the proportion adopting among successful communes was at least twice as high as the proportion among unsuccessful communes

celibacy or free love	daily group meetings
other abstinence	songs about community
nonresident members prohibited	average member rarely leaving community
property signed over at admission	rules for interaction with visitors
group assigns property to member	controls on sexual relations
clothing and personal effects owned by community	parent-child separation
	families not sharing dwelling unit
no compensation for labor	common ethnic background
no charge for community services	new members segregated from old
communal work efforts	instruction in community doctrines
defectors not reimbursed for property	regular confession, confession upon joining
defectors not reimbursed for labor	members distinguished on moral grounds
special term for outside	formally structured deference to those of superior moral standing
outside conceived as evil and wicked	
uniform worn	mutual surveillance by leaders
foreign language spoken	public denunciation of deviants
slang, jargon, other special terms	sanctions include removal of privilege, prohibition of participation in community function
outside newspapers ignored	
more than two thirds of typical day spent with other members	

Source: Kanter 1972: 80–112.

- enhanced connections with supply sources
- increase of available resources
- heightening of mutual attraction
- dissolution or insulation of dyads and cliques
- creation of a charismatic center (increased viability in short run, decrease in long run)

Table 3.2 lists each individual mechanism that Kanter's successful communes adopted at least twice as frequently as did unsuccessful communes. For example, six of Kanter's nine successful communes (67 percent) employed public denunciation of deviants, while only three of sixteen unsuccessful communes for which she had the necessary information (19 percent) denounced their deviants publicly. Any such single-point comparison runs the risk of running the causal arrow backward; communes that lasted longer for whatever reasons could, for example, have adopted public denunciation later in their careers. These largely agrarian communes, furthermore, all sequestered their own resources, hence except for recruitment of new members differences in resource acquisition disappear from the data. We should therefore use caution in drawing conclusions from these cross-sectional comparisons.

Still, the list of mechanisms makes the overall direction of differences inescapable. Many of the mechanisms employed more frequently by successful communes sharpened the boundary between inside and outside; obvious examples include special terms for the outside, conception of the outside as evil, wearing uniforms, speaking jargon or foreign languages, ignoring outside newspapers, and segregating new members from old. Others limited outside connections, notably by prohibiting nonresident members, signing over property to the commune, providing community-owned clothing and personal effects, and restricting contact of members with nonmembers. Internal control mechanisms divided roughly among equalization, socialization, monitoring, and defenses against clique formation. To the extent that we can translate Kanter's "survival" into my "viability," the evidence from nineteenth-century American communes confirms this book's general arguments on how internal changes affect the viability of trust networks. The greatest doubt arises over the question of charisma: boon or bane? As Kanter herself suggests, probably some of each, depending on the circumstances.

Two twentieth-century studies by Benjamin Zablocki permit us to follow up and refine conclusions from Kanter's evidence. During the communitarian 1960s, Zablocki joined or helped found several communes. He then began his professional study of communes with an ethnography of the Bruderhof, or Society of Brothers, a federation of three communities in Pennsylvania, Connecticut, and New York. The first Bruderhof community had formed in Germany during the turbulent postwar year of 1920. Its members professed a radical Anabaptist Christianity.

In 1931, the German-based Bruderhof affiliated with the Hutterian Church, a similar Anabaptist group based in Canada and the United States. The Bruderhof then adopted a number of Hutterian practices. After the German founder, Eberhard Arnold, died in 1935, a group of Brothers moved to England, only to be joined by the remainder when the Nazis dissolved the German branch in 1937. As England began interning Germans with the outbreak of war in 1940, the Brothers began scouting for places in

Canada and the United States, but ended up in Paraguay, the only country ready to admit them.

After difficult years in Paraguay, the Bruderhof first broke with the North American Hutterians (1950), then founded their own North American colony (1954). The Woodcrest, New York Bruderhof not only transplanted some members from Paraguay, but acquired new members from splits in established New York State communes. One of the splits brought the Brothers their main future source of income, a toy-manufacturing business called Community Playthings. Unlike the agrarian bases of the nineteenth-century communes studied by Kanter, the Brothers thereby acquired a commercial stream of sustaining resources.

Zablocki concentrated his attention on the Woodcrest community. By the time he began his study in 1965, a majority of Woodcrest's members were converts who had belonged to the commune fewer than ten years. With historical continuity from 1920 and even some members remaining from the 1920s, however, the commune easily met Kanter's criterion of success: survival for twenty-five years or more. In fact, Woodcrest built in most of the commitment-maintaining mechanisms Kanter identified in her successful communes: collective controls over external relations, boundary-sharpening mechanisms, and equalization, socialization, monitoring, and defenses against clique formation as devices for regulation of internal relations. "Theoretically," remarks Zablocki,

one could live one's whole life at the Bruderhof and, unless he had a job which required contact with the outside world, never see any money. Food, clothing, shelter, all material needs are provided free by the community. The individual must work at whatever community job is assigned him. This is true of all adult Bruderhof residents – members, novices, even short-term guests. But only full members give all of their previously acquired wealth to the community. When a person takes his baptismal vows, he signs over all he owns to the community forever. He is never entitled to get any of it back, even if he leaves, even if he is thrown out. Even the smallest piece of personal property is surrendered, but the Bruderhof never makes an issue out of this in practice. Unlike some monastics, the Bruderhof member is not required to say, '*our* cup,' '*our* toothbrush.' (Zablocki 1971: 114)

This description alone ticks off a number of mechanisms on Kanter's checklist. It also hints at more, notably the establishment of formal sanctions for misbehavior. The Brotherhood did, indeed, impose graded exclusions, beginning with admonition, passing through degrees of isolation, and ending with expulsion (Zablocki 1971, Chapter 5). They certainly organized

Table 3.3. *Reasons Given for Failure By Members of Dissolved Communes*

Reasons	Percent of rural	Percent of urban	Percent of total
External:			
legal, official	10.5	3.1	7.1
public opinion/action	10.5	0	5.7
environment, disaster	5.3	3.1	4.3
policy of sponsor organization	2.6	9.4	5.7
Internal:			
health and safety	5.3	3.1	4.3
economic failure	0	3.1	1.4
ideological schism, dispute	7.9	9.4	8.6
loss of ideological saliency	10.5	21.9	15.7
power, influence, dispute between leaders, followers	31.6	15.6	24.3
sexual relations	10.5	12.5	11.4
personal loss of interest	5.3	18.8	11.4
TOTAL	100.0	100.0	99.9
N	38	32	70

Source: adapted from Zablocki 1980: 153.

external contacts, boundary, and internal relations decisively and effectively. In addition, by means of Community Playthings the Bruderhof found the way to secure stable resources without involving its members dangerously in outside activity.

In a hugely ambitious second study, Zablocki drew a sample of 120 communes, ten per region, from a dozen American regions paired evenly between rural areas and nearby metropolitan centers. All the communes came into existence before 1975, and all were operating at some time between 1965 and 1975; fifty of them still existed in 1978. The numbers mean, of course, that seventy of them – thirty-eight rural and thirty-two urban – disintegrated before the study ended. Of the seventy failures, members reported their perceptions of reasons for disintegration as in Table 3.3.

Although former members of rural communes reported somewhat more often that their organizations had succumbed to external pressures, in both cases the vast majority described the reasons for failure as internal. Loss of ideological saliency and power struggles led the way. These are precisely the threats against which Kanter's commitment mechanisms presumably guard communes. But Zablocki's findings go beyond Kanter's in several fascinating regards. Zablocki found that up to a high level, membership turnover failed to threaten survival, just so long as new members continued to arrive. Turnover depended on three organizational characteristics, which Zablocki called "rationality in decision-making," "dyadic cathexis," and "dyadic partiality":

rationality in decision making: fieldworker judgment of public rationality in collective decisions
dyadic cathexis or *love density:* sociometric density of loving bonds within the commune, i.e., the extent to which dyads with highly positive effect are connected to each other
dyadic partiality: the extent to which pairs of commune members singled each other out for special relationships

Counterintuitively, both rationality in decision making and dyadic cathexis predicted positively to turnover, while dyadic partiality predicted negatively to turnover (Zablocki 1980: 155–162).

To state the relationship more crudely than Zablocki dared, where a loving central core of members prevailed and where the commune enforced publicly announced rules, members who remained outside the core tended to leave; we can easily imagine them sensing that insiders were pushing them around by means of arbitrary rules. Where members could pair off with like-minded others, however, peripheral members were more likely to stay. Yet the presence of a charismatic leader compromised those effects somewhat, especially by keeping turnover low in the presence of high love density. Charisma always presents risks for a commune: an influential leader can cause crises of meaning by contradicting the group's previously established moral codes. Such leaders lose credibility if they visibly fail to resolve a commune's newly pressing problems (Zablocki 1980: 322–334).

Zablocki sums up:

Both charismatic leadership and accumulated duration can increase commune stability, but, however they may achieve this, they do not do it by reducing cathexis. This fits with what we know about historical communes such as the Harmonists, Shakers, Oneidans, and Bruderhof. Their success was due to the channeling of cathexis, not its reduction or elimination.   (Zablocki 1980: 165)

Translated into this chapter's language, the "channeling of cathexis" depends on control over members' external connections, maintenance of an us-them boundary, and balancing between positive and negative effects of interpersonal attraction. More indirectly, it also depends on stabilizing control over resources that sustain the community's collective activities.

Notice one important implication of the trust networks examined in this chapter. Contrary to the obvious intuition that physical proximity matters, trust networks often survive and thrive over great distances. As in failed intentional communities, too much proximity or the wrong kind can actually destroy trust networks. Nor does solidarity-sustaining communication depend on face-to-face contact. We have already seen immigrants' letters enhancing coordination and sustaining intimacy over substantial blocks of space and time. What matters is the quality, structure, and dynamics of interpersonal connections within trust networks.

Evidence concerning chain migration, trade diasporas, and intentional communities confirms the importance of internal mechanisms for the survival, alteration, and collapse of trust networks, independent of their interactions with rulers and regimes. Of course changes in access to resources, external connections, and relations to public politics all produce significant shifts in how trust networks operate, and affect whether or not they survive. But so do their internal dynamics, especially their creation of mechanisms that reinforce the us-them boundary, maintain collective controls over sequestered resources, redistribute resources within the network, promote mutual attraction of members, limit the effects of clique formation, and insulate collective activities from the short-term effects of charisma. To the extent that these mechanisms weaken or reverse, trust networks become less viable. With this understanding in place, we can look more directly at encounters between trust networks and external predators, including political regimes.

4

Trust Networks Versus Predators

Born in Haverford West, Wales, on the Irish Sea, around 1682, John Roberts went to sea on merchant vessels. By 1719, he was the thirty-seven-year-old mate of a slave ship operating across the Atlantic. In June of that year, fellow Welshman and former slave ship officer Howell Davis, who had turned pirate in 1718, captured Roberts' vessel and enlisted Roberts in his crew. Davis' men, including Roberts, alternated among piracy (that is, seizure of commercial vessels, their goods, and sometimes their crews for private profit), privateering (that is, government-licensed piracy), and regular commerce for the next year. Then Davis' duplicity overreached itself. In the Portuguese slaving colony of Principé, the Portuguese militia received a credible report that Davis was planning to kidnap the governor. Prudently, they ambushed and killed Davis.

The marauders could not continue without a captain. The crew therefore gathered to drink, smoke, and deliberate about the succession. In his colorful *General History of the Pyrates*, first published in 1724, Daniel Defoe put this speech in the mouth of a pirate officer, Lord Dennis:

We are the Original of this claim (says he) and should a Captain be so sawcy as to exceed Prescription at any time, why down with him! it will be a Caution after he is dead to his Successors, of what fatal Consequence any sort of assuming may be. However, it is my Advice, that, while we are sober, we pitch upon a Man of Courage, and skill'd in Navigation, one, who by his Counsel and Bravery seems best able to defend this Commonwealth, and ward us from the Dangers and Tempests of an instable Element, and the fatal Consequences of Anarchy; and such a one I take Roberts to be. A Fellow! I think, in all Respects, worthy your Esteem and Favour.
(Defoe 1999: 194–195; the book appeared originally under the putative authorship of a certain Captain Charles Johnson; in a nice touch for the subject of pirating, scholars are still disputing whether Defoe or Johnson wrote it; Cordingly 1995: xix–xx)

Table 4.1. *Posted Rules of Bartholomew Roberts' Pirate Crew, 1719–1722*

1. Every man shall have an equal vote in affairs of moment. He shall have an equal title to the fresh provisions or strong liquors at any time seized, and shall use them at pleasure unless a scarcity makes it necessary for the common good that a retrenchment may be voted.
2. Every man shall be called fairly in turn by the list on board of prizes, because over and above their proper share, they are allowed a shift of clothes. But if they defraud the company to the value of even one dollar in plate, jewels or money, they shall be marooned. If any man rob another he shall have his nose and ears slit, and be put ashore where he shall be sure to encounter hardships.
3. None shall game for money, either with dice or cards.
4. The lights and candles shall be put out at eight at night, and if any of the crew desire to drink after that hour they shall sit upon the open deck without lights.
5. Each man shall keep his piece, cutlass and pistols at all times clean and ready for action.
6. No boy or woman to be allowed amongst them. If any man shall be found seducing one of the latter sex and carrying her to sea in disguise, he shall suffer death.
7. He that shall desert the ship or his quarters in time of battle shall be punished by death or marooning.
8. None shall strike another aboard the ship, but every man's quarrel shall be ended on shore by sword or pistol in this manner: at the word of command from the Quartermaster, each man being previously placed back to back, shall turn and fire immediately. If any man do not, the Quartermaster shall knock the piece out of his hand. If both miss their aim, they shall take to their cutlasses, and he that draws first blood shall be declared the victor.
9. No man shall talk of breaking up their way of living till each has a share of £1,000. Every man who shall become a cripple or lose a limb in the service shall have eight hundred pieces of eight from the common stock, and for lesser hurts proportionately.
10. The Captain and the Quartermaster shall each receive two shares of a prize, the Master Gunner and Boatswain, one and one half shares, all other officers one and one quarter, and private gentlemen of fortune one share each.
11. The musicians shall have rest on the Sabbath Day only, by right, on all other days, by favor only.

Source: Konstam 2002: 186–187.

The surviving crewmen duly elected Roberts captain of their Commonwealth. They then bombarded Principé's fort and escaped to sea.

Captain Roberts soon changed his name to Bartholomew. For his ruthlessness, Bartholomew Roberts acquired the nickname Black Bart. He also became something of a dandy, wearing a scarlet damask suit, a red feather in his three-cornered hat, and a gold chain from which hung a diamond-studded cross. For almost three years, Black Bart terrorized maritime traffic from Brazil to Newfoundland, among other exploits hanging the governor of Martinique from the yardarm of the governor's own ship. French, British, and colonial authorities stepped up their efforts to exterminate Black Bart. Back in West Africa, the British naval vessel *Swallow* found Roberts' ship at anchor near Cape Lopez, Gabon, on February 10, 1722. As Roberts attempted to sail away in "lightning and thunder and a small tornado," the *Swallow's* crew fired broadside at his ship, killing him instantly (Cordingly 1995: 215).

During his command, Roberts enforced a surprisingly strict code for a pirate. Black Bart himself rarely drank anything stronger than tea. Vigorously installing vigilance in his subordinates, he posted the rules in Table 4.1. His rules convey a remarkable combination of hierarchy, equality, and discipline. They qualify this chapter's title: trust networks versus predators. Clearly predators sometimes formed trust networks of a sort, and groups united by trust networks often preyed on others that likewise constituted trust networks. Pirates resembled bandits in this regard. Just as discharged privateers frequently became pirates, discharged mercenaries frequently became bandits. In either case, the risks they ran gave significant advantages to groups organized as trust networks. They could maintain their internal cohesion and discipline for risky attacks on others. But they did so at the usual cost: heightened distrust in both directions across the network boundary.

Remember how trust networks stand out among interpersonal networks in general. They carry on consequential, long-term collective enterprises that remain at risk to members' malfeasance, mistakes, or failures. They incorporate strong ties among at least three persons such that:

- the relation has a name mutually known to its participants
- involvement in that relation gives all participants some minimum of shared rights and obligations
- participants have means of communicating and representing their shared membership
- participants mark and maintain boundaries separating all members from outsiders
- interactions within the network place members' valued activities at serious risk to other members' malfeasance, mistakes, or failures
- the network operates exclusively and competitively: members of any particular network form a minority of the populations within which

they live, exclude most others rigorously from membership, and compete with other networks for control of resources
- the network makes exit difficult, costly, or even impossible

Like some mercantile networks and military units, pirates bend the final principle by imposing time limits. As Bartholomew Roberts' posted regulations and his own biography show us, pirates did not typically become members of the same band for life, but during a given voyage lived under stringent discipline coordinated by the captain and usually enforced by the full membership. Yet the main point is clear: although organized in trust networks, these predators typically preyed on members of other trust networks, including other groups of pirates.

Pirates first appear in the historical record shortly after 1220 BCE. At that point the maritime invaders Egyptians called the Sea Peoples controlled most of the eastern Mediterranean. Coming from the north, the Sea Peoples anticipated the much later Vikings: they raided, pillaged, and occasionally conquered. They survived by predation. They preyed on the merchant networks that had been organizing trade throughout the region for at least two millennia. They acted as pirates on the grand scale.

Sharply as we now draw the line between outlaws and honest traders, over most of human history, banditry, piracy, official military activity, and honest trade have blurred into each other. Speaking of the Mediterranean over the long run, Peregrine Horden and Nicholas Purcell put it this way:

Mercenaries have appeared to be as integral to an ecological history as other mobile groups. The same may be said of pirates and brigands. A normal manifestation of Mediterranean production and redistribution, piracy can be seen as the continuation of *cabotage* [coastal trade] by other means, although pirates can deal in high-value goods also. It has been a systemic epiphenomenon of connectivity, suppressed by powerful states only for brief intervals in Mediterranean history. Like other skilled manpower, pirates have been employed (as privateers) in the defence of polities, or even as their *raison d'être*. In the first century B.C., piracy, and especially that from Cilicia, was so far from being the accidental result of local criminal opportunism that it was represented as an organized threat to Roman supremacy. The elite of archaic Samos developed its own value-system of plunder and ransom, and, in the same period, the oracle of Apollo at Didyma advised that it was right for pirates to do as their fathers did. (Horden and Purcell 2000: 387)

People called the eighteenth-century pirates who operated from North Africa, Malta, and nearby Mediterranean locations *corsairs*, a term to distinguish entirely from buccaneers, which applies to Caribbean pirates of the seventeenth century. (The term buccaneer or *boucanier* stems from the Caribbean swashbucklers' practice of *boucan*, roasting whole animals in the fashion later called barbecue, when on shore.)

As Howell Davis' spells in privateering illustrate, corsairs, buccaneers, and other pirates long maintained love-hate relationships with Western states. They resembled mercenaries, who regularly hired themselves out to fight for kings, but just as regularly pillaged when pay was slow to come, and frequently turned to outright banditry in peacetime (Thomson 1994, Tilly 1992b: 80–84). Both pirates and mercenaries served as military reserves for rulers who could raise enough capital to hire them by the job, but not enough to sustain large standing armies and navies. As commercialization proceeded, as capital became more abundant, and as temporarily hired warriors became harder to manage, rulers turned increasingly to standing armies and navies. They financed them in the short run by loans and in the long run by taxes. At that point, pirates and mercenaries who preyed on a country's merchants themselves became prey to hunt down.

Piracy virtually disappeared from the Mediterranean during the nineteenth century. Backed by such external powers as Great Britain and the United States, states around the sea's perimeter consolidated legal control over maritime traffic. (Inland banditry persisted longer, and still recurs in the Mediterranean region from time to time.) In West African waters, the Red Sea, the Indian Ocean, and the Pacific, however, piracy may actually have increased since World War II with the rise of long-distance trade and the decline of colonial control (Konstam 2002: 181–183).

Pirates set this chapter's problem forcefully. Given the prevalence of predators – including predatory rulers – throughout history, how have members of trust networks defended themselves and their resources from predation? Pirates and bandits exemplify one answer; they have erected defenses by equipping themselves for predation, fighting fire with fire. More commonly, however, trust networks have defended themselves from predation, including predation on the part of rulers, by adopting some combination of three other strategies: concealment, clientage, and dissimulation. The *concealment* strategy, of which Waldensians have so far given us the purest example, fortifies the boundary between insiders and outsiders by means of secrecy and dissimulation. The *clientage* strategy, roughly illustrated by privateering, depends on some power holder's patronage, usually at a handsome price, for defense against other potential predators.

Dissimulation, illustrated by Howell Davis and his pirate crew during their intervals of masquerading as legitimate merchants, involves conceding just enough compliance with rulers' demands and regulations to hold off close surveillance and expropriation.

As we will see, the strategies of predation, concealment, clientage, and dissimulation all sometimes failed, especially as stronger centralized states emerged; determined predatory regimes succeeded in destroying autonomous trust networks or co-opting them, but in either case gained access to their previously sequestered resources. In those cases, trust networks chose implicitly among the alternative strategies of enlistment, bargaining, and dissolution.

Since predation is a risky, costly protective strategy – even bold Black Bart and his crew lasted less than three years! – the great bulk of historical trust networks that have sought to avoid governmental control have essayed combinations of concealment, clientage, and dissimulation. To the extent that expanding states extend their monitoring, incorporate or eliminate political middlemen, and impose strict controls on collective action, those three strategies also become risky and costly. Drawing opportunistically on scholars who have documented trust networks and their predators, this chapter helps explain how and why.

Who Preys on Whom?

Predators rely on externally effective coercion to extract resources from others. Coercion includes all concerted means of action that commonly cause loss or damage to the persons, possessions, or sustaining social relations of social actors. It features means such as weapons, armed forces, prisons, damaging information, and organized routines for imposing sanctions. Many organizations, down to households and family businesses, use internal means of coercion; parents punish their children, bosses dock their workers' pay, and teachers shame their students. Most of these organizations, however, lack effective means of *external* predation. Predation applies coercive means to outside people or organizations. In this sense, trust networks more often serve as prey than as predators.

Historically, nevertheless, some trust networks have preyed preferentially on other trust networks. The minority of trust networks that survive by predation must also meet the main organizational requirements of other trust networks; they must maintain their boundaries, secure their sustenance, stabilize their members' outside connections, and impose internal controls that maintain commitment and sustain collective activities. They differ from others in building coercive means and their renewal into the organization, and in acquiring resources from unstable prey.

Lineages that engage in blood revenge, for example, employ armed force as they do so. Their revenge cycles frequently begin with an abduction or a theft – with predation.[1] Organized ethnic and religious groups, which typically combine trust networks with authoritative organizations, sometimes prey on each other.[2] During the wild privatization and transformation of Russian business during the early 1990s, violent entrepreneurs whose organizations emerged from sworn criminal brotherhoods or from sportsmen's clubs spent almost as much energy killing off each other as they did in shaking down legal businesses (Varese 2001, Volkov 2002). Mutual predation occurs especially where adjacent networks are competing for the same resources.

Still, mutual predation does not constitute the greatest threat to most trust networks. Most trust networks lack effective means of preying on others. For those nonpredatory networks, the most frequently effective predators employ or consist of specialists in coercion (Tilly 2003b, Chapter 2). Although the boundaries blur and fluctuate, we can array those specialists from antigovernmental to semigovernmental to governmental:

antigovernmental: bandits, pirates, gangs, racketeers
semigovernmental: privateers, mercenaries, militias, private armies, paramilitaries
governmental: armies, navies, police forces

The list calls up some further nuances. At least temporarily, pirates, bandits, and gangs often organize as trust networks. Armies, navies, and police forces usually take the form of authoritative organizations, but units within them often create trust networks; indeed, fighting strength commonly depends on the trust-bearing solidarity that builds up within smaller combat units (Lynn 2003). Still other groups of coercive specialists – for

---

[1] Allcock 2000: 388–390, Boehm 1987, 1996, Gould 2003, Ikegami 1995: 244, Malcolm 1996: 18–21, Otterbein 1999, Ylikangas, Karonen, and Lehti 2001.

[2] Brass 1996, Brubaker and Laitin 1998, Ellis 2000, Horowitz 2001, Kakar 1996, Naimark 2001, Williams 2003.

example, some bandits and mercenaries – more closely resemble collaborative institutions in their a) mutual discipline when performing and b) sharing of benefits combined with c) relatively free exit (Blok 2001).

The story of Bartholomew Roberts has already taught us to treat any sharp distinction between pirate and privateer with skepticism. The same holds for privateers and legally constituted navies (Thomson 1994). Nor are police just police, the same all over.[3] Since 1989, the former Soviet Union has seen wild oscillations in the boundaries – and rapid movement of violent specialists across the boundaries – among government security forces, private protection agencies, thugs, and gangsters (Derluguian 1999, Varese 2001, Volkov 2002). Governmental agents who have coercion at their command frequently prey on vulnerable members of trust networks.[4] All sorts of violent specialists can become predators.

Although rulers usually deny it, over the long historical run trust networks' most persistent and effective predators have been duly constituted governmental agents who were just doing their jobs (Tilly 1985). In European experience of the last thousand years, organized anti-Semitism offers the most dramatic examples: expelling or massacring Jews before seizing their property, exacting large fees from Jewish communities to buy off expulsion or dispossession, requiring segregated residences or distinctive personal markers, imposing special taxes on them by virtue of their vulnerability.

The rise of Catholic power and of Catholic monarchs from the thirteenth to fifteenth centuries repeatedly exposed Jews to Christian predation. The Catholic Church's council of 1245 required Jews within its territory to wear skullcaps as distinguishing marks, French rulers banned Jews (only to recall them) four times between 1132 and 1321, while Edward I of England expelled Jews from his country in 1290. After massacres of Jews in Spain during 1391, Spain's and Portugal's expulsions of Jews and Muslims between 1492 and 1500 simply culminated a century of state-backed intolerance. Anti-Semitic predation waxed and waned across the following centuries, but never disappeared from European life. At times, Muslims, Protestants, and other religious minorities also felt the sting of government-directed predators.

---

[3] Brewer et al. 1988, Chalom and Léonard 2001, Chevigny 1999, Cunningham 2003, Deflem 2002, Huggins 1998, Kalmanowiecki 2000, Kraska and Kappeler 1997, Monjardet 1996.

[4] Bayart, Ellis, and Hibou 1999, Davis and Pereira 2003, Hochschild 1998, Romero 2003, Stanley 1996, Tishkov 2004.

Yet the great bulk of governmental predation on trust networks in Europe and elsewhere lacked this rationale of deliberate religious discrimination. From the first rise of substantial states five thousand years ago, the sheer effort to create militarily viable states, hold off rivals, crush opposition, and establish self-sustaining systems of rule has inevitably (if often inadvertently) threatened local trust networks. From the top down, of course, tribute, taxes, fines, forced loans, conscription, and wartime requisitioning look like legal measures that may have distasteful local consequences, but serve the public good by supporting essential activities of governments. Rulers often condemn popular resistance in precisely these terms.

As seen from the bottom up, in contrast, the same measures frequently attack trust networks directly by removing resources already committed to marriages, children's futures, long-term commercial ventures, provisions for burial, or religious obligations. Both elites and ordinary people have reasonable fears that if governmental agents grab hold of their trust networks and the resources embedded within them, their own abilities to preserve their network-based ways of life will decline catastrophically.

Political theorists will, of course, debate whether governmental taxation, conscription, and requisitioning on behalf of the common good qualify as predation. What characterizes governmental prerogative? What constitutes consent? From this book's perspective, however, two features of governmental intervention in trust networks certainly identify it as predation. First, it commonly employs externally effective coercion to produce compliance; you go to jail or pay fines for resisting governmental demands. Second, it removes from trust networks resources that otherwise would sustain routine relations and collective activities within the network. Over a wide range of circumstances, governmental expansion threatens network survival.

During the nineteenth and twentieth centuries, anarchists sensed that threat, and proposed alternatives. They recurrently formulated a dual program: dismantle central governments and create forms of self-government for small, local units organized as trust networks. In an optimistic passage of his 1840 treatise on property as theft, Pierre-Joseph Proudhon summarized human history in these terms:

Thus in a given society the authority of men over other men stands in inverse proportion to the intellectual level the society has reached, and the likely duration of that authority can be reckoned by the prevalence of demand for true government, that is government based on knowledge. Just as the law of force and the law of deception give way before the pursuit of justice and must therefore dissolve into equality, likewise the sovereignty of will gives way to the sovereignty of reason and will disappear with scientific socialism. Property and royalty have been under demolition since the world's beginning; as men seek justice in equality, society seeks order in anarchy.   (Proudhon 2003: 245)

Born in poverty, the largely self-taught intellectual worked as a printer before living precariously from his writings. His brief service as a member of the French National Assembly during the Revolution of 1848 and his prison term under the reaction led by President, then Emperor, Louis Napoleon did not shake his opposition to property and constituted authority. Proudhon considered it natural, desirable, and legitimate that people should voluntarily associate to solve common problems, but denied vehemently that anyone had the right to impose association upon them. His was an anarchistic creed.

Sixteenth-Century Parish Networks Face Predation

Long before anarchism, nevertheless, communities facing demands from expanding states repeatedly fought against governmental predation, sometimes escaped the worst by means of dissimulation or clientage, but frequently found their organizational and material supports for their ways of life crumbling under attack from governmental agents. Consider, for example, Henry VIII's intervention in the village of Morebath, Devonshire. Although he sometimes looked like a hero from the top down, King Henry greatly resembled a predator when seen from the bottom up. In 1521, at a time when Henry had allied England with the Habsburgs against France as well as laying claim to the French crown, he wrote a pamphlet against Martin Luther's doctrines. For his efforts, the pope dubbed Henry Defender of the Faith. Churchmen began voicing doubts about that title, however, no later than 1525. That year, Henry levied a major tax on church property to pay for his wars with Catholic France. Church officials passed much of the increased tax burden down the hierarchy to local parishes and ordinary people.

As the pope himself delayed in sanctioning Henry's divorce from Catharine of Aragon to marry Anne Boleyn, Henry sacked his papal legate Cardinal Wolsey and, after some maneuvering, declared the English church independent of Rome. The break with the pope brought Henry substantial church revenues. In 1534, Henry rammed through the Act of Supremacy, which made him and his successors heads of an independent English church. The same act rendered refusal to take an oath of recognition a capital crime of high treason. *Utopia* author and former chancellor Thomas More lost his head for just such a refusal.

By 1536, with the help of Thomas Cromwell, Henry was having Anne Boleyn executed on a trumped up charge of adultery, forcing dispossession of the monasteries, publishing William Tindale's translation of the Bible, and putting down major rebellions against his religious innovations. Henry VIII overcame extensive resistance to his organizational transformation of the English church. Doctrinally, however, Henry turned out to be less adventurous; by 1539, King Henry was issuing the Six Articles, which defined beliefs and practices greatly resembling those of the Catholic Church except in their substitution of the king for the pope.

Through all these gyrations, Henry's men missed no opportunity to seize church revenues or to raise money from church members. After Henry's death in 1547, English believers had to follow twists and turns through reigns of a rather more Protestant Edward VI, a quite Catholic Mary, and a warily Protestant Elizabeth I. The sixteenth century dragged ordinary English people through a maze of alternating religious and political identities. All exits from the maze led to greater royal power over English religious institutions and their resources.

In his dense, complex, but ultimately vivid reconstruction of parish life in sixteenth century Morebath, Eamon Duffy has demonstrated how deeply the top-down turmoil stirred by Henry VIII and his successors shook local social relations and practices. The lives of local people – and therefore whatever evidence we have of local trust networks – come to us mainly through Duffy's analysis of the village churchwardens' accounts from 1527 to 1596. Between 1527 and 1573, the long-serving vicar Sir Christopher Trychay copied the parish accounts, and much more information about local affairs, into a big 205-folio book.

Via Duffy's painstaking analysis, the big book tells us that the parish drew the major part of the money required for local devotions from two sources: gatherings organized by local groups and maintenance of parish sheep. Both depended on trust networks, especially the guilds of maidens and of bachelors, on one side, and the parishioners who raised parish sheep with their own flocks but turned all profits over to the church, on the other (Duffy 2001: 26–27). The election of two churchwardens each year, which drew from rich and poor alike, signaled another parishwide trust network; the wardens had not only to organize their own money-raising gathering (significantly named the Church Ale) and to supervise allocation of the parish sheep, but also to take responsibility in turn for the church's material possessions, including its silver plate. Since ten local men filled other offices, in any year a dozen of the parish's thirty to forty households had a man serving his rotation in religious administration.

Not that everything went smoothly in Morebath. In 1537, three years after Henry VIII broke the English church away from Rome, the parish split over the refusal of some parishioners to help pay for the parish clerk, the vicar's chief assistant. Without a clerk, the vicar could not (or at least refused to) perform some crucial services. For example, a poor parishioner named Marke and his wife suffered the death of their infant twins soon after their birth, but also after their baptism, which established them as full-fledged persons. When Marke and his party arrived at the church for a requiem mass that Father Trychay had scheduled on St. George's Day, they found the sanctuary locked for lack of a clerk (Duffy 2001: 60–61). Small potatoes, to be sure. "But," as Duffy comments:

the affair of the clerkship brings into sharp focus the extraordinary complexity of the concept of community in Morebath, and the interweaving of religious and secular considerations in the pursuit of peace. It discloses to us a small rural community in which the non-cooperation of a handful of poor men could paralyse the parish's decision-making and smooth working, and in which consensus, however achieved, rather than majority rule, was felt to be the essential basis for collective action. It discloses, too, a community in which economic division, though present, was not the fundamental principle of social organisation or hierarchy.   (Duffy 2001: 63)

A village of multiple trust networks felt the cold grip of royal predation.

Sir Christopher did his best to protect his initially Catholic parishioners from the opposite dangers of over-eager reform and dogged resistance. In conjunction with dissimulation, clientage worked for a while. But changing definitions of religious and political affiliation, with their accompanying obligations, impoverished the local church, destroyed the rough equality of household involvement in parish affairs that had characterized the early sixteenth century, and caused recurrent struggles of locals with outsiders who sought to profit from or to impose the new realignment of rural parish administration.

Henry's 1547 Injunctions, for example, combined an attack on votive lights and sacred images with dissolution of the chantries that had supported memorial masses, the proceeds going to pay for war with Scotland. In sheep-raising Morebath, such a reform simultaneously struck at practices that entwined religion with kinship and forced sale of the church sheep whose wool had provided the major income supporting local devotions. The Injunctions' local application severely damaged the village's existing trust networks.

Most of the time Morebath's people fought their battles with weapons of the weak (Scott 1985). In 1549, nevertheless, they paid the expenses of sending five local men to a rebel camp near Exeter in what came to be known as the Western Rebellion. More or less simultaneously Edward VI's regime had imposed the Protestant Book of Common Prayer plus new taxes on sheep and cloth to support the expanding wars against France and Scotland. The rebels of 1549 centered their demands on the restoration of religious life more or less as defined toward the end of Henry's reign – largely Catholic beliefs, practices, and identities within a Church of England. The king's forces, backed by foreign mercenaries, slaughtered the rebels. No commoners were going to decide the content of England's religious and political identities as imposed from the top down. Henry VIII and his successors worried little about the local trust networks on which their agents preyed. The outcomes of governmental actions proved, however, that Morebath's people and their vicar had rightly tried to insulate their trust networks from royal control.

The case of Morebath also illustrates a major difficulty in this book's enterprise. I have spoken confidently of the youth guilds, the arrangements for care of parish sheep, and the rotation of churchwardens as instances of trust networks in operation. Neither Duffy nor his readers know to what extent these obviously important social organizations actually contained trust networks: sets of strong social ties among people carrying on consequential long-term collective activities at risk to the malfeasance, mistakes, or failures of network members. We know only that they supported crucial local activities and joined most or all of the parish households in those activities.

Nor do we know what *other* valued long-term activities participants carried on by means of these networks. We can easily imagine that the networks supporting parish devotions also played prominent parts in courtship, marriage, credit, health care, and joint agricultural efforts. But it takes conjecture and analogy – always valuable as aids to theory, always dangerous as proof – to identify Morebath's local social relations as full-fledged trust networks. The further back in time we go, in general, the flimsier the evidence of concrete network operation. Yet in order to examine the range

91

from complete isolation to full integration of trust networks, we have little choice but to work with such historical evidence as remains. Morebath's story looks like one in which royal predators successfully pried resources from localized trust networks that had previously survived mostly through clientage and dissimulation.

Network Strategies

Remember the five strategies that members of segregated trust networks follow to reproduce and sustain their networks: 1) predation on external individuals or organizations, 2) concealment, 3) clientage, 4) dissimulation, and 5) combinations of 1 to 4. Pirates practiced predation, but so did bandits and military units living on the land. Predation could only work as a longer-term survival strategy if the supply of victims held up. Pirates concentrated along major shipping lanes, bandits along paths of merchants or pilgrims, military units in regions of viable agriculture or active food trade, small-time Russian gangsters in markets where they could terrorize operators of retail businesses.

Most segregated trust networks, however, do not survive by predation. Concealment, clientage, and dissimulation serve more often to sustain them. So long as it worked, concealment had the advantage of keeping resources within the network and thus sustaining its day-to-day doings. It had serious drawbacks, notably the network's vulnerability to a single malcontent, its need to conceal not only its routine operation but also its acquisition of new resources or members, and its lack of allies in the event of discovery and predation. Clientage mitigated these drawbacks, but at the (sometimes very large) cost of tribute to the patron. In the presence of constituted governments, dissimulation often worked best, simply because it facilitated accommodation with others who could damage the network but actually benefited somehow from its continued presence.

In Catholic countries, religious confraternities provide a remarkable example of variation and alternation among concealment, clientage, dissimulation, and direct incorporation into public politics by means of enlistment or bargaining.[5] As with Morebath's youth guilds, we have a reasonable presumption – both not a certainty – that confraternities usually

---

[5] Black 2000, Muir 1997, Nada Patrone and Airaldi 1986, Najemy 1982, Trexler 1981, Zink 1997.

contained or built on active trust networks. In early modern Italy, Nicholas Terpstra describes an evolution of confraternities from relative equality and autonomy:

Existing confraternities underwent an ennobling of membership that reflected a more general process of aristocratization in early modern society; this was further reinforced as reforming bishops like Carlo Borromeo and reforming orders like the Jesuits established new and exclusive confraternities on class, occupational, and gender lines in order to draw particular social groups into their reform programs. Networks of parish or peninsular confraternities emerged under the patronage and closer supervision of priests, bishops, or religious orders, with standardized statutes and with their energies directed to very specific social, educational, or devotional purposes; although not always successfully established, these reforms generated further reactions. Parochial and autonomous confraternities alike consolidated their resources and activities in order to protect and increase their traditional prerogatives.   (Terpstra 2000: 7)

Where the Catholic Church prevailed, confraternities occupied a privileged position among associations: ostensibly dedicated to worship and religiously tinged service, they benefited from a degree of ecclesiastical protection. By virtue of that protection, they easily became sites of mutual aid, social display, exclusion, and autonomous power going far beyond simple piety. They often hoarded wealth and social connections. As a result, they called forth fear, envy, and cupidity. If they did not already serve local rulers' programs, those rulers typically tried either to co-opt them or to suppress them while seizing their wealth. Like other trust networks, confraternities easily became vulnerable to predation.

In Tuscany, for example, Habsburg Grand Duke Peter Leopold decreed all confraternities closed in March 1785. He did so in part because many Florentine confraternities aligned themselves with reforms in the Catholic Church but also because they were hoarding wealth that, in his view, would better serve church and state directly. A census of confraternities he commissioned in 1783 duly reported that "the majority of the works of mercy carried out by confraternities were ... for their own benefit, and that in many of these organizations officers and members received special gifts (rations of pepper, candles, bread, etc.) and other hidden profits, again for their own benefit" (Eisenbichler 2000: 274). In 1784, the Duke established what he called the Ecclesiastical Patrimonies to administer parish revenues; the following year, those Patrimonies absorbed the banned confraternities' wealth (Eisenbichler 2000: 275).

When Peter Leopold wrote a memorandum on ruling the Grand Duchy for his son and successor Ferdinand III, it included the following indictment of Tuscan confraternities:

> They gathered on feast days and recited the Office, and for the most part they served to waylay the people from the parishes and from [Christian] instruction, and they constantly fomented dissension with the parish priests on account of the authority the brothers thought they had over churches, functions, processions, etc. In the countryside they served as a pretext for festive meals. In Florence, then, there were also many night companies, where they gathered to eat all night long, and even slept there, and they heard Mass on feast days very early, before daylight, and they spent the rest of the day hunting, or at the inn, or loafing around, and they did a thousand knavish things in the distribution of the many dowries that were given out by these confraternities, and were of a respectable amount.   (Eisenbichler 2000: 277)

As usually happened in old regime settlements of this sort, the Duke finally allowed a few exemptions for confraternities that were actually providing public services. But he greatly narrowed their privileges. His regulations pushed confraternities away from autonomous operation as trust networks toward incorporation into the Duke's own authoritative organization, Tuscany's formal government.

We should not be surprised to learn that authorized confraternities "were no longer to use hoods and banners (*stendardi*), nor to take part in public processions, meet at night or on holy days, or bestow dowries on women" (Eisenbichler 2000: 275). Like many an Enlightenment monarch, Grand Duke Peter Leopold thought he knew the public good better than the wealthy, self-satisfied, and excessively independent members of Tuscan confraternities. He therefore used his power to dissolve them and seize their wealth. He destroyed the protection that had previously sustained them.

Confraternities Meet the French Revolution

Not all confraternities, by any means, enjoyed the opulence of Florentine associations or fell prey to Enlightenment improvers. Through much of Catholic Europe, trust networks organized publicly as devotional societies did a great deal of local work – not only prayers, memorial masses, and social services, but also control of the marriage market, provision for festivals, mutual aid, and, especially, burial insurance. Religious patronage offered partial protection from civil authorities; pious processions, Sunday masses, and saints' day celebrations offered occasions for popular assemblies that no secular association, much less any voluntary grouping of citizens, had the right to convene. Similarly, confraternities often enjoyed the protection of local civil authorities, who gained prestige and assistance in public ceremony from confraternity members, and therefore shielded them from plundering by higher-level governmental officials.

As a practical matter, formally organized confraternities shared parish work with other nonreligious or semireligious institutions such as night watches, trade guilds, and youth abbeys – the latter being organizations of young unmarried persons similar to the men's and women's guilds in Morebath. Trade guilds and youth abbeys commonly inflicted on local moral reprobates the shaming ceremonies variously known as donkeying, charivari, and rough music (Thompson 1991: 467–538). They also guarded their local jurisdictions and honor by battling similar groups from adjacent parishes who dared to infringe their territory or perquisites. They survived through a combination of clientage and dissimulation.

In villages and towns of eighteenth century Provence, Maurice Agulhon documents the central parts played in public life by religious confraternities, youth abbeys, militias, and similar organizations. Despite overlapping personnel, they organized around different activities, rights, and obligations – conducting saints' day processions, shaming immoral persons, providing military escorts for processions, collecting taxes on women's exogamous unions, and (literally) fueling celebrations at which bonfires warmed the festivities. The White Penitents of Toulon:

reported that up to the Revolution, not stopping at gifts to the poor and travel money for Frenchmen bought back from the Barbary Pirates who debarked at Toulon, they had taken over the Sailors' Fund founded by other people, which involved aid to widows and orphans of men lost at sea. As for the Gray Penitents, they visited prisons to give prisoners clothing and food, then accompanied each man under a death sentence from his cell to the scaffold to the cemetery. (Agulhon 1966: I, 209)

Over the region as a whole, nevertheless, during the eighteenth century confraternities drifted away from religious devotion to secular pursuits (Agulhon 1970: 232).

In Draguignan, the *corps de la jeunesse* (youth abbey) argued in 1751 that since they had ceded the fee called *pelote* (levied on women who married outside the locality) to the confraternity of the Holy Sacrament, the municipality should pay for repair of the ballfield used by local youths and previously maintained by the corps (Agulhon 1966: I, 107). Likewise in Draguignan, during July 1783:

> the police commission received word of a charivari in the market place on the occasion of a wedding. A great crowd of peasants, householders and artisans gathered, making a racket with a drum and many other noisy instruments. Someone shouted out an insulting parody of a wedding announcement. The crowd then hooted the police inspector who tried to end the proceedings. The police arrested one of the young people and put him in jail for a day. But despite its bourgeois composition the police commission divided over whether to punish anyone, and we can see why: charivari was a tradition, not a misdemeanor. (Agulhon 1966: I, 134)

At the parish and village levels, publicly visible trust networks ran a significant share of local affairs, especially those affairs that did not connect local residents with the national church or government.

The French Revolution forcibly incorporated some of these trust networks, destroyed others, and drove still others underground. The Revolution swept religiously authorized trust networks including confraternities from public life, substituting government-controlled authoritative organizations including patriotic clubs, National Guard units, revolutionary committees, and officially constituted municipalities. In Draguignan, the White Penitents held their last recorded meeting in September 1791, but kept on managing funerals until November 1792 (Agulhon 1966: II, 478). Especially when it came to death benefits, members of confraternities often continued their activities in secret (Agulhon 1966: II, 479–502). They survived by shifting from clientage and dissimulation to concealment.

From 1793 onward, Jacobins in power closed down or co-opted autonomous organizations – including both religious societies and secular political associations – as best they could. The Jacobin legislature of 1793 sought to substitute government-organized assistance for the private assistance and religiously sanctioned mutual aid they abhorred, but those measures fell away with the financial exigencies of war. Workers' confraternities disappeared from French public life during the early 1790s, and only recovered partially under the Napoleonic Empire (Woloch 1994: 290–293). Popular societies revived temporarily under the Directory in 1799, but again lost autonomy with Napoleon's rise to power (Woloch 1970, 1994). The Napoleonic Code decreed that "No association of more than twenty people whose aim is to meet each day or on certain set days to take up religious, literary, political, or other subjects may form except with governmental authorization, under such conditions as public authorities may choose to impose" (Agulhon 1977: 21). Although Masonic lodges thrived as connectors under Napoleon, they faded badly with the Restoration of 1815.

Temporary resurgence of church-based organizations under the same Restoration did not stem the long-term decline of the old regime's associational forms (Agulhon 1970: 414–425). During the nineteenth century, secret political societies bedeviled French authorities, workers' mutual aid associations lived mostly underground until the legalization of private-sector unions in 1884, and nonpolitical voluntary associations waxed and waned from one regime to the next. But confraternities, youth abbeys, and similar religiously sanctioned popular organizations never recovered anything like their eighteenth-century prominence in local affairs (Tilly 1986: 245–312). Indeed, religious objects, activities, and personnel became favorite targets for direct action by France's clandestine political activists during the nineteenth century (see e.g., Beaubernard 1981: 129–180).

On balance, the French Revolution reduced the segregation of France's interpersonal trust networks from public politics. It did so in the three usual ways: by destroying some trust networks, by integrating some previously existing trust networks into public politics, and by creating new networks that connected their members directly with public politics. Despite some concealment, most religiously certified confraternities simply disbanded under Jacobin repression.

Vignettes of Viability

In the absence of firm integration into government or solid protection from patrons, what makes trust networks viable? We saw earlier that trust networks change through internal processes whether or not they encounter predators. Changes in boundary definition and control, in relation to outsiders other than predators, in connection with sustaining resources, and with regard to internal controls over members all affect the viability of trust networks. But encounters with predators matter especially because predators so regularly seek not simply to fasten on their hosts like run-of-the-mill parasites, but to suck out their sustenance and thus destroy them; pirates typically struck a victim only once.

Our historical vignettes of encounters between predators and trust networks suggest two important conclusions concerning the viability of segregation from governments as a defense of trust networks. First, despite the heroic records of clandestine faiths and political conspiracies, the viability of complete concealment from public politics as a defensive strategy

97

depends less on trust networks' internal character than on their relations to other organized groups, especially including governments at different scales. Second, the growth of high-capacity centralized states dramatically reduced the feasibility of trust networks' segregation from public politics while it increased the prominence of governmental agents as trust networks' principal predators.

A triple insight begins to dawn:

1. To some degree the four clumps of mechanisms that sustain trust networks – boundary, sustenance, external connection, and internal control – conflict with each other. Except where members of a trust network have sequestered an entirely self-renewing source of sustenance, for example, an absolute us-them boundary cuts off the network from resources that could sustain its membership and collective activities.

2. Bottom-up strategies such as concealment, dissimulation, clientage, and predation differ in their impact on the four clusters; under favorable circumstances, for example, predation provides sustaining resources, but incentives for defection and uncertainties in the supply of prey make internal controls crucial to a predatory network's survival.

3. Visibly, viability of various bottom-up strategies varies systematically with the type of regime; enlistment and bargaining threaten trust networks with destruction in regimes of low-capacity governments relying mainly on coercion rather than capital or commitment, but become much more attractive with high-capacity governments that stress capital and commitment as their inducements for collaboration. Clientage may work in either type of regime, but it has very different consequences for a trust network's internal operation when (as in most low-capacity regimes) an effective patron must provide a shield against coercion by other predators. Although holders of power employ predation in all sorts of regime, unless the networks themselves hold power predation only sustains trust networks in relatively low-capacity regimes.

To be sure, no one-way civilizing process drove nonstate predators steadily out of business; pirates and bandits prospered to the extent that their potential victims prospered. Predators' relation to governments therefore remained deliciously dialectical: the prosperity of predators' prey depended in part on governmental guarantees for economic activity (Lane 1973,

1975). The revival of piracy in West African coastal areas, the Red Sea, the Indian Ocean, and the Pacific as interstate trade intensified after World War II marks another phase in the dialectic. Nevertheless, the long-term trend runs from widespread predation on trust networks outside of governmental auspices to increasing centrality of governments in the coercive extraction of resources from trust networks.

As a strategy for maintaining trust networks' autonomy, predation itself therefore lost efficacy over the long run. Concealment, clientage, and dissimulation gained attractiveness as defensive predation became less feasible. Concealment could only work over any substantial length of time if a trust network had means not only of defending a tight boundary but also of renewing its membership and sustaining resources without public exposure. Such means remained much more readily available in worlds of hunting, gathering, pastoralism, or subsistence cultivation than in commercial economies. Clientage could work over a much wider variety of circumstances, but only so long as protectors had the capacity and interest to maintain their own political autonomy. Dissimulation became the rule for segregated trust networks in worlds of complex economies and intrusive governments. As *blat's* survival in post-Soviet Russia tells us, it may well have become the dominant strategy for segregated trust networks in our own time.

5

From Segregation to Integration

By 1720, French imperial forces had long since established a serious presence in North America. Although they had lost some ground to the aggressive English since 1700, the French still laid claim to the eastern part of what we now call Canada except for Hudson's Bay, Acadia, and Newfoundland, to northern sections of what we now call the American Midwest, and to a significant share of the Mississippi basin. Québec, Montréal, Detroit, St. Louis, Mobile, and New Orleans had all come into being as French cities and fortresses. French merchants, soldiers, and administrators controlled the major waterways linking the continental interior to Europe. Violence, intrigue, and venality intertwined in their imperial system of rule. The French held their ground until the 1760s under incessant pressure from Spanish and English competitors including frontier settlers. Defeat by the English in the Seven Years War (1756–1763) radically reduced France's North American territories. Up to then, nevertheless, the French still had some hope of becoming the dominant power in North America.

Despite their looming presence on the continent, the French never achieved more than contingent domination over the Indian populations they encountered from their earliest arrival in North America. They tried, but their very efforts to conquer Indian peoples or to push them aside for French settlements created new forms of connection among previously distinct villages, bands, tribes, and federations. Remember the three sorts of resources that rulers generally apply to subordinate populations:

> *coercion*: all concerted means of action that commonly cause loss or damage to the persons, possessions, or sustaining social relations of social actors

100

capital: tangible, transferable resources that in combination with effort can produce increases in use value, plus enforceable claims on such resources

commitment: relations among social sites (persons, groups, structures, or positions) that promote their taking account of each other

French authorities deployed combinations of all three. They used coercion aplenty as they conquered, but they also bought off Indians in generous ritual exchanges of gifts, and fostered commitment in their support of Catholic missionaries among the Indians as well as their toleration of French-Indian intermarriage.

Top-down French applications of coercion, commerce, and commitment transformed Indian life, but did not insert Indians neatly into the French system of rule. Interacting with French conquerors, Indians developed skill in concealment, clientage, dissimulation, and predation. In addition to general Indian reluctance to accept European rule, the French discovered that British and Spanish paymasters were often willing to offer hard-pressed Indians support for their resistance against the French. In compensation, French paymasters similarly sought to buy away Indian supporters of the English and French.

Up to the French defeat in the Seven Years War, repeated French efforts to subordinate Indians, to integrate them durably into patron-client relations, or even to bargain out brokered autonomy as if they were lesser sovereign states sometimes worked in the short run. Over the long run, however, those strategies usually generated not integration but concealment, predation, and (especially) dissimulation. As a consequence, French soldiers, administrators, and merchants expended a great deal of effort in negotiating coexistence with the Indian populations in their territories. That negotiation produced what Richard White calls a "middle ground" of understandings and practices linking nominally sovereign French authorities to Indian populations within their jurisdictions. In a more literal sense, the territory between areas of dense French settlement and those of largely Indian population shifted as a mixed middle ground of encounter. As of the 1690s, the middle ground extended around the Great Lakes.

French-Indian sexual relations, cohabitation, and marriages crisscrossed the middle ground. In 1694, for example, prominent trader and notorious libertine Michel Accault sought to marry Aremepinchieue, seventeen-year-old daughter of a leading Kaskaskia chief in the Illinois territory.

Aremepinchieue, a fervent Catholic in defiance of her father's opposition to the faith, refused to marry the nonpracticing Accault. She received backing from Jesuit Jacques Gravier, French missionary to the Illinois, who had allied himself with Accault's enemies. Despite this configuration of conflicts, the principals worked out an astonishing dénouement: with the support of Father Gravier, Aremepinchieue agreed to marry Accault. Her conditions: he would return to the Catholic faith and her parents would accept Catholic baptism. The parties accepted. After this stunning example, and following concerted efforts on the part of French missionaries, by 1711 the Kaskaskias had almost all become Catholic (White 1991: 74).

Aremepinchieue was not alone. By the 1720s, French men and Indian women had frequently been cohabiting, and sometimes marrying, for seventy years. Three generations or more of *métis* had therefore grown up in the middle ground. If White's identifications of the chief characters are right, the wedding of 1694 not only illustrated the creative character of French-Indian relations but also facilitated Indian intervention into French-on-French murders three decades later. In 1723, a French soldier insulted a French warehouse keeper named Perillaut, who replied by killing the soldier with his sword. French authorities condemned Perillaut to death. But Illinois Indians who had dealt extensively with Perillaut pleaded for his life. (As warehouse keeper, Perillaut took charge of distributing authorized gifts and military bounties to Indian groups.) First three Kaskaskia chiefs appeared with thirty warriors. Then followed a delegation of Cahokias including a much respected woman called Marie Rompiechoue, who – as her name suggests – was most likely the daughter or other close relative of the earlier Aremepinchieue.

The Kaskaskia chiefs had already allied their tribes closely with the French against their common enemies the Chickasaws and the Fox. The Indians offered the French a peace pipe. The French knew well that, by long-established Indian custom, to accept the pipe meant granting the giver's request. Led by a Catholic Indian spokesman, the Kaskaskias made a subtle, forceful argument: Chickasaws and Foxes would interpret the execution of Perillaut, friend of the Kaskaskias, as avenging their own dead in wars against the Kaskaskias and the French. In keeping with both Indian custom and Christian doctrine, they argued that the perpetrator's contrition, compensation to the victim's family, and a French pardon would resolve the situation more equitably. The chiefs reminded the French, furthermore, of the times that Kaskaskias had lost their lives avenging the French but, at French request, the Kaskaskias had not exacted blood revenge on their enemies.

French commander Boisbriant saw the point. He:

insisted that the affair set no precedent, but he agreed to petition the king for Perillaut's pardon and release. Those Kaskaskias who 'have died to avenge the Frenchman, cover the body of the one who has now been killed.' So ended the first recorded criminal case tried by the French in Illinois. Perillaut was free that May.   (White 1991: 92)

This negotiation occurred in a world in which French military units freely massacred their Indian enemies and in which Indians at war commonly tortured, scalped, burned, and ate captured enemies. The Kaskaskias and French were not adopting a general strategy of nonviolence, but bargaining out conditions of rule.

We know too little of day-to-day Indian life between the 1690s and the 1720s to say confidently that the Kaskaskias as a whole formed a single connected trust network. French losses during the Seven Years War meant that France never integrated the Kaskaskias or other North American Indian nations durably into its regime. But confrontations of Indians with French around the American Great Lakes during that period surely included repeated encounters between regimes and trust networks. They illustrate a middle ground between total segregation and complete integration of trust networks.

From the top down, we see French officials experimenting with different combinations of coercion, capital, and commitment, sometimes achieving patronage or brokered autonomy, but never reaching full integration of Indians' trust networks into their system of rule. From the bottom up, we see Indians and *métis* mixing concealment, predation, and dissimulation with contingent forms of protection by French patrons. We watch the early stages of colonial domination.

Unequal Encounters

So far we have looked at trust networks mainly from the perspectives of their members. In the background we have noticed rulers applying various combinations of coercion, capital, and commitment in efforts to control visible trust networks and to draw essential resources from those networks. We have witnessed repeated encounters between trust networks and predators, including agents of government. We have examined how changes in external connections, boundaries, sustenance, and internal relations affect the day-to-day operation of trust networks. But we have not yet confronted the major processes by which trust networks actually become integrated into public politics: disintegration of existing networks, multiplication of populations outside of existing networks, and so on. How do these processes actually produce their political effects? Once again, it helps to distinguish bottom-up and top-down components of the processes, then break each of them into finer mechanisms.

"Bottom up" means simply as seen from the perspectives of trust networks. Chapter 2 distinguished seven varieties of bottom-up strategies:

1. *concealment*: avoiding detection and manipulation by authorities
2. *dissimulation*: feigning conformity by adopting some available public identity, but minimizing both compliance and visibility of internal operations and resources
3. *clientage*: acquiring protection by intermediate authorities, thus reducing compliance and visibility, but usually at a price
4. *predation*: organizing enough externally effective force both to acquire resources and to defend against predation by others
5. *enlistment*: active integration into an existing regime's available niches
6. *bargaining*: establishing relations with major political actors on the basis of mutual contingent consent
7. *dissolution*: destruction of an existing network through either incremental departures or collective dismantling

Following encounters of a given trust network with political authorities over a substantial period, we often observe a sequence of these strategies, for example an integration process running *concealment – dissimulation – clientage – enlistment* for Val d'Aosta Waldensians as they went from clandestinity to membership in the Protestant establishment. In the opposite direction, *enlistment – clientage – dissimulation – dissolution* describes the changing position of many religious confraternities before and during the French Revolution.

Authorities deployed contrasting top-down strategies in seeking to control trust networks and resources within them. Figure 5.1 summarizes the main possibilities. Authorities first chose their *means of control*: a mixture of coercion, capital, and commitment ranging from exclusive reliance on coercion (nothing but application of means that damage and destroy) to

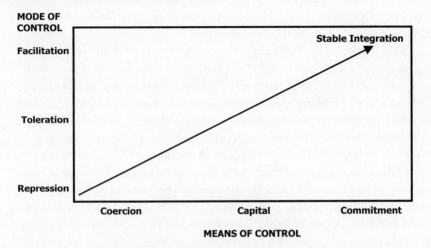

Figure 5.1 Top-Down Approaches of Rulers to Trust Networks

exclusive reliance on commitment (nothing but appeals to shared means of communication and solidarity). But they also chose a *mode* of control: whether to *facilitate* a trust network's operation, to *tolerate* it, or to *repress* it. Some combinations of means and mode – for instance, facilitation by coercive means – seem unlikely at first glance, and did in fact occur no more than rarely. Rulers did, however, sometimes facilitate by coercive means, as when French authorities in North America annihilated enemies of their Indian allies. To take the scheme's opposite corner, repression by means of commitment occurred every time the Catholic Church literally excommunicated a dissident, heretical trust network. Nevertheless, the diagonal arrow summarizes my main argument: stable integration of trust networks into systems of rule depends on a decline of coercive control combined with increasing reliance on capital and commitment. That shift entails movement from repression to toleration and facilitation.

Authorities' choices of means and modes obviously interacted with trust networks' strategies for dealing with authorities; however unequally, the two parties engaged in strategic interaction. Authorities faced with predatory trust networks such as pirates and bandits generally chose within a range running from repression by coercive means (attacking them directly) to facilitation by means of capital (enrolling them as privateers or mercenaries). Trade diasporas faced with regimes that stressed repression by coercive means generally chose within a range running from dissimulation by means of capital (bribery) to clientage by means of commitment (protection by

105

kin or coreligionists). Hence, incessant negotiation took place among trust networks, rulers, and other political actors.

These negotiations located particular trust networks in our relation-means space. They differentiated evasive conformity, brokered autonomy, particularistic ties to rulers, patronage systems, totalitarianism, democracy, and theocracy. Thinking about the negotiations brings out similarities and dissimilarities in relations of trust networks to public politics. Totalitarianism and theocracy resemble each other greatly, in this view, except that theocracy substitutes the commitment of common religious membership for totalitarian coercion. Brokered autonomy resembles other patronage systems, except that it involves the explicit recognition of a distinctive community and its representation. Evasive conformity and particularistic ties to rulers likewise operate in similar fashions, except that in evasive conformity the tie between ruler and trust network remains negotiated and contingent. Democracy differs from the rest, since all three of its ties – trust network to ruler, trust network to intermediary, and ruler to intermediary – work via negotiation and contingency. In that regard, we return to Margaret Levi's insight concerning contingent consent (Levi 1997: 21). Democracy entails contingent consent based mainly on combinations of material incentives with shared commitment.

Here is another way to interpret the range from high integration to high segregation. The top layer of high integration – totalitarianism, democracy, and theocracy – contains zones of direct rule, in which agents of the central government extend its writ effectively to local communities. The middle layer of negotiated connection – patronage and brokered autonomy – contains zones of indirect rule, in which powerful intermediaries enjoy substantial autonomy within their own domains. The bottom layer of segregation – evasive conformity and particularistic ties – contains zones of thin political control, backed neither by effective central agents nor by powerful autonomous intermediaries. The diagram therefore offers a restatement of this chapter's twin problems: What processes locate trust networks in different zones within the space, especially zones of direct rule, indirect rule, and thin control? What processes move trust networks from one zone to another?

What do we find as we move up through the zones? At the bottom level, we find few people other than members of the ruling class relying on governmental agents for protection of their major valued long-term enterprises from risk. Instead, we find most people organizing such enterprises within autonomous trust networks and defending those networks as best they can from governmental intervention. In the middle level, we observe partial integration of trust networks into systems of rule, but always with protection by powerful intermediaries from the ruler's direct intervention. At the upper level, we discover people whose trust networks either extend into the government, depend on direct governmental intervention, or incorporate political actors (for example, trade unions, political parties, and commercial firms) that in turn depend on governmental connections for their continued operation. Only at the upper level do we therefore discover large numbers of citizens who regularly yield their children to military service, put their life savings into government-backed securities, and respond willingly to census takers. How and why do regimes at the top level ever come into existence?

This journey from bottom to top identifies some challenging difficulties in the analysis of segregation and integration. Rare is the trust network that migrates the whole distance from bottom to top or top to bottom without changing significantly in organization and membership. The forms, geographic locations, external relations, and very names of Indian villages and tribes altered continuously as they interacted with the conquering French. In the North American regions whose transformations during the seventeenth and eighteenth centuries Richard White studied, under today's U.S. and Canadian rule many tribes claim descent from entities that make appearances in White's account, but their organizations bear little relationship to those of their ancestors. We cannot hope for the neat experiment of observing the "same" trust network as it moves from level to level across the whole range.

If my arguments are correct, furthermore, at any given level we should see not only upward or downward movement of existing trust networks among segregation, negotiated connection, and integration but also creation of new trust networks and disintegration of old ones. We should observe effects of major transforming processes, processes in which segregated networks disintegrate or lose their members while politically connected trust networks form and expand. Despite these complexities, it will clarify our analysis if we break this chapter's task into segments. First, a look at actual trust networks inhabiting each of the three levels – segregation, negotiated connection, and integration – to see if they behave as the general argument says they should. Second, a broader survey of trust networks' disintegration and new creation. Finally, an examination of how the experiences of existing trust networks articulate with those larger processes of transformation.

Segregated Trust Networks

Let us start at the bottom and work our way to the top. Toward the bottom of our space, we should find rulers influencing trust networks by applying intermittent coercion or using particular ties of commitment. We should discover only thin political control, and should observe members of trust networks engaging in combinations of concealment, dissimulation, and predation. As we move toward the top, we should pass through a zone of indirect rule and negotiated connection on our way to another zone in which rulers are employing ample applications of capital and commitment as they establish direct rule. In that uppermost zone, we should notice trust networks adopting strategies of enlistment and bargaining, but also sometimes dissolving as rulers – including democratic regimes – encourage the formation of new, integrated trust networks.

One case per category will move us from significant segregation to extensive integration. We have already scrutinized Medieval Europe's segregated Waldensians, but today's world likewise yields revealing instances of segregation. The place of Islamist networks in most Middle Eastern countries provides a dramatic case in point. Through much of the Middle East, repressive regimes forbid political association and mobilization by means of formal organizations other than a few state-authorized political parties. They ban authoritative organizations that might dare to make public political claims. So doing, they increase the reliance of ordinary people on informal networks as vehicles for survival and influence (Singerman 1995, Chapter 3).

The same impoverishment of formal public life drives activism underground. As Diane Singerman observes,

The collusion among monarchical, dynastic regimes, the military, and intelligence forces has suffocated a wide range of mediating structures and formal organizations throughout the region, whether they are professional associations, regional clubs, neighborhood and community organizations, political parties, women's associations, human rights groups, youth groups, etc. The power and organizational vitality of society has been diminished by draconian laws of association and assembly, limitations on fund-raising, a censored press, and regulatory overkill. This has left the state, kinship, and religious institutions in place, offering few rights of citizenship, representation, voice, or political freedoms in return. Thus the ground for activism – no less Islamic activism – is littered with risks and formidable obstacles. (Singerman 2004: 148–149)

Nominally Islamic regimes have little choice, however, but to tolerate (and keep a wary eye upon) ostensibly nonpolitical Islamic organizations such as medical clinics, schools, charities, and cultural societies. In relatively open Jordan:

Informed by a concern with controlling religious discourse, the regime uses administration, repression, and legal mechanisms to create a web of disincentives for more critical Islamic groups, which as a result find formal organizations constraining in the struggle over sacred authority. Moderate Islamists with a strong relationship to the regime, on the other hand, are allowed to act through formal organizations, so long as they limit their activities in accordance with the conditions of participation and do not challenge the state's Islamic discourse.   (Wiktorowicz 2001: 83)

The same regimes, nevertheless, generally face covert opposition by networks of Islamists: activists who seek to impose strict religious rule over states they regard as having secularized and/or sold out to the secular West. Few Islamists plunge as deep into opposition as Osama Bin Laden and al-Qaeda, but many share Bin Laden's hope for a purified Islamic world.

As a consequence, Islamists themselves combine concealment and dissimulation; they keep their organized networks underground, but they infiltrate tolerated Islamic organizations, seeking both to influence those organizations and to recruit promising believers into their own networks. Shiites even have a word for outward but reluctant conformity to political authorities: *taqiyya* (Kepel 2002: 38). Jordan's Salafi enthusiasts gain most of their new members from existing circles of pious but politically inactive Muslims (Wiktorowicz 2001: 134–135).

One common path into ostensibly legitimate organization passes through religious discussion groups. In Yemen and elsewhere, religious women often participate in Qur'anic (Koranic) study groups, or *nadwas*. These nadwas, Janine Clark reports,

form an important part of women's informal networks. These Qur'anic study groups provide religious solace and guidance, an education in reading and in Islam, an emotional outlet, a social life outside of the home, and a support group for the women who attend them. They also provide an arena where a woman can go for advice or find out where (or to whom) she can go to alleviate her problem. Nadwas furthermore form an important link in the transmission of knowledge and education and education from female religious scholars to the next generation. While girls generally learn about Islam at home, those with a desire for broader knowledge seek out a nadwa in someone's home.   (Clark 2004a: 169)

These discussion groups typically have shifting memberships and lack formal structure. Yet they figure prominently in Islamist fundraising, charitable activity, and mutual aid. Nadwas establish "free spaces" where authorities that fear militant Islam have trouble entering and where women who

109

live mainly sequestered lives can mingle.[1] For all their justified worries about religious extremism, Yemeni authorities can hardly forbid middle-class women from gathering for religiously respectable sociability.

Nadwas do not qualify in themselves as trust networks, but they provide an opportunity for members of Islamist trust networks to enter safe spaces where they can advance their ideas and recruit new members. This they do, not so much recruiting openly in the course of Qur'anic discussions as spotting likely members and inviting them to other nadwas in which Islamists play larger parts (Clark 2004a: 178). Thus a subversive network combines concealment and dissimulation under the cover of evasive conformity.

Islamist trust networks do not always remain underground and are often segregated from the regimes within which they live. Much to the dismay of revolutionaries and secular reformers who had risen against Iran's Shah, a dissident Islamist network centering on the Ayatollah Ruhollah Khomeini seized power in Iran as the Shah's secular opposition fragmented (Kepel 2002: 36–42, 106–135, Parsa 2000: 247–250). Although the Algerian government's ruthless military action eventually drove back the Islamist Groupe Islamique Armé, those zealots and their massacres of civilians shook the regime mightily during the 1990s (Kalyvas 1999). Gold that passed through Muslim trading networks – *hawalas* – helped bring the very Islamist Taliban to power in Afghanistan (Farah 2004: 113). In these cases, precisely what conservative Muslim rulers throughout the Middle East feared actually materialized: previously segregated trust networks made military bids for national power. In Iran, Sudan, and Afghanistan, they even succeeded in building their own theocracies, at least for a while. The thin control, intermittent coercion, and particularistic ties that rulers exercise in our zone of segregation neither give rulers access to resources embedded in trust networks nor contain the political threats they sometimes pose.

Negotiated Connections

To exploit and contain trust networks, rulers across the world often reached into them by means falling far short of full integration. They struck deals with trust networks' patrons in two different ways: patronage systems and brokered autonomy. In patronage systems, trust networks remained under the protection and control of powerful intermediaries who took

[1] Evans and Boyte 1986, Polletta 1999, Singerman 1995, Tilly 2000, Wiktorowicz 2001.

responsibility for containing them, but also drew resources from them to meet their own obligations vis à vis the regime. Such patrons often came from outside the trust network. Chapter 2 showed us thirteenth-century villagers in Spain's Galicia, for example, protecting themselves from the demands of León's king by seeking the patronage of powerful local monasteries. The villages became clients of patrons who in turn kept their distance from the king.

Brokered autonomy likewise involves patronage, but with a significant difference. In brokered autonomy, rulers grant formal recognition to a trust network, which retains distinctive rights and representation in return for negotiated payoffs going directly to the regime. In many parts of the world, trade diasporas established one relationship or the other to rulers of major commercial centers; either they lived under the patronage of some regional magnate, or they acquired formal licenses to trade as recognized foreign communities.

Seen from the top down, trust networks receiving protection from patrons escape from the ruler's repression, but gain relatively little toleration and even less facilitation from rulers. Recipients of brokered autonomy, in contrast, acquire toleration and at least a modicum of facilitation from rulers. From the trust network's bottom-up perspective, either arrangement centers on clientage rather than on concealment, dissimulation, or predation. Members of trust networks always pay something for the protection they receive, but who receives the payment makes a difference to the network's autonomy. On the whole, brokered autonomy provides greater guarantees that members can maintain their collective way of life.

Long before the nationalism of our time, Europeans frequently called beneficiaries of brokered autonomy "nations," with the implication of shared nativity rather than attachment to a particular nation-state. In Medieval Europe, the "nation" commonly meant a corporate group from the same geographic region, although it could also refer to members of a recognized religion. Among its several definitions of nation, the *Oxford English Dictionary* offers this one:

In the mediaeval universities, a body of students belonging to a particular district, country, or group of countries, who formed a more or less independent community; still retained in the universities of Glasgow and Aberdeen, in connexion with the election of the Rector. ("nation," definition 1c.)

In universities, cities, and other centers of consumption, such nations often elected their own officials and public representatives, provided for their own security, judged their own members' derelictions, and, in time of want, took responsibility for their own food supply. At their interfaces with local authorities, these common-origin trust networks created authoritative organizations. The very arrangement gave authorities pretexts and means for expelling whole communities – including religious minorities organized as nations – in times of famine, epidemic, or war (Tilly 1975: 437–440).

As we might expect, brokered autonomy often formed through an initial act of patronage by some authority. During the European Middle Ages, for example, regional potentates often recruited their own Jewish communities in order to organize their finances, promote trade, benefit from international connections, and produce taxable revenue. Polish rulers often welcomed Jews for their commercial skills and connections. Royal invitations to Poland's cities promoted a substantial movement of German-speaking Jews eastward. Yiddish (a dialect built largely on German) then became a common language in important parts of Northeastern Europe. Similarly, many Iberian Jews moved to North Africa and the Ottoman Empire, where their Muslim hosts opened special niches for them. (Iberian-origin Jews more often spoke the dialect called Ladino than Yiddish.)

A number of Jews also migrated to the more tolerant Italian city-states. Venice opened a new residential area for Jews, who had previously lived on the island of Giudecca – meaning "Jewish district" – in 1516. People called the new space Ghetto, "foundry" in Venetian, for the metal-working industry already established there. Afterward, the word *ghetto* applied to any city's Jewish quarter. From the two movements toward Poland and the Mediterranean springs the still common distinction between Ashkenazi and Sephardic Jews.

Lois Dubin has painstakingly reconstructed the acquisition of brokered autonomy by the Jewish community of Trieste. In 1382, the port city of Trieste, on the Adriatic's northeast coast, turned to the Habsburgs (by then hereditary Holy Roman Emperors) for protection from predatory Venice. During centuries of Venetian power and, to the south, Ottoman expansion, Trieste remained a small, minor connection between Vienna and the bustling Adriatic. During the early eighteenth century, however, Habsburg emperors began building their commercial presence in the Mediterranean region, including an expansion of trade with the still-formidable Ottoman Empire. Between 1719 and 1769, step by step the Habsburgs created, then expanded a tax-free port with open access to merchants of many nations. The effort succeeded: Trieste became a prosperous city, and the Habsburg empire's chief maritime center.

Jews lived in Trieste as early as the thirteenth century, and served as the city's authorized public bankers for centuries:

In the sixteenth and seventeenth centuries, certain Jewish individuals and families, such as the Levis in 1556 and Ventura Parente in 1624, resided in Trieste on the basis of the privileges granted them by Holy Roman emperors in return for their services of 'goods and blood' in time of war. These privileges promised sovereign protection and justice; unmolested practice of Judaism; the right of residence in any town where Jews already lived, including Vienna; unrestricted economic activities, including ownership of real property; the right of travel without distinguishing signs or special taxes; and immunity from any taxes not imposed on Christian merchants. (Dubin 1999: 18–19)

For their time, the Catholic Habsburgs were granting Trieste's Jews generous privileges. In Metz, for example, the French crown imposed stiff head taxes, additional fees, and obligations to supply and lodge royal troops on the Jewish community, yet did not give its Jewish merchants the secure right to travel within the kingdom (Miskimin 2002: 48–50).

Both Habsburg rulers and Trieste's municipal authorities were engaging in deliberate toleration, with a dollop of facilitation thrown in. The authorities were offering Trieste's Jews a measure of protection against the exploitation, violence, and vindictive anti-Semitism to which Jews elsewhere in Europe often fell prey. From the perspective of the city's Jews, full enlistment in the empire's public life set too high a price even if it were possible, since it would have required assimilation and conversion to Catholicism. Nor were concealment, dissimulation, or predation viable strategies for the Jews of Trieste. Clientage was the price they paid for protection.

Protection had its limits. Like their French cousins, the Habsburgs tried to contain the empire's Jewish populations. In 1697, after much wrangling with leaders of the Jewish community, the city established a formal ghetto, surrounded by three streets and protected by three gates, in the Portizza di Riborgo quarter. But free port activity spurred Jewish migration to Trieste, increased the Jewish community's prosperity, and multiplied the number of Jewish households enjoying particular permission to reside outside the ghetto. By the time of the ghetto's formal abolition in 1785, the majority of Trieste's Jewish population had long since lived elsewhere.

Nevertheless, the Jewish community maintained its brokered autonomy into the nineteenth century. Jews could not become citizens of Trieste, or serve on its governing council; they counted among the city's multiple recognized *nazioni*. (The regime used the revealing term *Università* to designate the Jewish and other such nations.) They maintained authorized but separate communal institutions. Calling its members *li Hebrei di Trieste*, the Jewish community conducted religious services, maintained a Jewish cemetery, controlled Jewish immigration, and imposed discipline on its unruly members. As the community grew, however, it formalized its relation to the regime. In 1746, it proposed and received government approval of an elaborate statute centering on an assembly of all tax-paying heads of households run and represented by two elected Capi. The 1746 Statute also institutionalized the offices of scribe, chancellor, rabbi, cantor, and beadle (Dubin 1999: 22–23). Within Trieste's Jewish trust network, they created an authoritative – and officially recognized – organization.

By 1782, the community was creating its own regime-authorized normal school: the *Scuola Pia Normale sive Talmud Torà*. The school took up space in the same ghetto building that also contained community offices, a kosher butcher, and a synagogue (Dubin 1999: 103). In 1788, when the Habsburg state became the first European power to draft Jews into its army, Trieste's Jews received exemption despite their leaders' expressed willingness to collaborate with the measure (Dubin 1999: 148–152). Meanwhile, Trieste's Jews successfully resisted the Habsburg state's efforts to impose German names and regulate marriage according to civil law. Not for another half century did the formal vestiges of brokered autonomy disappear.

Integrated Networks

Because we have until now concentrated on distant and contingent relations between trust networks and regimes, extensively integrated trust networks have rarely appeared in this book so far. We saw them in:

- the temporary integration of locally recruited military units into the Confederate Army
- accommodations between communities formed by chain migration and their local governments
- pirates who became privateers
- the (often reluctant) integration of parishes and confraternities into Europe's state churches

With the exception of migrant communities, none of these tells us much about integration between trust networks and the powerful states of our own time. Unexpected news on the subject comes from Russia's world of crime and violence. At considerable risk to his own safety, Vadim Volkov entered the world of violent entrepreneurs in the mid-1990s. He begins his book on the subject:

This book was triggered by an observation. In 1995, on my way to work, I used to walk past a mansion in central Petersburg that housed the headquarters of the Northwestern Regional Anti-Organized Crime Directorate (RUBOP). Each time I would observe the same scene: people of formidable physical proportions, with very short haircuts, wearing leather jackets or long dark overcoats, walked out of the RUBOP headquarters, got into black cars with tinted windows, and departed in various directions. Others parked nearby and entered the mansion. What struck me each time was that these people looked, moved, and gesticulated very much like those whom they were supposed to be fighting – members of organized criminal groups, the so-called bandits. (Volkov 2002: ix)

That observation led Volkov to a remarkable journey through the underside of the Soviet Union's disintegration.

In Soviet times, the government maintained a huge domestic security force, of which the KGB – the Committee for State Security – was best known outside the country. But in the interstices of the authoritarian system lurked petty criminals and enforcers who often came from sporting clubs: wrestlers, boxers, weight lifters, and martial arts experts. Mikhail Gorbachev's reforms of the 1980s produced four major changes in Russia's domestic security situation. First, the government greatly reduced its own professional security forces, throwing a large number of specialists in the use of force onto the private labor market. Second, the government consequently relaxed its surveillance and policing, giving more scope to criminals on the small scale and the large. Third, the withdrawal of the large Soviet army from its stalemate in Afghanistan poured thousands of combat-hardened veterans into the civilian labor force, where legitimate employment was hard to find. Finally, private businesses multiplied at all scales from local markets to privatized national industries. In the absence of effective policing, opportunities for extortion and protection rackets increased throughout Russia's commercially active regions.

At the bottom and the top, the enforcers who offered protective services at a price commonly belonged to trust networks: sworn bands of criminals, groups of sportsmen, former colleagues in the shady work of government security services, and veterans who had fought together in Afghanistan. Russian rates of reported extortion soared between 1989 and 1992, leveled off, and only started to decline in 1996 (Volkov 2002: 2–3). In a large Petersburg market, according to one of Volkov's informants:

In 1989 in Deviatkino all brigades stood side by side; initially, there were no clear divisions between *tambovskie, malyshevskie, Kazanskie* [gang names] and so forth, as happened later. Each brigade *poluchala* [received tribute] from *kommersanty* [businessmen, traders] who were not involved with other brigades. There was plenty of room for everyone. We also set up our own *kommersanty*, provided them with trading spots, and then protected them for a fee. The only rule was that we not assault or rob each other's *kommersanty*. (Volkov 2002: 15)

Later, in Petersburg and elsewhere, gangs began killing each other off as they competed for larger shares of the protection racket. In the process they developed increasingly elaborate hierarchies and divisions of labor.

Enforcers did not only engage in extortion and protection rackets. They also went into the businesses of debt collection, illegal commodities, sexual services, and physical protection for businessmen. A rough three-way division of labor emerged among 1) old fashioned bandits, thugs, and thieves, 2) local racketeers and, 3) increasingly organized operators of private protective services in major cities and at a national scale. Through the later 1990s, Volkov argues, category 3 moved increasingly into the public sphere as legitimate business, essentially substituting commercial services for the policing, protection, and contract enforcement the state itself had ceased to provide. They also began to operate their own legitimate businesses, whether legally or illegally acquired. Their leaders came disproportionately, in fact, from the ranks of retired state specialists in law enforcement. In the process, the more successful among them were using their trust networks to create formidable, and increasingly recognized, authoritative organizations.

Some sportsmen also made it to the top. Volkov tells the tale of Boris Ivaniuzhenkov, who became the Russian minister of sports in 1999:

it took him four days to accept the offer by then prime minister Sergei Stepashin (former head of the MVD and then of the FSB) that he become minister of sports. In police files, Ivaniuzhenkov is known as 'Rotan,' the right-hand man of Sergei Lalakin ('Lutchok'), the leader of the Podol'skaya criminal group. Born in the suburban town of Podol'sk near Moscow, Ivaniuzhenkov embarked on a dual career, achieving the title of master of sports in wrestling and a leading position in the local racketeering group. Podol'sk, he claims, 'is the only town where there were never any feuds. The situation was always stable.' In other respects, *podol'skie* went through the same evolution as many other similar organizations. They took control of the local market, trades, and businesses, consolidating power in the locale and expanding beyond it. The ability to maintain order and to give generously to charity... brought the

116

violent entrepreneurs popular support: Lalakin 'Lutchok' was made an honorary citizen of Podol'sk, and Ivaniuzhenkov ('Rotan') was elected to the Moscow *oblast'* legislature in 1997. (Volkov 2002: 187)

In the career of wrestler-gangster Lutchok we witness the integration of formerly criminal trust networks – those of the Podol'skaya gang – into public politics.

The violence-wielding trust networks studied by Vadim Volkov pursued spectacular paths toward integration into Russian public politics. As Margaret Levi's analysis of conscription should remind us, most paths toward the same sort of integration have a more familiar air. They include governments' establishment of veterans' benefits, recognition or incorporation of mutual benefit organizations, protection of religious congregations, institutionalization of craft-based interest groups, formation of ties between governmental service providers and their clienteles, development of solidarities within political parties or publicly active voluntary associations, and political sponsorship of musical groups, sports teams, or ethnic clubs. All these paths to integration move away from the concealment, dissimulation, and predation that prevail at the bottom of our range from segregation to integration. Some pass through the clientage of the middle zone. Some respond to the dissolution of previously existing trust networks. But all of them involve enlistment and bargaining to a far larger extent than the bulk of the trust networks we have examined so far.

Origins of Integration

Let us step away from the trajectories of particular trust networks to survey processes by which such networks become integrated into public politics. As Chapter 1 said, when that integration occurs, we should expect to find people creating publicly recognized associations, mutual-aid societies, parties, unions, congregations, and communities, or seeking recognition for similar organizations that have existed underground, pursuing friendship, kinship, shared belief, security, and high-risk enterprises within such organizations, and a whole series of other things connecting locally consequential long-term activities and interpersonal ties to the vagaries of public politics. Historically, such reliance on public political actors and governmental agents for support of risky activities and relations has rarely occurred.

In our sweep across history, nevertheless, we have already encountered some historical circumstances in which that rare outcome actually emerged.

117

Trust networks in the form of religious sects, kinship groups, or mercantile networks have occasionally established their own systems of rule (example: John Calvin's religious conquest of Geneva). Regimes have sometimes conquered other regimes that were already run by trust networks (example: Canadian or U.S. conquest and incorporation of intact Indian tribes). Political actors organized as trust networks have sometimes seized state power in established regimes (example: the Taliban in Afghanistan). Once in power, rulers have often created their own trust networks in the forms of dynastic marriage alliances and internal patronage systems (examples: almost all European monarchies before the nineteenth century).

High levels of integration have actually occurred. At least temporarily, totalitarian and theocratic regimes have managed extensive incorporation of existing trust networks into authoritarian systems of rule (example: Italian Fascist integration of those craft organizations they did not destroy). Democracies, finally, accomplish partial integration of trust networks into public politics (example: the repeated extension of benefits to U.S. military veterans from the Civil War onward, which not only created individual rights but tied veterans' organizations directly to the state; Skocpol 1998).

Reculer pour mieux sauter: Having stepped back, we make a heroic leap. Among these marvelously varied historical circumstances, do some common processes occur? The *outcomes* certainly have some common properties. In all of them, a government and/or a political actor exercising regular relations with that government (for example, a state church or trade unions with their own internal networks of mutual aid) connects trust networks to public politics. In all of them (as Figure 5.1 predicts), facilitation by rulers combines with rulers' reliance on commitment in addition to coercion and capital, with the result of a relatively stable integration of trust networks into political regimes.

How, in general, could that rare historical occurrence actually happen? Among all the possible transforming processes, here are the most promising candidates:

1. Existing segregated trust networks shrivel, disintegrate, or lose capacity to sustain their members' vital activities, thus making their constituencies more readily available for politically connected trust networks.
2. New risks and risky activities appear against which existing trust networks are incapable of defending their members.

3. Populations multiply outside of existing trust networks, thereby becoming available for politically connected trust networks.
4. Rulers or major political actors destroy existing trust networks, with similar effects.
5. Rulers or major political actors effectively integrate existing networks into public politics.
6. Rulers or major political actors create politically connected networks and recruit people to them.

We have seen how energetically members of trust networks across history have fought off these six processes, striving both to maintain their own networks and to shield them from political intervention. We have seen them defending their boundaries, securing external resources, monitoring members' external connections, and exerting control over internal social relations that might disrupt their networks' collective activities.

The major exceptions were members of ruling classes, who could bend the state to their own ends instead of fearing that its intervention in their trust networks would frustrate those ends. Even they typically moved into relations with governments and other major political actors tentatively, often relying on intermediaries with whom they had already established relations of trust as their initial connectors. Such intermediaries often included kin, churchmen, commercial collaborators, landlords, and local power holders who also occupied positions of power at a national scale. Those intermediaries served as brokers in the process of integration.

Marjolein 't Hart points out that the new Dutch state, unlike its European rivals, already enjoyed excellent credit during the seventeenth century. The Netherlands' seventeenth-century revolt against Spain led to an ordering of public finances in that supremely commercial regime. In the process, Dutch burghers began investing furiously in government securities, thus tying their families' fates to that of the regime:

In part, the Dutch success must be explained by the fact that the chief investors were magistrates and politicians themselves. They were close enough to their local receiver with whom they had contracted loans. At times, they were urged to invest by their political leaders so as to stimulate other buyers. The federal structure implied also a large degree of local political control. Other secure investments were found in land and houses, but already by 1700 the capital invested in government bonds exceeded all other. ('t Hart 1993: 178)

The segmented structure of the Dutch Republic, 't Hart reminds us, facilitated the work of brokers who simultaneously occupied municipal,

119

provincial, and national positions of power. They helped make the Dutch Republic precocious in its integration of elite trust networks (Adams 1994, 1994b, Davids and Lucassen 1995, Glete 2002). It took another two centuries before ordinary Europeans and North Americans began investing major parts of their savings in government securities.

Sooner or later, however, it happened widely. Ordinary people face risks and carry on risky long-term enterprises even when their available trust networks fail to give them adequate protection. In those circumstances, governments or political actors that can either shore up existing networks or create new alternatives to them become more attractive – or at least less unattractive – allies. As the Dutch example suggests, some additional circumstances increase the attractiveness of politically connected trust networks to a broad public: creation of external guarantees for governmental commitments, as when a peace treaty or an occupying power backs up a defeated government's finances; increase in governmental resources for risk reduction and/or compensation of loss, as when commercial expansion generates new tax revenues; and visible governmental meeting of commitments to the advantage of substantial new segments of the population, as when noncitizens not only become eligible for welfare benefits but actually receive them.

The Integration of Proletarians

In Western history of the last half millennium, one large process has swamped all others in its promotion of items 1 to 3 on our list of transforming processes: failure of existing trust networks, appearance of new risks, and multiplication of populations outside of existing trust networks. That process is proletarianization, an increase in the share of the total population depending on wages for survival and/or working at means of production over which they exercise little or no control. Europe experienced stupendous growth in its proletarian population after 1500. My own best guesses of total European population by category from 1500 to 1900 appear in Table 5.1. They suggest massive proletarianization, with a surprising proportion of it occurring in small towns and rural areas before the urban proletarianization of the nineteenth century.

Three major factors converged in producing this explosive growth: capitalist consolidation of control over the means of production, including agricultural land; multiplication of opportunities for wage labor in agriculture, cottage industry, and (later) in urban production of goods and services;

Table 5.1. *Estimated Proletarianization of the European Population, 1500–1900*

	Millions of people		
	1500	1800	1900
total population	56	150	285
nonproletarians	39	50	85
proletarians in cities	1	10	75
rural proletarians	16	90	125
% of total proletarian	30.0	66.7	70.2

Source: Tilly 1984: 36.

and a natural increase in a proletariat that, on the average, married earlier and had more children than its counterparts in land-owning and tool-owning labor (Levine 1984, Tilly 1984).

Wage-earning proletarians became even more vulnerable to seasonal and longer-term economic swings than were most peasants and artisans. They survived more or less well when landlords and merchants hired them, but did badly in times of unemployment. Yet landlords and merchants could not do without them. Thus poverty became a problem for public policy at the municipal and national scales. Critics of the poor, including rulers, created a public mythology castigating vagabonds, wastrels, beggars, and idle layabouts for their lack of prudence and self-discipline. At the same time, however, authorities organized disciplined provision for the labor force in times of need. "In sum," comment Catharina Lis and Hugo Soly,

during the late fifteenth and early sixteenth centuries the criticism of idleness and its counterpart, the exaltation of work, became major themes in the writings of both prominent men and middling people, laity and clergy, and Catholics and Protestants throughout western Europe. Their reaction was not limited to mere words. In the Netherlands (1531), France (1534), England (1531 and especially 1536), Scotland (1535), and Spain (1541), the central authorities proclaimed ordinances concerning begging and/or poor relief; detailed regulations were, however, relegated to the local governments. Between 1522 and 1545 some 62 towns created a coordinated system of public assistance: at least 30 in Germany, 15 or 16 in the Low Countries, 8 in France, 6 in Switzerland, and 2 in northern Italy. In nearly all towns two principles dominated: strict prohibition of begging for the able-bodied poor, regardless of age and sex, in order to compel them to accept work at any wage, and centralization of existing funds into a 'common box' to enable the selection and control of the 'true needy.' (Lis and Soly 1984: 168; see also Lis and Soly 1979)

121

The distinction between the worthy and unworthy poor hinged especially on the readiness of the worthy to perform disciplined low-wage work when the opportunity arrived. Moralists and authorities alike condemned idleness and improvidence. They both blamed poor people for profligacy. But at least local authorities recognized the necessity of tiding the worthy over recurrent bouts of unemployment, seasonal or longer term.

Few historians, alas, have documented interactions among proletarianization, poor relief, and trust networks. In a painstaking study of Amsterdam's poor relief between 1800 and 1850, Marco van Leeuwen has nevertheless established several crucial points. He uncovers an elaborate system of poor relief divided chiefly among Catholic, Calvinist, Jewish, and municipal authorities. Each one kept meticulous records of its clientele; hence the possibility of van Leeuwen's analysis. Each one imposed extensive conditions of membership, worthiness, and eligibility: were the applicants faithful and upright members of their religious congregations? Did they genuinely lack opportunities to earn wages honestly? Did they have secret accumulations of wealth? Could other people take responsibility for their welfare?

In 1809, such rules produced a clientele of 1,968 adults for the Ashkenazi Charity; two thirds consisted of the elderly, the infirm, widows with children, and/or families with three or more children (van Leeuwen 2000: 107). Even in these cases, van Leeuwen shows, poor relief usually amounted to no more than a supplement, far short of enough money for survival. Amsterdam's poor households were surely relying on local trust networks, however fragile, for much of the rest.

Because Amsterdam's poor Jews concentrated in street vending, garment making, domestic service, and a few other low-paying trades, Jewish charities' clientele differed from those of other charitable organizations. Dockers led by far among the men aided by the municipal and Lutheran charities (van Leeuwen 2000: 112). As an important port, Amsterdam swung from intense economic activity during the warm months to a frequent standstill during the winter. Van Leeuwen argues persuasively that Amsterdam's authorities adopted an implicit policy of fixing a mobile labor force in place by supplying just enough poor relief in the off season to allow dockers and similar workers to get through the year without emigrating. The same system permitted the authorities to exercise moral surveillance and control.

Not all of Amsterdam's workers, however, depended on public poor relief. Craftsmen generally belonged to guilds, which paid benefits far higher than poor relief to their sick, disabled, and aged members as well as to widows and children of deceased craftsmen. In 1811, Amsterdam had about 14,000 guild members in a total city population of about 200,000 (van Leeuwen 2000: 167). As the nineteenth century wore on, voluntary mutual-aid societies, sickness benefit groups, and burial associations all became popular; by century's end, some 40 percent of the city's population belonged to a mutual-benefit association of some kind (van Leeuwen 2000: 166). But all these varieties of trust networks operated with official sanction, under public scrutiny. Although van Leeuwen does not put it this way, he is describing the integration of popular trust networks into public politics. He is describing the early phases of a momentous transformation, a reversal of age-old segregation.

Citing van Leeuwen along the way, Peter Lindert has greatly generalized the story. Looking at a large number of countries, he has established how regularly economic expansion has led to formation of redistributive systems of social spending, especially as ordinary workers acquired political voice. "Since the eighteenth century," he remarks,

the rise of tax-based social spending has been at the heart of government growth. It was social spending, not national defense, public transportation, or government enterprises, that accounted for most of the rise in governments' taxing and spending as a share of GDP over the last two centuries. (Lindert 2004: I, 20)

But wage-labor became more central to economies, first in the West and then across the world. As it did so, redistributive social spending skyrocketed. Most of that increase has occurred recently. Before the twentieth century, as the Amsterdam case illustrates, social spending never sufficed to maintain poor people in idleness, much less to entice them away from viable employment. Conservative critics to the contrary notwithstanding, Lindert challenges the view that welfare benefits sap initiative.

Lindert concludes that social spending stabilized the labor force and increased its productive capacity. Because it did so, even very high levels of expenditure occurred at little or no net cost to the whole economy. Amsterdam's city fathers were anticipating a strategy that eventually attracted capitalists and public authorities across the world. But capitalists and public authorities did not simply drift in an irresistible river. Which policies governments adopted, Lindert continues, depended closely on the organization of public politics. Great Britain led Europe in poor relief between the 1780s and 1834 because its great landlords invested in retaining their agricultural labor force. But when the Reform Act of 1832 gave industrial capitalists new voice, a dramatic cutback in benefits occurred (Lindert 2004: I, 67–86).

Nevertheless, a rapidly urbanizing and industrializing Great Britain also raised its levels of social spending during the later nineteenth century, and became a world leader in redistributive programs during the twentieth century. Where the Roman Catholic Church wielded great political influence, to take another case in point, its opposition to public programs slowed their expansion until after World War II. Then an increasingly anti-Communist Church began to support social spending as it fashioned Christian democracy into a competitive political strategy (Lindert 2004: I, 216–217).

To be sure, Lindert neither uses the language of trust networks nor shows us in detail how connections between trust networks and public politics proliferated during the momentous shifts he does document. Let us leave it as a plausible pair of conjectures: proletarianization overwhelmed existing trust networks wherever it occurred, but in response major political actors and governments created trust networks of their own. That meant establishing boundaries between insiders and outsiders, monitoring connections between members and outsiders, securing resources to maintain the networks' collective activities, and exerting control over internal relations that could disrupt those collective activities.

Lindert's analysis also identifies another strong force for integration of trust networks over the last century or so: democratization. The acquisition of political voice by ordinary people, he shows, promoted increases in social spending. The expansion of public education, social services, income guarantees, and various forms of insurance backed by political guarantees, in its turn, offered ordinary people attractive alternatives to reliance on kin, fellow migrants, coreligionists, and other members of private trust networks for the buffering of risk. Although the next chapter will portray some minimum integration of trust networks into public politics as a necessary condition for democratization, the relationship surely runs in both directions: under favorable conditions, politically backed trust networks and democratic institutions reinforce each other.

6

Trust and Democratization

History performed a nasty experiment in Ireland. Through English arms and anglophile landlords' exploitation, it produced two colonies where colonizers and subjects shared broadly similar culture, language, and genetic heritage, where the vast bulk of the population lacked political voice, where religious divisions formed part of governmental structure, but where in two separate regions those divisions produced contrasting alignments vis à vis rulers across the Irish Sea. Centuries before Irish independence, differences between mainly Protestant Ulster and Ireland's overwhelmingly Catholic remainder deeply marked Irish politics.

In both regions, trust networks formed chiefly within channels of religious affiliation. In Ulster, Scottish settlers had planted a Presbyterian church that still retains a substantial following. During the sixteenth century, English conquerors established the Church of Ireland, a counterpart to the Church of England, and granted it the right – like its English counterpart – to draw revenues from the entire population. (For convenience and as a reminder of its special standing, I will call the Church of Ireland "Anglican.") In Ulster and elsewhere, the rest of the population stuck mainly with the Roman Catholic Church. Starting with England's sixteenth-century conquests, vitriol and violence flowed in both directions across Irish regional and religious boundaries. On one side occurred extensive integration of Protestants into the system of rule; on the other, enforced segregation of Catholics.

During his 1835 tour of Ireland, Alexis de Tocqueville asked the Catholic bishop of Carlow one of his standard questions: whether having the British government pay salaries to Ireland's Catholic clergy would improve their living standards and ease political conflict. Both Tocqueville and the bishop understood the question's background: Ireland's Anglican clergy were collecting tithes from Protestants and Catholics alike, Catholic clergy were living on much lower incomes than Anglicans, and Catholic activists were agitating against the Anglican tithe. The bishop denied that salaries would work well:

The Catholic clergy would then lose its influence over ordinary people. I don't know what's right for other countries, but I have no doubt that in Ireland the clergy would lose badly from such a change, and religion itself could only suffer. In this country, incredible solidarity exists between the clergy and the common people.

(Tocqueville 1991: 528)

Five days later, on July 25, 1835, Tocqueville spoke with John Patrick Prendergast – Tocqueville wrote *Pointdergast* – Dublin Protestant lawyer and historian. The French visitor asked his question again. "I don't think so," replied his informant.

In every country, and especially in Ireland, the Catholic clergy seeks domination. It has decided to expel the Protestants and rule Irish society single-handedly. It will never give up that ambition, whatever we do. It will not sacrifice its aims for money and instead will use any money it receives to pursue its ends.

(Tocqueville 1991: 548–549)

Both sides exaggerated. Catholic peasants had their differences with a demanding church hierarchy, and Catholic churchmen repeatedly settled for their pieces of Irish power. But in 1835 both sides clearly saw a yawning chasm between a privileged Protestant minority and a stigmatized Catholic majority. Prodded by Tocqueville's questioning, Prendergast conceded that his faction excluded the few rich Catholics from the national elite and staffed the Irish government almost entirely with Protestants (Tocqueville 1991: 549). By excluding Catholic elites, power-holding Protestants reinforced the religious division and drove Catholics into the arms of their clergy.

No doubt recalling the revolutionary fate of the French aristocracy to which his family had belonged, Tocqueville reflected on Irish polarization. In any society where the aristocracy had done what the Irish Protestant aristocracy had done:

You will surely have terrible social conditions: conditions in which the aristocracy will have all the defects and all the doctrines of oppressors and the people will have all the vices and weaknesses of slaves; where the law will destroy what it should protect, violence will protect what elsewhere it seeks to destroy; where religion will seem to gain its strength from the very passions it should be combating, existing only to maintain hatred and to keep men from establishing the brotherhood it endlessly preaches.

(Tocqueville 1991: 556)

In a language Tocqueville never employed, Protestant and Catholic trust networks confronted each other across the chasm, the one set of networks built into the apparatus of rule, the other supported by a well connected church but driven at best to evasive conformity. Yet somehow over the next century and a half the polarized zone shrank to the contested territory of Northern Ireland, and the rest of the country created a more or less viable democracy. What happened in Ireland?

What happened was a series of civil wars ending in a revolutionary transfer of power. Table 6.1 provides a crude chronology of Protestant-Catholic struggles in Ireland over the last five centuries. After assimilation of earlier Anglo-Norman conquerors and colonists, Ireland settled into several centuries of competition among indigenous chiefs and kings. Beginning with Henry VIII, however, Tudor invasions generated a new round of armed resistance. Thus began almost five centuries during which some group of Irish powerholders has always aligned with Great Britain, and multiple other powerholders have always aligned against Great Britain. Between the 1690s and the 1780s, even propertied Catholics lacked any rights to participate in Irish public politics. From the 1780s to the 1820s, they still suffered serious political disabilities. Since the sixteenth century Ireland has rarely moved far from virulent, violent rivalries. The island has repeatedly careened into civil war.

Not until the nineteenth century did Ireland become a democratizing country. From the viewpoint of democratization, we might single out 1801, 1829, 1869, 1884, and 1919–1923 as crucial dates. In 1801, dissolution of the exclusively Protestant Irish Parliament and absorption of 100 Irish Protestants into its United Kingdom counterpart actually de-democratized an already oligarchic regime; it shattered the unequal accommodations that Ireland's Catholic elites had established with their Protestant rulers. Even elite networks of kinship and religion lost connection with the Irish system of rule. Passage of the Catholic Emancipation in 1829 (which followed similar political concessions to non-Anglican Protestants by a year) reversed that segregation. It gave Ireland's wealthier Catholics formal representation and rights to hold most public offices in the United Kingdom.

During the nineteenth century, demands for Irish autonomy or independence nevertheless swelled. Conflict between tenants and landlords was exacerbated and public shows of force on either side repeatedly generated street violence in Northern Ireland (Tilly 2003b: 111–127). A campaign for home rule brought disestablishment of the previously official Church of Ireland in 1869. Despite the eventual backing of prime minister William

Table 6.1. *Landmark Dates of Irish Protestant-Catholic Relations*

1520–1603	Tudor invasions, plantations, rebellions, civil wars, establishment of Irish Protestant Church
1610–1640	Stuart dispossessions, English and Scottish settlements in Ireland, especially Ulster
1641–1650	rebellions and civil war in England and Ireland, ending with Cromwell's brutal conquest of Ireland
1689–1691	Glorious Revolution in England, civil war in Ireland, reconquest by William III, sharp abridgement of Catholic political rights, massive seizure of Catholic property continuing to 1703
1782–1783	partial restoration of Irish political autonomy, Catholic rights to acquire land and to teach (but Irish Parliament still exclusively Protestant)
1791–1795	United Irishmen (autonomist, increasingly Catholic) and Orange Order (loyalist, Protestant) form
1798	United Irish risings, civil war, massacres, French invasions, bloody suppression
1801	creation of United Kingdom (England, Wales, Scotland, Ireland), abolition of Irish Parliament, incorporation of 100 Irish Protestant MPs into U.K. Parliament
1813–1829	repeated campaigns for Catholic Emancipation in England and Ireland, mass mobilizations for Emancipation in Ireland, against it in England, final passage of parliamentary acts expanding (but not entirely equalizing) Catholic political rights, raising property requirements for the Irish franchise, and dissolving Daniel O'Connell's Catholic Association
1830s–1890s	numerous antilandlord and antitithe actions, failed agitation for Irish home rule
1845–1850	potato famine, leading to large-scale emigration
1843–	major Protestant-Catholic violence in Belfast, especially 1843, 1857, 1864, 1872, 1886, 1893
1848	Young Ireland uprising in Munster
1858	founding of Irish Republic Brotherhood (Fenians) in Dublin and New York
1867	Fenian risings in Ireland, Clan na Gael founded in New York
1869	Church of Ireland (Anglican) disestablished
1884	Franchise Act greatly expands rural (and almost entirely Catholic) electorate
1916	Easter Rising, with German support
1919–1923	civil wars, first producing separate governments and parliaments for North and South (1921), then creation of Irish Free State excluding Northern Ireland (1922)
1923–2004	intermittent Protestant-Catholic struggles in Northern Ireland, frequent involvement of British troops, suspension and restitution of successive Northern Ireland governments
1949	declaration of independent Irish Republic, still excluding Northern Ireland

Gladstone, however, Home Rule itself failed to pass the U.K. Parliament. Irish Protestants rallied against such measures to the theme that "Home rule is Rome rule" (McCracken 2001: 262). The Franchise Act of 1884, simultaneous with Great Britain's Third Reform Act, awarded the vote to most of the adult male Irish population, and thus greatly expanded the rural Catholic electorate. By that time, however, each major party had attached itself to a single religious segment. Catholic-based parties had committed themselves decisively to Irish autonomy or independence.

After multiple anti-British risings over the previous sixty years, the question of military service on behalf of the United Kingdom split Ireland profoundly during World War I. In 1919, wartime divisions broke into civil war. The Treaty of 1922 established a largely autonomous and overwhelmingly Catholic Irish Free State with dominion status parallel to those of Canada and Australia. Meanwhile, a Protestant-majority Northern Ireland remained closely attached to the United Kingdom, but divided even more sharply along religious lines than before.

In the rest of Ireland, direct-action segments of the Irish Republican Army continued to attack Protestants and suspected British collaborators for another year (Hart 1998). Militantly republican forces lost both the Irish Free State's general election of 1922 and the civil war that followed it. Yet republican militants survived, and eventually got the full independence from Great Britain for which they had fought. Since the 1920s, the IRA has repeatedly made armed incursions into Northern Ireland (for surveys, see Keogh 2001, White 1993). Stable democracy has by no means arrived in the North. But the Irish Free State gained virtual independence (as Eire) in 1937 and became the fully independent Irish Republic in 1949. Those increasingly autonomous southern regimes worked more or less democratically from the peace settlement of 1922 onward.

Trust Networks and Irish Democratization

How will we recognize democracy and democratization? Let us not settle for mere competitive elections, which leave open great possibilities for oppressive rule, not to mention manipulation of the elections themselves (Engelstad and Østerud 2004). Here, democracy means the extent to which subjects of a given government enjoy relatively broad, equal rights and obligations vis à vis that government's agents, exercise binding consultation with regard to that government's personnel, policies, and resources, and receive protection from arbitrary action by governmental agents

129

(Tilly 2004a, Chapter 1). Note the watchwords: equality, breadth, consultation, and protection. Consultation includes not only voting but also referenda, lobbying, interest group membership, social movement mobilization, and direct contact with politicians.

Democratization means movement toward greater breadth, equality, consultation, and protection of mutual rights and obligations between citizens and governmental agents. De-democratization means movement away from breadth, equality, consultation, and protection. By these standards, Ireland was a very undemocratic place at the start of the nineteenth century, and had democratized significantly by the 1920s. Ireland's democratization occurred through mighty, bloody struggle (Tilly 2004a: 136–164).

How do trust networks figure in this turbulent history? We have little direct evidence on Irish trust networks as such, but we do know something about configurations of kin groups, religious congregations, fraternal orders, sporting clubs, and militant nationalist organizations. Close studies of local conflict, furthermore, provide graphic evidence concerning the involvement of these sorts of organizations in public politics.[1] In his superb close study of Cork between 1916 and 1923, for example, Peter Hart shows how the Irish Republican Army drew on previously existing youth networks, and took on their forms:

I.R.A. units were a natural extension of this youth subculture and its body of unspoken assumptions and bonds. Usually benign events and practices became vehicles for political mobilization, and customs such as 'strawing' became part of the political struggle. The family resemblance between the majority of I.R.A. 'operations' and the actions of the Straw Boys is close and clear: the same use of masks or blackened and painted faces, often the same 'queer clothes,' the same-sized gangs of young bachelors acting anonymously under a 'captain,' the same pseudo-military posturing, and the same nocturnal raiding and petty intimidation.

(Hart 1998: 180)

Let us therefore make two strong assumptions: that the visible forms of popular connection contained trust networks, and that their overall segregation from or integration into systems of rule tells us about trust and rule in Ireland.

On that assumption, each of the critical dates – 1829, 1869, 1884, and 1919–1923 – created new ties between Catholics' trust networks and the ruling regime. Each transition shook earlier control of the regime by

---

[1] Broeker 1970, Bryan 2000, Clark and Donnelly 1983, Conley 1999a, 1999b, Farrell 2000, Jarman 1997, Jupp and Magennis 2000, O'Neill 2001, Palmer 1988.

elite Protestant networks. Under the Free State, Eire, and the Republic, integration of trust networks operated mainly through intermediary organizations such as political parties, trade unions, and religious congregations rather than through direct connections between governmental agents and trust networks. Contrary to the earlier fears of Protestant militants, nothing like a theocracy emerged in Ireland. The Catholic Church as such never acquired either an intimate connection with the national government or a dominant position in Irish public politics. Instead, both the church hierarchy and local priests exercised their influence through authority among the faithful.

That authority, to be sure, remained impressive. Ireland's government took care not to offend ecclesiastical authorities and Catholic popular sentiment. The only significant clash between the church hierarchy and the government occurred in 1951, when prelates objected to the terms of the government's new maternal health scheme. A new plan soon mollified the church (Lynch 2001: 285). As a result of the church's influence, Ireland has moved more slowly than its European neighbors on such religiously tinged policy questions as contraception, abortion, and divorce. But it has moved in the same directions.

A Dutch ethnographer's remarkable study of an Irish rural area during the later 1960s provides evidence for brokered integration of local trust networks into national politics. In the (unnamed) region where Mart Bax lived, political parties did not represent distinct class or sectoral interests, but assiduously aggregated local interests. Both county and national legislators fought for their positions by using their governmental connections to do concrete favors for their actual or prospective constituents. As much as possible, they undercut the ability of their competitors to do similar favors.

A successful Irish politician, Bax tells us, used and created multiple ties of friendship, kinship, and voluntary association membership with constituents. He (the vast majority were male) also maintained a cadre of local brokers, most frequently within his party's clubs. Students of politics elsewhere will recognize some standard patterns of patronage systems (see e.g., Auyero 2000, Fox 1994, Willerton 1992). Irish patronage, in Bax's account, provided many of the most important connections between citizens and government. Only so long as a politician delivered governmental goods to local trust networks did he maintain his following.

Among his many tales of connections, Bax tells of Patricksville broker Tadgh O'Sullivan. A shoemaker, electric meter reader, and journalist, O'Sullivan participated actively in the Gaelic Athletic Association, became general secretary of the regional Fianna Fail party organization, and helped the incumbent member of parliament win election. Much of his day-to-day business consisted of doing favors by exercising his personal influence within governmental agencies. "One night," reports Bax,

a businessman from a nearby town dropped in at the O'Sullivans. The man was in trouble: the importation of a shipment of commodities was delayed at the Customs. It was of vital importance for the man to have it next day. O'Sullivan was asked whether he could help. He promptly rang up one of the ministers living close to the harbour; he was in and told Tadgh to bring the businessman down to his home. The two drove to the minister's house, the man explained his case and the minister told him he would do his best. Next evening the businessman was back at the O'Sullivans and he told him that he was delighted that the matter was fixed.

(Bax 1976: 96–97)

Later, the businessman arranged O'Sullivan's purchase of a motorbike at half price, and promised support in future elections. O'Sullivan was exercising "pull" – capacity to deliver services from the government. In the Irish system, if a politician loses pull, he loses influence and office. But that pull connects local trust networks of kinship, friendship, sport, and fraternity with the regional and national governments.

Trust in Democracy

How do such connections affect democracy? Robert Putnam's work on Italy and the United States puts the connections between trust and democracy prominently on the agenda of democratic theory without actually stating a clear argument concerning the causal chain between trust and democracy. Putnam's *Making Democracy Work* provides evidence of a significant relationship between the perceived effectiveness of governmental institutions in an Italian region and the extent of participation in nongovernmental civic associations in the same region: the greater the participation, the higher the effectiveness. A theoretical slide then occurs at each end of Putnam's argument. On the side of governmental institutions, Putnam drifts into interpreting more effective institutions as more democratic. On the side of civic engagement, Putnam begins to treat organizational networks, social capital, norms of reciprocity, and fabrics of trust as an indissoluble block. This double glissando leads to his book's final sentence: "Building social capital will not be easy, but it is the key to making democracy work" (Putnam 1993: 185).

Similarly, in the United States, Putnam moves hurriedly from civic involvement to democracy:

Modern society is replete with opportunities for free-riding and opportunism. Democracy does not require that citizens be selfless saints, but in many modest ways it does assume that most of us much of the time will resist the temptation to cheat. Social capital, the evidence increasingly suggests, strengthens our better, more expansive selves. The performance of our democratic institutions depends in measurable ways upon social capital. (Putnam 2000: 349)

At best, then, we can draw from Putnam's analyses a much more modest conclusion: *within already relatively democratic regimes*, people who engage in civic organizations (or perhaps only in organizations oriented to the public good) are more likely to meet their collective obligations, to press for better government performance, and to trust their fellow citizens (Bermeo 2000). Such an argument may well be valid, but it tells us little about the causal connections between democracy and trust.

Recent democratic theorists have made four main claims about the bearing of trust on democracy as such:

1. As Margaret Levi's analysis of contingent consent indicates, collaboration with government on the basis of commitment rather than coercion depends on expectations that others will bear fair shares of the governmental burden – pay their taxes, perform their military service, and so on.
2. Democracies are supposed to require higher levels of trust in government than other sorts of regimes because the voluntary delegation of powers to representatives and officials can only occur on the basis of extensive trust.
3. Alternation of factions in power depends on the trust of current non-incumbents that their turn will come, or at least that incumbents will honor their interests.
4. From the perspectives of most political actors democracy is inherently a riskier, more contingent system than others; therefore only actors having significant trust in the outcomes of democratic politics will collaborate with the system at all.

All four claims make a certain level of trust a necessary condition for democracy and imply that a significant decline in trust threatens democracy. All four imply that authoritarian and patronage-based regimes can survive with much lower levels of trust than democracies.

133

Mark Warren neatly knits together the four claims by pointing out the contradictions between public politics and trust. Politics, for Warren, combines conflicts over goods, pressures to associate for collective action, and attempts to produce collectively binding decisions (Warren 1999: 311). All these processes – goods conflicts, collective action, and bids for collectively binding decisions – occur more widely in the public politics of democracies. But precisely those processes threaten naturally accumulated trust: goods conflicts generate dissension, collective action brings us-them boundaries into play, and collectively binding decisions mean unequal realization of individual and group interests. Thus democracies require greater trust – at least with regard to outcomes of political struggle – than other sorts of regimes. We might call Warren's formulation *the democratic dilemma of trust*.

Warren identifies three competing theoretical solutions to the democratic dilemma: neoconservative, rational choice, and deliberative. The neoconservative view, typified by Francis Fukuyama, declares that the only way to mitigate the dilemma is to minimize the number of collective decisions made by political institutions and maximize those lodged where trust of one kind or another already exists: natural communities and markets. Rational choice approaches, exemplified by Russell Hardin, make trust a belief that another (a person or an institution) has an interest in one's own welfare; hence institutions that guarantee beneficial performance help resolve the democratic dilemma. The deliberative solution, which Warren himself prefers, bridges the gap by making democratic deliberation and trust mutually complementary: the very process of deliberation generates trust, but the existence of trust facilitates deliberation. The neoconservative theory identifies no necessary connection between democracy and trust, whereas the rational choice and deliberative theories make trust uniquely indispensable to democracy.

My argument likewise addresses the democratic dilemma, but radically recasts it and proposes a fourth solution. By now, readers who have traveled with me this far should find the recasting and resolution familiar. They consist of:

- treating trust as a relationship in which at least one party places valued enterprises at risk to the errors, failures, or malfeasance of another party
- recognizing that such relationships cluster in distinctive networks, especially as the duration and stakes of the valued enterprises increase

134

- further recognizing that although historically most trust networks have grown up outside of public politics, sometimes they originate within major political actors (e.g., trade unions) or in government itself (e.g., veterans' pension systems)
- denying that associations as such hold the key to democratic participation
- asserting instead that relations between trust networks and public politics matter deeply
- reinterpreting the democratic dilemma as how to connect those valued enterprises and the networks that sustain them to public politics without damaging either trust networks or public politics
- deducing that the connection will only work well with contingent consent on the part of trust network members
- arguing that a governmental shift away from coercion toward combinations of capital and commitment promotes contingent consent
- noting that the trajectory of democratization therefore differs greatly depending on whether the previous relationships between trust networks and rulers are those of authoritarianism, theocracy, patronage, brokered autonomy, evasive conformity, or particularistic ties

As an exit from authoritarianism, for example, democratization depends on movement away from coercion and relaxation of governmental controls over visible trust networks. From a starting point of patronage, in contrast, democratization depends on weakening of patrons' mediation and on more direct integration of trust networks into public politics.

Of breadth, equality, consultation, and protection, integration of trust networks into public politics most directly affects consultation. To the extent that people integrate their trust networks into public politics, they come to rely on governmental performance for maintenance of those networks. They also gain power, individual and collective, through the connections to government those networks mediate. They acquire an unbreakable interest in governmental performance. The political stakes matter. Paying taxes, buying governmental securities, yielding private information to officials, depending on government for benefits, and releasing network members for military service cement that interest and promote active bargaining over the terms of its fulfillment.

Interested citizens participate more actively, on the average, in elections, referenda, lobbying, interest group membership, social movement mobilization, and direct contact with politicians – that is, in consultation.

135

Conversely, segments of the population that withdraw their trust networks from public politics for whatever reasons weaken their own interest in governmental performance, hence their zeal to participate in democratic public politics. To the extent that rich, powerful people can buy public officials or capture those pieces of government bearing most directly on their interests, furthermore, they weaken public politics doubly: by withdrawing their own trust networks and by undermining the effectiveness of less fortunate citizens' consultation.

Three main processes, all of them by now quite familiar, integrate trust networks into public politics: dissolution of segregated trust networks, integration of previously segregated trust networks, and new creation of politically connected trust networks. These processes qualify, I argue, as necessary conditions for democratization. They are necessary because without them citizens lack incentives to face the adversities of democratic politics and can easily exit from public politics when things go against them. In Albert Hirschman's terms, integrated trust networks encourage citizens to choose voice and loyalty over exit (Hirschman 1970).

Integration of trust networks into public politics is not, however, a *sufficient* condition for democratization; authoritarian regimes and theocracies, after all, likewise integrate trust networks. For a full explanation of democratization, we also have to consider two other clusters of processes: 1) insulation of categorical inequalities (for example, by class, gender, and race) from public politics and 2) transformation of public politics itself through a) broadening of political participation, b) equalization of political participation, c) enhancement of collective control over government, and d) inhibition of arbitrary power by political actors, including agents of government (Tilly 2004a: 15–23). Together, these transformations of public politics, insulation of categorical inequalities, and integration of trust networks produce the broad, equal, binding, and protective relations between citizens and governmental agents that characterize democracy.

Ireland certainly experienced the requisite transformations of public politics after the 1820s: step-by-step political participation broadened and equalized, binding consultation of citizens increased dramatically as the country moved away from tight British control, and protections for citizens expanded significantly along the way. Insulation of public politics from categorical inequality likewise increased greatly as both gender distinctions and the Protestant-Catholic divide lost their formal presence in political rights and obligations. But here we focus on shifts in relations between trust networks and public politics. In the case of Ireland – always excluding the North – we witness some dissolution of trust networks as old solidarities of kinship and religion disintegrate. We see substantial integration of existing trust networks into public politics, notably as Catholics become organized political actors. We notice creation of new politically connected trust networks as the Irish state takes on the sorts of social security programs widely adopted by Western states during the twentieth century.

Although the evidence at hand falls short of clinching the case, it looks as though integration of Irish networks in public politics played a significant part in advancing Irish democracy. Let us see whether the same framework helps make sense of a very different history: that of Mexico.

Mexican Democratization

Like Ireland, Mexico fought its way to a relatively democratic regime through constant struggle, occasional civil war, and many a reversal (McAdam, Tarrow, and Tilly 2001: 290–302). Repeatedly, popular mobilizations challenged the state only to succumb under a wicked synthesis of repression and co-optation. Mexico's experience with trust networks and public politics matched the complexity of Ireland's, but followed a very different trajectory. Most dramatically, successive Mexican regimes dispossessed, sidelined, or at least contained the Roman Catholic Church. With the revolution of 1910, Catholic activists began to form Catholic Workers' Circles and even formed a National Catholic Party. But by 1914 revolutionaries were actively attacking the church and seizing its properties (Bailey 1974: 17–26).

Despite small accommodations during the following years, the election of revolutionary general Plutarco Elías Calles to the presidency in 1924 reinforced the government's anticlericalism and drove the church out of national politics:

[T]he post-revolutionary state broke with the Church in the 1920s, as it implanted itself in the countryside, provoking a wave of violent uprisings throughout the south and centre of the country in which peasants and clergy rose up to demand land and the reopening of the Churches. The repression was brutal, and although a sweeping land reform was implemented in the early 1930s and the Churches were allowed to reopen, for fifty years Mexican governments behaved outwardly as if the Church did not exist. The Church for its part, confined firmly to civil society, has avoided the crises brought about by commitment to social and political causes, and has lived comfortably with a popular religious practice embedded in the daily life of the people.   (Lehmann 1990: 145)

137

Much more broadly, the revolution of 1910 to 1919 fostered popular mobilization, both urban and rural, that Calles and his allies finally contained. In Veracruz, for example, a remarkable tenants' movement formed after stevedore and labor organizer Rafael García became the city's mayor in 1921. Until Calles' election of 1924, tenants' organizations played central parts in Veracruz politics. But soon after Calles' inauguration, federal officials arrested tenant leader and anarchist Herón Proal; Proal's imprisonment brought the beginning of the end (Wood 2001, Chapters 4–8). Tenants, dockers, and other workers continued to struggle in municipal politics, but lost their connections with the national level of public politics. Even more so than with regard to Ireland, any analysis of Mexican democratization must distinguish sharply between the national and local levels.

Nationally, Mexico installed some of the conventional democratic apparatus, such as formally competitive elections, political parties, and manhood suffrage, about the same time as many of its European counterparts (Caramani 2000, 2004, Tilly 2004a: 213–217). Civil wars, rebellions, coups, and authoritarian regimes repeatedly curtailed democratic rights at a national scale, only to be reversed with surprising rapidity and followed by periods of renewed democratization. At the local and regional scales, however, much of Mexico experienced only highly selective integration into national politics, much less into democratic rights and obligations, before the last few decades of the twentieth century. In particular, the surviving indigenous population – about a tenth of the national total at the twentieth century's end – remained largely excluded from national public politics.

Table 6.2 lays out a rough chronology of national events affecting Mexican democratization and de-democratization from 1848 to 2000. Despite omitting many an insurrection and smaller-scale civil war, the chronology portrays a century and a half of tumultuous politics. My task here is not to provide a complete description and explanation of Mexican democratization and de-democratization, but to ask whether the segregation and integration of trust networks played the parts assigned to them in my causal account. Answer: a plausible connection exists. Before the revolution that began in 1910, the Mexican regime operated from the top down almost entirely through patron-client ties. For half a century after the revolution, the government provoked resistance repeatedly, but successfully insulated it from national politics. More so than in Ireland, sharp disjunctions developed between national and local politics. As a result, the state looked much more powerful from the top than from the bottom. During the twentieth century's final decades, however, workers, peasants,

Table 6.2. *Democratization and De-Democratization in Mexico, 1848–2000*

1848	as part of war settlement, Mexico cedes California, Arizona, and New Mexico plus parts of Utah, Nevada, and Colorado to the United States
1855–1861	period of liberal reforms under caudillo Juan Alvarez and minister, then president Benito Juárez; universal male suffrage (1857), nationalization of church property, separation of church and state (1859)
1861–1864	French invasion, conquest, installation of Maximilian as emperor, followed by his defeat and execution
1884–1910	dictatorship of Porfirio Díaz, liberalization of economy, dispossession and extermination of Indians
1910–1919	insurrection against Díaz begins revolution and civil war, radical constitution (1917), universal primary education, right to strike, return of peasant lands, oil declared national property
1926–1929	prochurch Cristero rebellion crushed, subordination of Catholic Church
1928–1929	assassination of president Alvaro Obregón, insurrections, settlement with church and labor
1934–1940	Lazaro Cárdenas president, land expropriations, redistribution to peasants as collective property, emergence of organized labor movement, nationalization of U.S. and British oil properties, formation of Party of the Mexican Revolution, predecessor of PRI
1946–1952	consolidation of PRI power, repression of labor and peasant organizations
1953	female suffrage
1958–1959	suppression of nationwide strike, jailing of labor leaders
1968	army puts down student demonstrations for democracy, kills 500, arrests more than 1500; widening of guerrilla activity
1976	landless peasants seize land in Sonora, president López Portillo grants peasants 250,000 acres
1982	nationalization of fifty-nine Mexican banks
1988	dubiously elected Carlos Salinas de Gortari undertakes neoliberal privatization program
1989	opposition parties PAN (liberal) and PRD (left) make gains in regional elections
1992	NAFTA signed with Canada and the United States (implemented January 1994)
1993	Zapatistas seize four towns in Chiapas, begin international campaign
1994	further PAN gains in regional elections
1999	PRI holds first presidential primary after Ernesto Zedillo ends practice of president's naming successor
2000	PAN candidate Vicente Fox Quesada wins presidency, but PRI keeps control of legislature

and indigenous people began to escape from patronage, brokered autonomy, and evasive conformity into direct involvement with national politics.

Despite the relatively early establishment of manhood suffrage (1857), before the revolution Mexico's national politics revolved around competition among warlords who backed their claims to power – and their control over electoral processes – with military might. Between 1910 and 1930, regionally organized workers and peasants united repeatedly behind populist leaders, both clerical and anticlerical, but no firm integration of their trust networks into national public politics occurred. From the 1930s onward, however, Lazaro Cárdenas and his successors performed the organizational miracle of building selective patron-client chains into a hegemonic national party, first known as the Party of the Mexican Revolution. Under Cárdenas, the government initiated a long-term practice of nationalizing large estates and redistributing them to compliant peasants as agricultural cooperatives, or *ejidos*. During the postwar years the Party of the Revolution mutated into the significantly named *institutional* revolutionary party (Partido Revolucionario Institucional), or PRI.

The party eventually commanded electoral support from important segments of the peasantry and organized workers by means of a brokered distributional network. From that point to the 1960s, except at the very summit the Mexican regime ran largely as a patron-client system, with indigenous communities connected to the regime only through evasive conformity, particularistic ties to rulers, or (more rarely) brokered autonomy. Meanwhile, breakaway segments of the PRI, organized students, fragments of organized workers, and some peasant groups intermittently tried to contest PRI-dominated public politics, but with little success.

Depending on employment opportunities in the United States, Mexican peasants alternated between migration north, movement into the edges of major cities, and patronized seizures of agricultural land (Sanderson 1984). Although landless peasants who seized land in northern Mexico did get substantial concessions from outgoing President Luis Echeverría in 1976, in general the government met public claim making that bypassed PRI's patrons with armed repression. Historian Enrique Krauze speaks of a 1971 massacre of students that he witnessed personally from a Mexico City rooftop where he had fled for shelter:

Although there were fewer killings that day than there were at Tlatelolco in 1968, Mexico's most notorious student massacre, in many ways it was a repeat performance: the government had violently suppressed students. President Luis

Echeverría spoke that night on television, promising to open an investigation 'no matter who is found guilty.' A few days later, he fired two officials and the promised inquiry was never begun. Years later, the weekly news magazine Processo explained why: Mr. Echeverría had orchestrated the killings himself.   (Krauze 2004: A21)

By 2004, anti-PRI President Vicente Fox was filing charges of genocide against ex-President Echeverría for that incident and calling for a truth commission to investigate PRI's abuses while in office (Thompson 2004). PRI had not, however, relied on repression alone. The party grew adept at absorbing protest groups that had gained enough organizational strength to threaten party control. It did so through judicious combinations of patronage and governmental repression.

Nevertheless, a series of social changes undermined PRI hegemony from the 1960s onward. Booming oil exports supported economic expansion, creation of an independent bourgeoisie, migration to cities, and new demands for technocratic public administration. Peasant migration to the United States created opportunities and connections outside of existing patron-client chains through remittances, flows of information, and political activity on the part of emigrants. Greater involvement of Mexico in the international economy accelerated the same processes, but also promoted domestic liberalization and increased responsiveness to international scrutiny of electoral politics; the initiation of the North American Free Trade Agreement (NAFTA, 1994) simply reinforced Mexico's neoliberal forces. Under these conditions, the once dominant government response to challenge – co-opt and repress – became less and less feasible. Opposition parties of left and right began to make significant inroads on PRI support during the 1980s. In 2000, the neoliberal PAN (Party of National Action) finally won the Mexican presidency, even if it could not capture control of the legislature.

Trust Networks in Mexico

What evidence do we have concerning connections between trust networks and Mexico's public politics over the long run of 1848 to 2000? Not much. Still, Carlos Forment has assembled a catalog of 2,291 named voluntary groups that were active in Mexico at one time or another during the nineteenth century. They include groups devoted to development, fraternal orders, mutual aid, patriotic causes, artisans, ethnic protection, education, literary and scientific causes, professional privilege, charity and welfare, religion (both Catholic and heterodox), leisure, hobbies, holidays, credit, and savings. Forment's analysis reveals an impressively vigorous nineteenth-century civic life in Mexico's cities and towns. A number of the groups participated actively in local politics, and even came to power at the municipal level. But, Forment insists, they stayed out of national politics. "We have centralized public life," declared Manuel Rejón, a Mexico City activist, in 1846,

and have been forced to deposit our sovereignty in a single place without allowing citizens to divide it among different locales . . . This has left the nation cold, inert and in a state of complete paralysis. Our country is vast. The state cannot attend to our interests without also extinguishing all our energies. In any case, the administrators they have sent to manage our local affairs are uninterested in them. This is the cause for all the rebellions that have taken place in the country. Citizens now regard the government as a foreign power. (Forment 2003: 163)

Forment argues that such nineteenth-century activists created municipal democracy, but shielded it as much as possible from national intervention. That description seems to hold for most of Mexico well into the twentieth century. Not only civic associations, but trust networks as well, remained segregated from the regime except for the selective integration of patron-client chains headed by major political figures. In Mexico's federal system, furthermore, the pattern repeated itself at regional and local levels: warlords eventually gave way to political bosses, but patron-client politics operated in most states and municipalities (Cornelius 2001).

During the twentieth century's final decades, however, Mexico's economic expansion and international integration produced a powerful new combination of changes:

- increasing proportions of the population felt the pressure of market expansion without sharing in its gains
- the capacity of PRI-backed regional bosses to contain those populations declined
- governmental programs designed to continue the decades-old strategy for co-optation of newly mobilized populations failed to incorporate all their targets and actually provided bases for new organization
- trust networks built into peasant cooperatives and indigenous communities connected increasingly with regional and even national political actors outside of patron-client networks and PRI

In his close study of Mexican food policy and its political ramifications, Jonathan Fox gives the example of the largely indigenous highland Montaña

142

region in Guerrero, the Pacific Coast state south of Mexico City. A national program of food distribution initiated in 1980 connected there with a decade-old peasant movement (led in part by radical schoolteachers) that had been gaining strength in municipal politics. By 1984 leaders of local food councils had formed a Production Consultation Committee coordinating local activities in about a third of the region's communities (Fox 1992: 188). Among other things, they distributed government-subsidized maize through their own local food stores, thus using national political means to serve local ends.

Mobilization and organization went even farther in the central valleys of adjacent Oaxaca. There, old local trust networks provided the basis for effective organization:

Behind this traditional defense of local autonomy is a complex web of communitarian institutions. The still widespread *tequio* system of unpaid obligatory community labor, for example, was often used to build the village stores themselves. The roles of rural food committee and store managers also often fit smoothly into the traditional civil-religious authority system known as *cargos*, which organized essential village services such as water, agrarian matters, and parent-teacher associations as well as religious festivals. The cargo system ran parallel to the formal municipal authorities, whose main task was to settle local disputes and to represent the community to outside institutions.   (Fox 1992: 199; more generally, see Fox 1994)

In 1984, the coordinating committee of Oaxaca food councils hosted the first national meeting of the National Union of Autonomous Regional Peasant Organizations. They were thereby integrating themselves into public politics via a newly formed national political actor. Contrary to its PRI-based authors' intentions, the national program of food distribution provided means and incentives for regionally based political entrepreneurs to enter the national scene.

Elsewhere in Oaxaca, Jeffrey Rubin has documented a parallel process in the predominantly Zapotec city of Juchitán. In that city, a largely indigenous Coalition of Workers, Peasants, and Students of the Isthmus (COCEI) came to power in 1989. After widespread protests of workers and peasants from the late 1960s onward, PRI sought to reassert control in Juchitán by imposing political boss Mario Bustillo. Mobilization against Bustillo began characteristically not in Oaxaca but with the Mexico City activities of an Association of Juchiteco Students. Lower-income students from the region gained influence in the association, pressing programs of Zapotec identity and collective self-improvement in place of the integration and personal advancement pursued by their middle-class

143

predecessors. They began to win association elections in 1973. By the end of that year, the student association was allying with local activists in Juchitán as it organized to oust a hospital director and create new health programs there (Rubin 1997: 105–107). COCEI emerged from that citywide mobilization.

The Coalición (as participants called it) worked opportunistically, identifying groups of aggrieved peasants or workers and supporting their demands for recognition and redress. Although it straddled the boundary between legal and illegal making of claims, COCEI retained the support of local moderates:

COCEI's militant and at times illegal approaches were potentially acceptable to moderates in Juchitán in light of the failure of earlier reform efforts, and, equally important, because of their local origin and their embeddedness in Zapotec language and cultural forms. COCEI was seen as a genuine response on the part of the pueblo to the economic and political exploitation that the moderates themselves had exposed. As a result, faced with a local world at odds with their convictions, moderates discussed and rethought their positions on basic political issues, such as democracy, opposition, and violence. Their willingness to support a radical grass-roots movement, even as most middle-class and elite Juchitecos fiercely opposed radical politics and tacitly supported ongoing repression, strengthened COCEI at key moments in its development, bringing votes, degrees of local tolerance, and support from some officials in Mexico City. (Rubin 1997: 110)

In Juchitán, we watch indigenous groups of peasants and workers exiting from patronage, brokered autonomy, and evasive conformity toward democracy through unexpected alliances with university students and local moderates. We watch durable connections forming between indigenous trust networks and national public politics.

Distrust and De-Democratization

If integration of trust networks into public politics promotes democratization, their withdrawal from public politics weakens democracy. Withdrawal can occur either voluntarily or involuntarily. Voluntarily, groups of citizens can sever their commitments to public politics at large by creating their own alternatives to government services or acquiring private control over different pieces of government. White segregationists that created private school systems during the American civil rights era did the first, whereas regulated industries that co-opt their regulators do the second. Involuntarily, previously connected groups can suffer categorical exclusion or termination of

144

the institutions that previously tied them to the regime. Japanese-Americans endured the first fate during World War II, while wholesale contraction of welfare programs probably had a similar effect on low-income American families during the 1990s.

De-democratization occurs more frequently than democratic theorists generally allow. In most theories of democracy, democratization is hard to achieve, but also difficult to reverse. Nancy Bermeo therefore performs a double service in analyzing the places of ordinary people in de-democratization: she shows how much more emphatically elites defected from democratic regimes than did ordinary citizens, and she shows that Western history has included many major reversals. She concentrates on cases in which authoritarian government displaced functioning democratic regimes. Her interwar European "casualties" to democracy (Bermeo 2003: 23) include:

1922: Italy	1923: Bulgaria
1926: Lithuania, Poland, Portugal	1929: Yugoslavia
1933: Austria, Germany	1934: Estonia, Latvia
1936: Greece, Spain	1938: Romania

Although it would have changed the pivot of her analysis, Bermeo could also have included the replacement of democracy by authoritarian rule in Finland, Denmark, Norway, the Netherlands, Belgium, Luxembourg, and France through Soviet and German conquests of 1939 and 1940.

In Latin America after World War II, Bermeo identifies major reversals of democracy in Argentina (1976), Brazil (1964), Chile (1973), and Uruguay (1973) (Bermeo 2003: 68). Not counting the conquests of 1939–1940, that makes seventeen catastrophic collapses of democracy over half a century in Europe and mainland Latin America alone.

Using a less demanding standard for democracy than Bermeo, Adam Przeworski and his collaborators likewise found an impressive frequency of reversals. The group analyzed year-to-year survival and reversal of democracy in 135 countries throughout the world over the period from 1950 to 1990. Democracy, for the Przeworski team, took an electoral form: "all regimes that hold elections in which the opposition has some chance of winning and taking office" (Przeworski, Alvarez, Cheibub, and Limongi 1997: 295). Over the forty-one years under investigation, fifty transitions from nondemocracy to democracy occurred in the 135 countries under study (in some countries more than once), but so did forty transitions from democracy to nondemocracy. It would be worth knowing what relationship between distrust and de-democratization, if any, appeared in those transitions.

Let us be clear what we want to know about democratic reversals. If my argument is correct, we should often find that a) voluntary withdrawals of trust networks from public politics by major political actors or segments of the citizenry precede and promote de-democratization and b) involuntary severing of connections between trust networks and public politics accompanies or follows de-democratization, and further insures de-democratization.

Neither Bermeo, Przeworski, nor anyone else has done the detailed studies of trust networks and public politics to establish the correctness or falsity of my arguments. Nevertheless, one of Bermeo's cases – Spain – offers us food for thought. Spain's repeated transit of the boundary between authoritarian and democratic government and its dramatic regional variation in relations to the national government provide a laboratory full of natural experiments (Ortega Ortiz 2000). Robert Fishman has made the case, for example, that when the Spanish socialist party held power during the early 1990s while the Communist Party belonged to the opposition, among socialists personal ties of labor leaders to intellectuals served political brokerage without making much difference to world views, whereas among their communist counterparts ties to intellectuals promoted significantly more global world views. For the opposition communists, Fishman concludes, ties to intellectuals generated transforming conversations about the world and the future:

The clear implication of these findings is that where political (or social) forces external to state power attract the collective energies and hopes of those politically engaged, and where ties such as the linkages we examine between intellectuals and workers take the form of conversation, those ties can substantially transform public rhetoric. (Fishman 2004: 166)

Fishman's findings do not, of course, tell us what changes in integration or segregation of trust networks occurred during Spain's earlier periods of democratization and de-democratization. But at least they suggest that variation in interpersonal networks affects political orientations today.

From World War I to the late twentieth century, Spain made a spectacular series of shifts between democratization and de-democratization. Table 6.3 supplies the chronology of major events. It makes three things clear about Spanish experience with democracy. First, democracy remained a fragile flower in Spain until at least the 1970s; multiple reversals occurred.

Table 6.3. *Democratization and De-Democratization in Spain, 1917–1981*

1917	under constitutional monarchy, military regime suspends constitutional guarantees, Catalans agitate for home rule, workers stage general strike
1923	military coup of Primo de Rivera, weakened monarchy
1925	partial civilianization of Primo de Rivera dictatorship, but continuation of military rule under weak monarchy with Primo de Rivera prime minister
1930	resignation and death of Primo de Rivera, interim government of Damaso Berenguer
1931	municipal elections produce landslide for republicans, king flees country without abdicating, provisional government declares republic, establishes universal male suffrage for ages 23+
1932	military rebellion quelled, Catalan charter of autonomy
1933	elections produce center-right rule; female suffrage established
1934	Catalan declaration of independence, radical risings, miners' insurrection in Asturias, all repressed
1936	Popular Front victory in national elections, strike waves and occupations in agricultural and industrial sectors, Spanish government grants home rule to Basque region, military rising in Morocco spreads to Spain, civil war begins, rebels name Franco chief of state, Germany and Italy aid rebels
1939	Franco's forces win civil war, establish authoritarian state
1969	Franco names Juan Carlos de Borbón his eventual successor as head of state
1975	Franco dies, Juan Carlos becomes king
1976–1978	under prime minister Adolfo Suarez, Spain initiates democratic reforms, elects new parliament, adopts democratic constitution, with voting age lowered first to 21, then to 18
1979	Basque and Catalan autonomy statutes
1981	attempted military coup defeated, new regional autonomies, beginning of continuous (if often turbulent) democratic rule

Second, as had been true long before 1917, military intervention in Spanish national politics occurred frequently, and almost always damaged democracy. Third, demands for regional autonomy or independence dogged national democratic programs throughout the century.

A fourth fact eludes the chronology, but shapes it: both agricultural and industrial workers organized and politicized in Spain to a remarkable degree from the end of the nineteenth century onward; on the whole, integration of organized workers into Spain's national public politics marked the country's periods of democratization, just as their collective exclusion signaled periods of de-democratization. Once the Primo de Rivera dictatorship ended in 1925, for example, the number of organized workers shot up rapidly, then accelerated with the peaceful revolution of 1931 (Soto Carmona 1988: 303–305). In that abrupt transfer of power, republicans won overwhelming majorities of Spain's urban voters in the municipal elections of April 12, 1931, and the king (no longer assured of support by an increasingly unenthusiastic general staff) fled the country.

Eduardo González Callejo argues that the transition presented a "revolutionary face that is hard to deny" because:

> the regime's collapse produced a sharp legal break, with no formal act transmitting power from the last monarchical cabinet to the National Revolutionary Committee. When the inevitable arrived, no representative of the old regime made a significant effort to support an orderly and legal cession of ruling power.
>
> (González Callejo 1999: 627)

Nevertheless, the revolutionary bases remained quite narrow. Popular attacks on churches, disestablishment of the Catholic Church, and extensive land reform soon alienated both rural landlords and the Catholic hierarchy (Malefakis 1970, Chapter 6).

Despite shrinking the army's active officer corps rapidly, the new regime continued to apply the old regime's instruments of exclusion and control (Payne 1967: 268–276). The provisional government installed on April 14, 1931 pursued an exclusive line, denying the right of public assembly to monarchists, anarchists, and communists alike (Ballbé 1985: 318). The bourgeois republic that then came to power regularly used military force to repress leftist and striking workers, thus excluding them from the new regime (Ballbé 1985, Chapter 11). The small Spanish Communist Party, in any case, took the position that the revolution of 1931 could at best serve as an entering wedge for a true proletarian revolution and that collaboration with bourgeois rulers would delay the coming revolution (Cruz 1987: 127–128).

Yet on the whole workers – especially those represented by the Socialist Party – stuck with the republic. Significantly, the first group of workers to defect from the republican coalition and align themselves with the military in 1935 and 1936 was the small but active Catholic Workers' Union (Soto Carmona 1988: 313). Peasants and agricultural workers benefited from the extensive land reforms of 1931, and generally continued to support the regime. Indeed, they soon went beyond it by occupying uncultivated fields and striking against low-wage landlords. By 1936, rural strikes and land occupations were threatening the precarious republican regime as the regime also faced military opposition from Francisco Franco and his collaborators (Malefakis 1970, Chapter 14). In Aragon:

Although under the Restoration and the Primo de Rivera dictatorship agrarian protest had been traditionally treated as a simple problem of public order, irruption of the republic's legal protection into the rural sector changed things substantially. Introduction of a labor regime corresponding more closely to the patterns of European agrarian capitalism, therefore limiting the previously absolute liberty and omnipotence of the landholding oligarchy, permitting large-scale unionization, the opportunity to demonstrate on behalf of demands, and the chance to strike were not well received by those people, little used to having laws shake their positions, who felt the threat of agrarian reform in their very flesh.

(Casanova, Cenarro, Cifuentes, Maluenda & Salomón 1992: 86–87)

In that one province, counterrevolutionaries eventually killed 8,628 suspected supporters of the republican cause (Casanova, Cenarro, Cifuentes, Maluenda, and Salomón 1992: 213). The Franco regime's violent repression snuffed out Aragon's previously energetic democratic mobilization.

Spain's political history during the 1930s makes plausible a sequence of this sort: 1) from 1931 to 1933, substantial integration of workers' and peasants' trust networks into national public politics through the mediation of unions and political organizations combined with partial exclusion of military; 2) from 1933 to 1935, confrontations between partially integrated workers, peasants, and regionalists, on one side, and national authorities, on the other; 3) in 1936, new mobilizations of workers, peasants, and regionalists, countermobilization of military; 4) from 1936 to 1939, incremental (and violent) exclusion of worker, peasant, and regionalist trust networks from national politics.

Between 1939 and 1975, according to this scenario, we would observe a return to the prevailing patronage, particularistic ties, and evasive conformity of the 1920s, now coupled with authoritarian integration of the military and the Catholic Church into Franco's system of rule. With the 1960s, continues the speculation, we would witness processes resembling those that were accelerating in Mexico about the same time: undermining of old local trust networks by economic expansion, relaxation of repression, and expansion of trust networks within workers' organizations. The rapid democratization of 1976–1978 would then rest on and facilitate integration of popular trust networks into national public politics and partial extrusion from the regime of trust networks based in the church and the military.

Threats to Democracy

Plausible, perhaps, but certainly not proven. In the twentieth-century histories of Ireland, Mexico, and Spain we discover not certainties, but a promising research program. The next round of inquiries into democratization should take seriously the segregation and integration of trust networks into public politics. Even if my analyses of how segregation and integration work contain serious errors, at least they establish the interest and importance of such connections. Surely connections between interpersonal trust networks and public politics strongly affect the viability of democratic institutions. But how strongly and how remain open to investigation.

Suppose, however, that I have it right. Two worrisome conclusions loom. First, even in rich, powerful countries democracy remains vulnerable to withdrawal of trust networks from public politics, especially if the networks that withdraw have subjected the rich and powerful to the give and take of contention. Private and home schooling, exclusive clubs and religious sects, gated communities, and capture of governmental agencies or offices for private profit all provide means for elites to secure their own advantages without subjecting themselves to the costs and constraints of public politics.

Second, to the extent that members of trust networks in relatively undemocratic countries manage either to subordinate government to those networks or to maintain themselves without integration into public politics, prospects for democracy will remain dim in those countries. In those countries, totalitarianism, theocracy, and patron-client politics seem more likely futures than democracy.

7

Future Trust Networks

They told us so! The U.S. State Department's annual report "Patterns of Global Terrorism" for 2000, issued on April 30, 2001, contained this description of al-Qaida:

Established by Usama bin Ladin in the late 1980s to bring together Arabs who fought in Afghanistan against the Soviet invasion. Helped finance, recruit, transport, and train Sunni Islamic extremists for the Afghan resistance. Current goal is to establish a pan-Islamic Caliphate throughout the world by expelling Westerners and non-Muslims from Muslim countries. Issued statement under banner of "the World Islamic Front for Jihad Against the Jews and Crusaders" in February 1998, saying it was the duty of all Muslims to kill US citizens – civilian or military – and their allies everywhere. (State 2001: 2450)

The report went on to say that al-Qaida had organized the bombings of U.S. embassies in Kenya and Tanzania (1998), engineered the assault of the USS Cole in Yemen (2000), and plotted numerous attacks on Westerners elsewhere. The document singled out South Asia as a base for vindictive violence directed toward U.S. interests, calling special attention to the Afghan Taliban's provision of safe haven for Usama bin Ladin and his network.

When State issued its report on 2000's terror attacks in April 2001, most of the nineteen men – four pilots and fifteen "muscle hijackers" – who would ram fuel-packed, passenger-filled American airliners into the World Trade Center, the Pentagon, and a Pennsylvania field on September 11th had already entered the United States. (Al-Qaida had actually recruited nine or ten more men for the operation, but for various reasons they ended up not participating; Commission 2004: 235.) Without knowing exactly where, when, or with whom they would strike, the nineteen suicide bombers were then rehearsing their parts in the coup, for example by working out regularly in American gyms to keep themselves fit (Commission 2004: 215–253).

Despite the fact that only a few of them had met before 1999, by the spring of 2001 they formed a lethal trust network carrying on a consequential collective activity as they placed their very lives at risk to the mistakes, failures, or malfeasance of other network members.

In his address to Congress nine days after the devastating attacks of 9/11, U.S. President George W. Bush declared that "Our war on terror begins with al-Qaida, but it does not end there. It will not end until every terrorist group of global reach has been found, stopped, and defeated" (State 2002: i). "In this global campaign against terrorism," echoed Secretary of State Colin L. Powell in May 2002:

no country has the luxury of remaining on the sidelines. There *are* no sidelines. Terrorists respect no limits, geographic or moral. The frontlines are everywhere and the stakes are high. Terrorism not only kills people. It also threatens democratic institutions, undermines economies, and destabilizes regions.   (State 2002: iii)

After the attacks, U.S. government statements and American media generally shifted the spelling to al-Qaeda. They continued, however, to portray Usama bin Ladin (or Osama Bin Laden!) as mastermind of a worldwide terror network, now American public enemy Number 1. The hunt for Bin Laden soon helped justify ill-considered American invasions of Afghanistan and Iraq.

The name al-Qaeda means simply "foundation" or "base" in Arabic; it referred initially to the computerized database of contacts that Bin Laden maintained for support of his Islamist projects (Gregory 2004: 36–38). After Bin Laden moved from Sudan back to Afghanistan in May 1996, he started to remake his contacts. No doubt the most important renewal cemented his relations with Ayman Zawahiri, leader of the Egyptian Islamic Jihad, an organization devoted to making Egypt a pure Islamic state. The alliance combined Bin Laden's remarkable access to oil-rich supporters with Zawahiri's widespread Islamist connections. In 1998, the two formalized their alliance in the World Islamic Front for Jihad Against the Jews and Crusaders, which announced its intentions to attack the United States and American allies across the world.

Although western media soon started calling Zawahiri Bin Laden's "deputy," on his own he provided crucial ties to Middle Eastern religious zealots and potential recruits (Commission 2004: 67, Stern 2003: 261–267). As they existed in 2001, the Bin Laden-Zawahiri composite connections as a whole did not qualify as a trust network by this book's demanding standards. By no means all the people linked through them were placing their

152

valued long-term enterprises at risk to the failure, mistakes, or malfeasance of other network members. But at the center of the World Islamic Front, within the Advisory Council (Shura), stood a small group of followers who had sworn personal fealty (bayat) to Bin Laden himself (Commission 2004: 56, 67). They formed a powerful, lethal trust network.

Ideologically inspired, conspiratorial networks organized for attacks on political enemies came into existence well before the twenty-first century. The term "terror" took on a political meaning in 1793, as French revolutionaries sought to impose virtue by top-down repression (Greer 1935, Guenniffey 2000, Mayer 2000). That top-down terror eventually generated a bottom-up terror, both of them often organized through conspiratorial networks either backed by existing states or opposed to those states. Unlike encounters of army with army or demonstrators with police, both forms of terror operated very asymmetrically and in secret. They used violence or threats of violence selectively but dramatically against the enemy's personnel, property, or symbols. During the mass migrations of the nineteenth century, connections provided by trust networks of emigrants started supporting bottom-up terrorism back home (Hanagan 1998, 2002). Both sorts of terror – top-down and bottom-up – continued into the twentieth century.[1] Hitler and Stalin deployed the top-down version, many a nationalist network the bottom-up version.

From the start of the Cold War and the rise of anticolonial independence movements, American authorities worried about terror as a threat to American interests at home and abroad. By congressional mandate, in fact, the State Department started producing annual catalogs of terrorist groups and attacks during the 1980s. State's compilations generally excluded state-sponsored terror and domestic terrorists such as American militias and assassins of abortion doctors. Instead, they concentrated on what American authorities defined as terror: clandestine deployment of force by foreign nonstate actors against holders, possessions, and symbols of national or international power (Tilly 2002b, 2004d).

---

[1] Caddick-Adams and Holmes 2001, Crenshaw 1983, 1995, Derluguian 1999, Ellis 2000, Enders and Sandler 2002, Farah 2004, Futrell and Brents 2003, González Callejo 2002a, 2002b, Kalyvas 1999, Kushner 2001, Mason and Krane 1989, Mazower 2002, Mommsen and Hirschfeld 1982, Naimark 2001, Oliverio 1998, della Porta and Pasquino 1983, Rapoport 1999, Ruby 2002, Schmid 2001, Schmid and de Graaf 1982, Senechal de la Roche 2004, Smelser and Mitchell 2002a, 2002b, Stanley 1996, Stern 2003, Taylor 1999, Tilly 2002b, 2004d, Turk 2004, Waldmann 1993, Walter 1969.

As a political strategy pursued by network-connected conspirators, then, terror has been with us a long time. The terror of 1998 to 2004 nevertheless stood out from earlier rounds in several regards:

- It connected increasingly with international flows of contraband: drugs, arms, precious minerals, and more.
- Despite continued struggles for national power in such places as Colombia, Sri Lanka, the Caucasus, Spain, and Northern Ireland, terrorist attacks shifted significantly toward transnational actors and targets.
- Terror employed by nonstate and antistate actors rose relative to state-sponsored and state-administered terror.
- Committed Islamists – demanding the imposition of Islamic law in predominantly Muslim countries and sometimes seeking restoration of the transnational Muslim caliphate as well – played increasingly prominent roles in terror.
- Well beyond 9/11, American property, armed forces, and interests across the world attracted larger shares of serious terrorism – terror that inflicted extensive damage on persons and property.

Note the implications of these shifts. Over the long history of trust networks and politics this book has traced, both the networks and the governments in question have operated at local, regional, or national scales. We have been looking mainly at segregation or integration of trust networks with regard to national regimes. But in the terror of 1998 to 2004 we see internationalization on both sides: in the networks of terrorists and in the objects of their violence. Could globalization, American hegemony, or the reorientation of Islam be producing a shift toward a global political arena? If so, integration or segregation of trust networks at the national scale would start to matter less for public politics than they have for thousands of years.

Outrageously extrapolated, the recent history of terrorist networks therefore points to a surprising possible future for trust networks: their expansion to transnational scale, their detachment from particular national regimes to international politics, their acquisition of autonomous political power, and their occasional takeover of a national government. (After all, Islamists did at least temporarily seize power in Iran, Sudan, and Afghanistan.) If those changes were to operate at a worldwide scale, they would, among other effects, seriously menace democracy wherever it now prevails. If they represented a more general political trend, alterations in the character of terror would point to a surprising new history for trust networks.

Thinning, Displacement, and Withdrawal

Another quite different but still possible future for trust networks in politics emerges from recent trends in transnational social movement activity. Although ad hoc coalitions, authoritative organizations, and established institutions such as churches have fed social movements from their eighteenth-century origins onward, substantial movements have almost always relied on trust networks as recruiting grounds and suppliers of resources.[2] Trust networks anchored temporary mobilizations in local politics and interpersonal concerns. Despite the use of telephone trees and mass media, clusters within social movements remained in touch through routine contact and personal acquaintance. The aiming of movement claims at local, regional, and national targets facilitated reliance on established, geographically concentrated trust networks.

Now we see signs of change. At least in rich countries, activists operating in national politics and those who form international alliances rely increasingly on electronic communication, most recently the internet and portable communications devices. At the same time, transnational targets such as multinational corporations, the World Trade Organization, and the European Union have become ever more frequent objects of claims. Could activists' widespread use of electronic communication and a shift of focus to transnational targets together detach previously integrated trust networks from national public politics and substitute thinner, more fleeting relationships among geographically separated activists for the mobilizing capacity of trust networks?

Many observers of recent changes in social movement activity worldwide have claimed one, the other, or both. Technology analyst Howard Rheingold, for example, describes what he calls Smart Mobs: "people who are able to act in concert even if they don't know each other" (Rheingold 2003: xii). Speaking of the 2001 mobilization in and around Manila that backed the ouster of President Joseph Estrada, Rheingold stresses the enormous enthusiasm of Filipinos for Short Message Service (SMS) since its introduction in 1995. At least superficially, such mobile communications

---

[2] Diani 1995, 2003, Fernandez and McAdam 1988, Ohlemacher 1993, Passy 1998, 2001, Polletta 2002, Riles 2000.

systems have the populist attraction of not falling easily under governmental control.

Rheingold goes farther, however. He argues that smart mobs connected by text messaging are already taking over from conventional twentieth-century social movements. He cites these four examples:

On November 30, 1999, autonomous but internetworked squads of demonstrators protesting the meeting of the World Trade Organization used 'swarming' tactics, mobile phones, Web sites, laptops, and handheld computers to win the 'Battle of Seattle.' In September 2000, thousands of citizens in Britain, outraged by a sudden rise in gasoline prices, used mobile phones, SMS, email from laptop PCs, and CB radios in taxicabs to coordinate dispersed groups that blocked fuel delivery at selected service stations in a wildcat political protest. A violent political demonstration in Toronto in the spring of 2000 was chronicled by a group of roving journalist-researchers who webcast digital video of everything they saw. Since 1992, thousands of bicycle activists have assembled monthly for 'Critical Mass' moving demonstrations, weaving through San Francisco streets en masse. Critical Mass operates through loosely linked networks, alerted by mobile phone and email trees, and breaks up into smaller, tele-coordinated groups when appropriate.

(Rheingold 2003: 158)

Undoubtedly early twenty-first-century social movement activists have integrated fresh new communications media into their organizing and into their very claim-making performances (Deibert 2000, Koopmans 2004, Rafael 2003, Rucht 2003). Significant changes in social movement technologies are, indeed, occurring during the early twenty-first century.

How extensively? Lance Bennett's reviews of transnational activism (Bennett 2003, 2004) argue that digital media are now changing international activism in several important ways: 1) making loosely structured networks, rather than the relatively dense networks of earlier social movements crucial to communication and coordination among activists; 2) weakening the identification of local activists with the movement as a whole by allowing greater scope for introduction of local issues into movement discourse; 3) reducing the influence of ideology on personal involvement in social movements; 4) diminishing the relative importance of bounded, durable, resource-rich local and national organizations as bases for social movement activism; 5) increasing the strategic advantages of resource-poor organizations within social movements; 6) promoting the creation of permanent campaigns (e.g., antiglobalization or for environmental protection) with rapidly shifting immediate targets; and 7) combining older face-to-face performances with virtual performances. Bennett concludes that these changes, in turn, make social movements increasingly vulnerable to problems of coordination, control, and commitment.

Does the internet change everything? In a thoughtful, comprehensive recent survey of internet use, Caroline Haythornthwaite and Barry Wellman offer a summary concerning social impact in general:

> Even before the advent of the Internet, there has been a move from all-encompassing, socially controlling communities to individualized fragmented personal communities. Most friends and relatives with whom we maintain socially close ties are not physically close. These ties are spread through metropolitan areas, and often on the other side of countries or seas. Mail, the telephone, cars, airplanes, and now email and the Internet sustain these ties. Most people do not live lives bound in one community. Instead, they maneuver through multiple specialized partial communities, giving limited commitment to each. Their life is 'glocalized': combining long-distance ties with continuing involvements in households, neighborhoods, and worksites.   (Haythornthwaite and Wellman 2002: 32)

Of course, these observations apply with greater force to rich Western countries than to the world as a whole. But they clarify the sense in which integration of communications innovations into existing social relations and practices extends projects that people already have under way, and especially accentuates connections that were already in play but costly to maintain. In the measured Haythornthwaite-Wellman view, trust networks are not dissolving, but reorganizing.

In any case, we should beware of communications determinism. Long before the internet and SMS, the telephone, radio, and television became available to social movement organizers and activists. In general, they reduced communication costs as they increased the geographic range covered by social movement communications. They also tied social movement participants more firmly to other users of the same technologies as they separated participants from nonusers of those technologies; they had significant selection effects in that regard.

In their times, similarly, transportation breakthroughs such as intercity steam trains, electrical street cars, and jet aircraft facilitated social movement contact at a distance, but actually impeded contact with like-minded people who lived away from major transport lines. Neither in communications nor in transportation, however, did the technological timetable dominate alterations in social movement organization, strategy, and practice. Shifts in the political and organizational context impinged far more directly and immediately on how social movements worked than did technical transformations as such.

What is happening to the political and organizational context of social movements, and how is it affecting movements' relations to trust networks? As a result of shifts in the context, some internationalization is occurring. As compared with the twentieth century, internationally organized networks of activists, international nongovernmental organizations, and internationally visible targets such as multinational corporations and international financial institutions all figure more prominently in recent social movements, especially in the richer and better-connected parts of the world.[3] Jackie Smith and her collaborators count "transnational social movement organizations" for human rights, the environment, peace, and other international causes operating in at least three countries across the world from 1973 to 2000. They find 183 in 1973, 348 in 1983, 711 in 1993, 959 in 2000, and still increasing (Smith and Bandy 2004: 6). Activist organizations are going global (Anheier and Themudo 2002).

Above and beyond formal organizations, international networks of activists are also forming. During the early twenty-first century, peace and antiglobalization movements began coalescing against American military power and its economic underpinnings. Activist Tom Mertes put it this way:

With the bombardment of Afghanistan – and, even more so, with the Anglo-American occupation of Iraq – the 'movement of movements,' if it is to go forward, needs to generate an understanding of how US military and political power operates not just in Iraq but across the Middle East, Asia, Africa and Latin America; to discern the superpower at work behind the multilateral screens of the UN Security Council, just as much as those of the IMF, World Bank or WTO; to build a global opposition capable of inflicting defeats on Washington's neo-imperialist ambitions as well as its neoliberal goals. (Mertes 2004: x–xi)

Even anti-American mobilization, in this sympathetic reading, takes an international form. Domestically oriented movements such as the anti-Estrada campaign in the Philippines now also receive, on the average, more international attention and intervention – including attention and intervention from transnational social movement organizations – than their twentieth-century counterparts. In much more circumspect academic language than Mertes, Joe Bandy and Jackie Smith report that global action is actually swelling:

---

[3] Boli and Thomas 1997, Chandhoke 2002, Imig and Tarrow 2001, Keck and Sikkink 1998, 2000, O'Neill 2004, Riles 2000, Jackie Smith 1997, 2002, 2004, Tarrow 2002, Tilly 2004e, Trif and Imig 2003, Wood 2004.

Liberalization and its tidal wave of social transformations have given rise to popular resistance movements throughout the world, and thus it is the source of social crises and a target of social alternatives. More than ever, movements are seeking to communicate across borders, to develop common grievances, and to organize in the pursuit of international alternatives – a "globalization from below." Any effective challenge to the liberalizing forces of transnational capital must be global, broad based, cross-sectoral, and capable of collective action.

(Bandy and Smith 2004: 231)

Organizationally speaking, these are costly forms of collective action. Unless the total pool of time, energy, and other resources available from activists greatly increases, the shift that Mertes, Bandy, and Smith describe will divert time, energy, and resources from local, regional, and national public politics. To that extent it will weaken connections between activists' trust networks and those smaller-scale sites of public politics. It may even make trust networks less significant for the maintenance of social movement activity.

As the previous chapter's discussion of de-democratization indicates, a worrisome parallel appears in the possible withdrawal of trust networks from public politics in local, regional, and national arenas. It is hard to know whether to worry more about the withdrawal of popular or elite trust networks. Withdrawal of networks from public politics occurs when participation in them declines and when they shift to private provision of benefits previously gained through public politics. On the popular side, that can occur through increasing apathy, impoverishment, fear of political participation, preoccupation with private affairs, or professionalization of the relevant services.

On the elite side, it can occur through capture of relevant governmental activities outside of public politics or through private provision of benefits. Direct capture includes purchase of favors from bureaucrats and politicians, subversion of elections and appointment procedures to secure public offices for private interests, and creation of governmental agencies devoted entirely to the advantage of specific groups. Private provision of benefits includes creation of private security forces, private and home schooling, involvement in clandestine sects, formation of private clubs, and establishment of gated communities. Both sorts of changes promote withdrawal of elite trust networks from public politics.

On the popular side, Robert Putnam's widely read *Bowling Alone* – which identifies me by name as a member of the last American participatory generation; Putnam 2000: 255 – has raised the specter of declining participation and trust as twinned threats to American democracy. After initial dissent, Theda Skocpol has discerned a similar threat in the increasing professionalization of the organizations running American civic life (Skocpol and Fiorina 1999, Skocpol 2003). Skocpol argues that a shift away from recruitment into civic life via interpersonal networks and toward issues favored by the upper middle classes is undermining the quality of public politics and threatening democracy. Optimists who cheer the rise of middle class issues do not see, she declares:

that gains in some kinds of social equality could be accompanied by erosions of cross-class fellowship and inclusive civic mobilization equally portentous for our democracy.

Despite the multiplicity of voices raised within it, America's new civic universe is remarkably oligarchic. This is true in the world of voluntary associations – those 'combinations' that Alexis de Tocqueville posited as central to democratic vitality – and even more true in realms of national politics and public policymaking that are thoroughly intertwined with associational life.   (Skocpol 2003: 222–223)

As we have seen, Nancy Bermeo (2003) has argued that, contrary to concerns about mass apathy or fickleness, elite withdrawal figures importantly in historical cases of democracy's reversal. "Advances in communication," concludes Bermeo,

give today's political elites better capacities to understand and to shape the preferences of ordinary people. History gives elites the capacity to learn from the deadly mistakes of the past. Whether elites use these capacities in the interests of democracy may depend as much on strength of conviction as on economic strength or on any other measure of performance. Where the experience of dictatorial rule has strengthened elite convictions about the merits of democracy, there is reason for hope. Where dictatorship has had other effects and where elected elites still fail to distance themselves from anti-democratic actors, ordinary people may once again be caught up in the drama of democratic breakdown.   (Bermeo 2003: 256)

Of course, none of these authors uses the language of trust networks, and all of them might reject this book's analyses. As I read them, however, the threats about which they warn could easily result not simply from attitudinal shifts but from active alterations in the connections between trust networks, popular or elite, and public politics.

Simultaneous with the proliferation of international terror networks, then, trust networks might be thinning, internationalizing, and detaching themselves from national public politics. If the two together marked major trends, they would signal significant threats to the hard-won integration of trust networks into national regimes, and therefore to democracy across the world.

More of the Same

Before letting two sensational sets of (possibly temporary) changes color the entire future, accordingly, we must think more generally about factors producing change in trust networks. From an interior perspective, we must consider what will affect the boundaries, connections, sustenance, and internal controls of trust networks. From an exterior perspective, we must consider what will cause some trust networks to disappear, some to integrate with public politics, others to form anew as an outgrowth of public politics, and still others to escape from integration into public politics, at least public politics at a national scale. The long history we have surveyed suggests that so long as high-capacity states relying especially on capital and commitment as inducements for participation survive, so too will the contingent integration of trust networks into public politics.

Major questions about the future of politics arise at precisely that point: Is globalization dissolving the capacity of states as we have known them? Does American economic and military hegemony threaten the autonomous power of all other regimes, hence their capacity to serve or dominate their citizens? Is the Muslim world finally reuniting in opposition to the non-Muslim West? Will victims of liberalism across the world heed Tom Mertes' call and others like it? Or will capitalism and democracy inexorably prevail throughout the globe? This book's historical survey of trust networks offers no answers to these pressing questions. But if my arguments are correct, they predict that any of these futures entails significant changes in connections between interpersonal trust networks and public politics everywhere.

In the short term, we are likely to witness more of the same: the partial integration of trust networks into national public politics produced by the twentieth-century combination of proletarianization, expansion of governmental capacity, incomplete democratization, and extension of government-backed social provision will continue through much of the world. In a pessimistic scenario, more of the same means continuation of the forms of inequality, injustice, and oppression that still exist in the world. In an optimistic scenario, it means incremental democratization, which should erode inequality, injustice, and oppression without eliminating them entirely. The future is ours to make.

References

Adams, Julia (1994): "The Familial State: Elite Family Practices and State-Making in the Early Modern Netherlands," *Theory and Society* 23: 505–540.

Adams, William M., Dan Brockington, Jane Dyson, and Bhaskar Vira (2003): "Managing Tragedies: Understanding Conflict over Common Pool Resources," *Science* 302: 1915–1916.

Agulhon, Maurice (1966): *La sociabilité méridionale (Confréries et Associations dans la vie collective en Provence orientale à la fin du 18e siècle)*. Aix-en-Provence: Publications des Annales de la Faculté des Lettres. 2 vols.

Agulhon, Maurice (1970): *La vie sociale en Provence intérieure au lendemain de la Révolution*. Paris: Société des Etudes Robespierristes.

Alapuro, Risto and Markku Lonkila (2004): "Russians' and Estonians' Networks in a Tallinn Factory" in Risto Alapuro, Ilkka Liikanen, and Markku Lonkila, eds., *Beyond Post-Soviet Transition. Micro Perspectives on Challenge and Survival in Russia and Estonia*. Saarijärvi: Kikimora Publications, pp. 101–127.

Allcock, John B. (2000): *Explaining Yugoslavia*. New York: Columbia University Press.

Anderson, Grace M. (1974): *Networks of Contact: The Portuguese and Toronto*. Waterloo, Ontario: Wilfrid Laurier University Publications.

Anderson, Richard D., Jr., M. Steven Fish, Stephen E. Hanson, and Philip G. Roeder (2001): *Postcommunism and the Theory of Democracy*. Princeton, NJ: Princeton University Press.

Anheier, Helmut and Nuno Themudo (2002): "Organisational Forms of Global Civil Society: Implications of Going Global" in Marlies Glasius, Mary Kaldor, and Helmut Anheier, eds., *Global Civil Society 2002*. Oxford: Oxford University Press, pp. 191–216.

Anthony, Denise and Christine Horne (2003): "Gender and Cooperation: Explaining Loan Repayment in Micro-Credit Groups," *Social Psychology Quarterly* 66: 293–302.

Armitage, David (1994): " 'The Projecting Age': William Paterson and the Bank of England," *History Today* 44: 5–10.

Audisio, Gabriel (1999): *The Waldensian Dissent. Persecution and Survival, c. 1170– c. 1570.* Cambridge: Cambridge University Press.

Auyero, Javier (2000): *Poor People's Politics: Peronist Survival Networks and the Legacy of Evita.* Durham, NC: Duke University Press.

Avritzer, Leonardo (2002): *Democracy and the Public Space in Latin America.* Princeton, NJ: Princeton University Press.

Bailey, David C. (1974): *Viva Crísto Rey! The Cristero Rebellion and the Church-State Conflict in Mexico.* Austin: University of Texas Press.

Ballbé, Manuel (1985): *Orden público y militarismo en la España constitucional (1812– 1983).* Madrid: Alianza. 2nd edn.

Bandelj, Nina (2002): "Embedded Economies: Social Relations as Determinants of Foreign Direct Investment in Central and Eastern Europe," *Social Forces* 81: 411–444.

Bandy, Joe and Jackie Smith (2004): "Factors Affecting Conflict and Cooperation in Transnational Movement Networks" in Joe Bandy and Jackie Smith, eds., *Coalitions Across Borders: Transnational Protest and the Neoliberal Order.* Lanham, MD: Rowman & Littlefield.

Barbalet, J. M. (2001): *Emotion, Social Theory, and Social Structure: A Macrosociological Approach.* Cambridge: Cambridge University Press.

Barber, Bernard (1983): *The Logic and Limits of Trust.* New Brunswick, NJ: Rutgers University Press.

Bates, Robert H., Avnet Greif, Jean–Laurent Rosanthal, Margaret Levi, and Barry R. Weingast (1998): *Analytical Narratives.* Princeton, NJ: Princeton University Press.

Bax, Mart (1976): *Harpstrings and Confessions: Machine-Style Politics in the Irish Republic.* Amsterdam: Van Gorcum.

Bayart, Jean-François, Stephen Ellis, and Béatrice Hibou (1999): *The Criminalization of the State in Africa.* Oxford: James Currey.

Bayat, Asef (1997): *Street Politics: Poor People's Movements in Iran.* New York: Columbia University Press.

Bayon, Denis (1999): *Les S.E.L., "Systèmes d'échanges locaux": Pour un vrai débat.* Levallois-Perret: Yves Michel.

Bearman, Peter S. (1991): "Desertion as Localism: Army Unit Solidarity and Group Norms in the U.S. Civil War," *Social Forces* 70: 321–342.

Bearman, Peter S. (1993): *Relations into Rhetorics: Local Elite Social Structure in Norfolk, England, 1540–1640.* New Brunswick, NJ: Rutgers University Press.

Beaubernard, R. (1981): *Montceau-les-Mines: Un "laboratoire social" au XIXe siècle.* Clamecy: Éditions de Civry.

Benedict, Philip (2002): *Christ's Churches Purely Reformed: A Social History of Calvinism.* New Haven, CT: Yale University Press.

Bennett, W. Lance (2003): "Communicating Global Activism," *Information, Communication & Society* 6: 143–168.

Bennett, W. Lance (2004): "Social Movements beyond Borders: Understanding Two Eras of Transnational Activism" in Donatella della Porta and Sidney Tarrow, eds.,

References

Transnational Protest and Global Activism. Lanham, MD: Rowman & Littlefield, pp. 203–226.

Bermeo, Nancy (2000): "Civil Society after Democracy: Some Conclusions" in Nancy Bermeo and Philip Nord, eds., *Civil Society before Democracy: Lessons from Nineteenth-Century Europe.* Lanham, MD: Rowman & Littlefield.

Bermeo, Nancy (2003): *Ordinary People in Extraordinary Times: The Citizenry and the Breakdown of Democracy.* Princeton, NJ: Princeton University Press.

Besley, Timothy (1995): "Nonmarket Institutions for Credit and Risk Sharing in Low-Income Countries," *Journal of Economic Perspectives* 9: 169–188.

Biggart, Nicole Woolsey (2001): "Banking on Each Other: The Situational Logic of Rotating Savings and Credit Associations," *Advances in Qualitative Organization Research* 3: 129–53.

Biggart, Nicole Woolsey and Thomas D. Beamish (2003): "The Economic Sociology of Conventions: Habit, Custom, Practice, and Routine in Market Order," *Annual Review of Sociology* 29: 443–464.

Biggart, Nicole Woolsey and Richard P. Castanias (2001): "Collateralized Social Relations: The Social in Economic Calculation," *American Journal of Economics and Sociology* 60: 471–500.

Black, Christopher F. (2000): "The Development of Confraternity Studies Over the Past Thirty Years" in Nicholas Terpstra, ed., *The Politics of Ritual Kinship: Confraternities and Social Order in Early Modern Italy.* Cambridge: Cambridge University Press, pp. 9–29.

Blok, Anton (2001): *Honour and Violence.* Cambridge: Polity.

Bodnar, John (1985): *The Transplanted: A History of Immigrants in Urban America.* Bloomington: Indiana University Press.

Boehm, Christopher (1987): *Blood Revenge: The Enactment and Management of Conflict in Montenegro and Other Tribal Societies.* Philadelphia: University of Pennsylvania Press. First published by University Press of Kansas, 1984.

Boehm, Christopher (1996): "Emergency Decisions, Cultural-Selection Mechanisms, and Group Selection," *Current Anthropology* 37: 763–793.

Boli, John and George Thomas (1997): "World Culture in the World Polity: A Century of International Non-Governmental Organization," *American Sociological Review* 62: 171–190.

Borges, Marcelo J. (2003): "Network Migration, Marriage Patterns, and Adaptation in Rural Portugal and Among Portuguese Immigrants in Argentina, 1870–1980," *History of the Family* 8: 445–479.

Braddick, Michael (2000): *State Formation in Early Modern England c. 1550–1700.* Cambridge: Cambridge University Press.

Bradley, Joseph (2002): "Subjects into Citizens: Societies, Civil Society, and Autocracy in Tsarist Russia," *American Historical Review* 107: 1094–1123.

Brass, Paul R., ed. (1996): *Riots and Pogroms.* New York: New York University Press.

Brewer, John D., Adrian Gualke, Ian Hume, Edward Moxon–Browne, and Rick Wilford (1988): *The Police, Public Order and the State: Policing in Great Britain, Northern Ireland, the Irish Republic, the USA, Israel, South Africa and China.* New York: St. Martins.

Broadbent, Jeffrey (1998): *Environmental Politics in Japan: Networks of Power and Protest*. Cambridge: Cambridge University Press.

Broeker, Galen (1970): *Rural Disorder and Police Reform in Ireland, 1812–36*. London: Routledge & Kegan Paul.

Brubaker, Rogers and David D. Laitin (1998): "Ethnic and Nationalist Violence," *Annual Review of Sociology* 24: 423–452.

Bryan, Dominic (2000): *Orange Parades: The Politics of Ritual, Tradition and Control*. London: Pluto Press.

Buchan, Nancy R., Rachel T. A. Croson, and Robyn M. Dawes (2002): "Swift Neighbors and Persistent Strangers: A Cross-Cultural Investigation of Trust and Reciprocity in Social Exchange," *American Journal of Sociology* 108: 168–206.

Buck, Andrew D. (1999): "Networks of Governance and Privatization: A View From Provincial Russia," *Political Power and Social Theory* 13: 81–108.

Burt, Ronald S. and Marc Knez (1995): "Kinds of Third-Party Effects on Trust," *Rationality and Society* 7: 255–292.

Caddick-Adams, Peter and Richard Holmes (2001): "Terrorism" in Richard Holmes, ed., *The Oxford Companion to Military History*. Oxford: Oxford University Press, pp. 906–907.

Caramani, Daniele (2000): *The Societies of Europe. Elections in Western Europe since 1815: Electoral Results by Constituencies*. New York: Grove's Dictionaries.

Caramani, Daniele (2004): *The Nationalization of Politics: The Formation of National Electorates and Party Systems in Western Europe*. Cambridge: Cambridge University Press.

Casanova, Julián, Ángela Cenarro, Julita Cifuentes, Pilar Maluenda, and Pilar Salomón (1992): *El pasado oculto: Fascismo y violencia en Aragón (1936–39)*. Madrid: Siglo Veintiuno de España.

Castrén, Anna-Maija and Markku Lonkila (2004): "Friendship in Finland and Russia from a Micro Perspective" in Anna-Maija Castrén, Markku Lonkila, and Matti Peltonen, eds., *Between Sociology and History: Essays on Microhistory, Collective Action, and Nation-Building*. Helsinki: SKS/Finnish Literature Society.

Chaliand, Gérard and Jean-Pierre Rageau (1997): *Penguin Atlas of Diasporas*. New York: Penguin.

Chalom, Maurice and Luce Léonard (2001): *Insécurité, Police de proximité et Gouvernance locale*. Paris: l'Harmattan.

Chambers, John Whiteclay II (1987): *To Raise an Army. The Draft Comes to Modern America*. New York: Free Press.

Chandhoke, Neera (2002): "The Limits of Global Civil Society" in Marlies Glasius, Mary Kaldor, and Helmut Anheier, eds., *Global Civil Society 2002*. Oxford: Oxford University Press, pp. 35–54.

Chevigny, Paul (1999): "Police Brutality," in Lester Kurtz, ed., *Encyclopedia of Violence, Peace, and Conflict*. San Diego: Academic Press, pp. III, 1–10.

Clark, Janine A. (2004a): *Islam, Charity, and Activism. Middle-Class Social Networks and Social Welfare in Egypt, Jordan, and Yemen*. Bloomington: Indiana University Press.

References

Clark, Janine A. (2004b): "Islamist Women in Yemen: Informal Nodes of Activism" in Quintan Wiktorowicz, ed., *Islamic Activism. A Social Movement Theory Approach*. Bloomington: Indiana University Press.

Clark, Samuel and James S. Donnelly, Jr., eds. (1983): *Irish Peasants: Violence and Political Unrest, 1780–1914*. Madison: University of Wisconsin Press.

Conley, Carolyn A. (1999a): *Melancholy Accidents: The Meaning of Violence in Post-Famine Ireland*. Lanham, MD: Lexington Books.

Conley, Carolyn A. (1999b): "The Agreeable Recreation of Fighting," *Journal of Social History* 33: 58–72.

Cook, Karen S., ed. (2001): *Trust in Society*. New York: Russell Sage Foundation.

Cordero-Guzmán, Héctor R., Robert C. Smith, and Ramón Grosfoguel, eds. (2001): *Migration, Transnationalization, and Race in a Changing New York*. Philadelphia: Temple University Press.

Cordingly, David (1995): *Under the Black Flag: The Romance and the Reality of Life Among the Pirates*. San Diego: Harcourt Brace.

Cornelius, Wayne (2001): "Huecos en la democratización: la politica subnacional como un obstáculo en la transición mexicana" in Reynaldo Yunuen Ortega Ortiz, ed., *Caminos a la democracia*. Mexico City: El Colegio de México, pp. 241–266.

Crenshaw, Martha, ed. (1983): *Terrorism, Legitimacy, and Power: The Consequences of Political Violence*. Middletown, CT: Wesleyan University Press.

Crenshaw, Martha, ed. (1995): *Terrorism in Context*. University Park: Penn State University Press.

Crépin, Annie and Philippe Boulanger (2001): *Le Soldat-citoyen. Une histoire de la conscription*. Paris: Documentation Française. Documentation Photographique 8019.

Cruz, Rafael (1987): *El Partido Comunista de España en la II Republica*. Madrid: Alianza.

Cunningham, David (2003): "Understanding State Responses to Left- versus Right-Wing Threats: The FBI's Repression of the New Left and the Ku Klux Klan," *Social Science History* 27: 327–370.

Curtin, Philip D. (1984): *Cross-Cultural Trade in World History*. Cambridge: Cambridge University Press.

Darr, Asaf (2003): "Gifting Practices and Interorganizational Relations: Constructing Obligation Networks in the Electronics Sector," *Sociological Forum* 18: 31–51.

Davids, Karel and Jan Lucassen, eds. (1995): *A Miracle Mirrored: The Dutch Republic in European Perspective*. Cambridge: Cambridge University Press.

Davis, Diane E. and Anthony W. Pereira, eds. (2003): *Irregular Armed Forces and Their Role in Politics and State Formation*. Cambridge: Cambridge University Press.

Deflem, Mathieu (2002): *Policing World Society: Historical Foundations of International Police Cooperation*. Oxford: Oxford University Press.

Defoe, Daniel (1999): *A General History of the Pyrates*. Mineola, NY: Dover.

Deibert, Ronald J. (2000): "International Plug 'n Play? Citizen Activism, the Internet, and Global Public Policy," *International Studies Perspectives* 1: 255–272.

Derluguian, Georgi (1999): "Che Guevaras in Turbans," *New Left Review* 237: 3–27.

de Tocqueville, Alexis (1991): André Jardin, ed., *Oeuvres I*. Paris: Gallimard.

Diamond, Larry (1999): *Developing Democracy: Toward Consolidation*. Baltimore, MD: Johns Hopkins University Press.

Diani, Mario (1995): *Green Networks: A Structural Analysis of the Italian Environmental Movement*. Edinburgh: Edinburgh University Press.

Diani, Mario (2003): "Introduction: Social Movements, Contentious Actions, and Social Networks: 'From Metaphor to Substance'?" in Mario Diani and Doug McAdam, eds., *Social Movements and Networks: Relational Approaches to Collective Action*. Oxford: Oxford University Press, pp. 1–20.

Diani, Mario and Doug McAdam, eds. (2003): *Social Movements and Networks: Relational Approaches to Collective Action*. Oxford: Oxford University Press.

Dietz, Thomas, Elinor Ostrom, and Paul C. Stern (2003): "The Struggle to Govern the Commons," *Science* 302: 1907–1912.

DiMaggio, Paul, ed. (2001): *The Twenty-First Century Firm. Changing Economic Organization in International Perspective*. Princeton, NJ: Princeton University Press.

DiMaggio, Paul, Eszter Hargittai, W. Russell Neuman, and John P. Robinson (2001): "Social Implications of the Internet," *Annual Review of Sociology* 27: 307–336.

DiMaggio, Paul and Hugh Louch (1998): "Socially Embedded Consumer Transactions: For What Kinds of Purchases Do People Most Often Use Networks?" *American Sociological Review* 63: 619–637.

Dolšak, Nives and Elinor Ostrom, eds. (2003): *The Commons in the New Millennium: Challenges and Adaptation*. Cambridge: MIT Press.

Dryzek, John S. (1996): "Political Inclusion and the Dynamics of Democratization," *American Political Science Review* 90: 475–487.

Dubin, Lois C. (1999): *The Port Jews of Habsburg Trieste: Absolutist Politics and Enlightenment Culture*. Stanford, CA: Stanford University Press.

Duffy, Eamon (2001): *The Voices of Morebath: Reformation & Rebellion in an English Village*. New Haven, CT: Yale University Press.

Ebaugh, Helen Rose Fuchs (1988): *Becoming an EX: The Process of Role Exit*. Chicago: University of Chicago Press.

Edwards, Bob, Michael W. Foley, and Mario Diani, eds. (2001): *Beyond Tocqueville: Civil Society and the Social Capital Debate in Comparative Perspective*. Hanover, NH: University Press of New England.

Eisenbichler, Konrad (2000): "The Suppression of Confraternities in Enlightenment Florence" in Nicholas Terpstra, ed., *The Politics of Ritual Kinship: Confraternities and Social Order in Early Modern Italy*. Cambridge: Cambridge University Press.

Eliasoph, Nina (1998): *Avoiding Politics: How Americans Produce Apathy in Everyday Life*. Cambridge: Cambridge University Press.

Ellis, Stephen (2000): *The Mask of Anarchy: The Destruction of Liberia and the Religious Dimension of an African Civil War*. New York: New York University Press.

Elster, Jon (1989): *Nuts and Bolts for the Social Sciences*. Cambridge: Cambridge University Press.

References

Elster, Jon (1999): *Alchemists of the Mind: Rationality and the Emotions.* Cambridge: Cambridge University Press.

Elster, Jon, Claus Offe, and Ulrich K. Preuss (1998): *Institutional Design in Post-communist Societies: Rebuilding the Ship at Sea.* Cambridge: Cambridge University Press.

Enders, Walter and Todd Sandler (2002): "Patterns of Transnational Terrorism, 1970–1999: Alternative Time-Series Estimates," *International Studies Quarterly* 46: 145–165.

Engelstad, Fredrik and Øyvind Østerud (2004): "Democracy and Power" in Fredrik Engelstad and Øyvind Østerud, eds., *Power and Democracy: Critical Interventions.* Aldershot: Ashgate, pp. 1–10.

Evans, Sara M. and Harry C. Boyte (1986): *Free Spaces: The Sources of Democratic Change in America.* New York: Harper & Row.

Farah, Douglas (2004): *Blood from Stones: The Secret Financial Network of Terror.* New York: Broadway Books.

Farrell, Sean (2000): *Rituals and Riots: Sectarian Violence and Political Culture in Ulster, 1784–1886.* Lexington: University Press of Kentucky.

Feige, Edgar (1997): "Underground Activity and Institutional Change: Productive, Protective, and Predatory Behavior in Transition Economies," in Joan Nelson, Charles Tilly, and Lee Walker, eds., *Transforming Post-Communist Political Economies.* Washington: National Academy Press, pp. 21–34.

Fernandez, Roberto and Doug McAdam (1988): "Social Networks and Social Movements: Multiorganizational Fields and Recruitment to Mississippi Freedom Summer," *Sociological Forum* 3: 357–382.

Fishman, Robert M. (2004): *Democracy's Voices: Social Ties and the Quality of Public Life in Spain.* Ithaca, NY: Cornell University Press.

Forment, Carlos A. (2003): *Democracy in Latin America 1760–1900. Volume I: Civic Selfhood and Public Life in Mexico and Peru.* Chicago: University of Chicago Press.

Fox, Jonathan (1992): *The Politics of Food in Mexico: State Power and Social Mobilization.* Ithaca, NY: Cornell University Press.

Fox, Jonathan (1994): "The Difficult Transition from Clientelism to Citizenship: Lessons from Mexico," *World Politics* 46: 151–184.

Fox, Jonathan (1996): "How Does Civil Society Thicken? The Political Construction of Social Capital in Rural Mexico," *World Development* 24: 1089–1103.

Fussell, Elizabeth and Douglas S. Massey (2004): "The Limits to Cumulative Causation: International Migration from Mexican Urban Areas," *Demography* 41: 151–171.

Futrell, Robert and Barbara G. Brents (2003): "Protest as Terrorism: The Potential for Violent Anti-Nuclear Activism," *American Behavioral Scientist* 46: 745–765.

Gambetta, Diego (1993): *The Sicilian Mafia: The Business of Private Protection.* Cambridge, MA: Harvard University Press.

Glasius, Marlies, Mary Kaldor, and Helmut Anheier, eds. (2002): *Global Civil Society 2002.* Oxford: Oxford University Press.

Glete, Jan (2002): *War and the State in Early Modern Europe: Spain, the Dutch Republic, and Sweden as Fiscal-Military States, 1500–1660*. London: Routledge.

González Callejo, Eduardo (1999): *El Máuser y el sufragio: Orden público, subversión y violencia política en la crisis de la Restauración (1917–1931)*. Madrid: Consejo Superior de Investigaciones Científicas.

González Callejo, Eduardo (2002a): *El terrorismo en Europa*. Madrid: Arco/Libros.

González Callejo, Eduardo, ed. (2002b): *Políticas del miedo. Un balance del terrorismo en Europa*. Madrid: Biblioteca Nueva.

Gould, Roger V. (1995): *Insurgent Identities: Class, Community, and Protest in Paris from 1848 to the Commune*. Chicago: University of Chicago Press.

Gould, Roger V. (1999): "Collective Violence and Group Solidarity: Evidence from a Feuding Society," *American Sociological Review* 64: 356–380.

Gould, Roger V. (2003): *Collision of Wills: How Ambiguity about Social Rank Breeds Conflict*. Chicago: University of Chicago Press.

Granovetter, Mark (1995): "The Economic Sociology of Firms and Entrepreneurs" in Alejandro Portes, ed., *The Economic Sociology of Immigration: Essays on Networks, Ethnicity, and Entrepreneurship*. New York: Russell Sage Foundation, pp. 128–165.

Green, Nancy L. (2002): *Repenser les migrations*. Paris: Presses Universitaires de France.

Greer, Donald (1935): *The Incidence of the Terror During the French Revolution: A Statistical Interpretation*. Cambridge, MA: Harvard University Press.

Gregory, Derek (2004): *The Colonial Present: Afghanistan – Palestine – Iraq*. Oxford: Blackwell.

Greif, Avner (1994): "Cultural Beliefs and the Organization of Society: A Historical and Theoretical Reflection on Collectivist and Individualist Societies," *Journal of Political Economy* 102: 912–950.

Grimson, Alejandro (1999): *Relatos de la diferencia y la igualdad: Los bolivianos en Buenos Aires*. Buenos Aires: Editorial Universitaria de Buenos Aires.

Guenniffey, Patrice (2000): *La Politique de la Terreur: Essai sur la Violence Révolutionnaire, 1789–1794*. Paris: Fayard.

Guiso, Luigi, Paola Sapienza, and Luigi Zingales (2004): "The Role of Social Capital in Financial Development," *American Economic Review* 94: 526–556.

Haber, Stephen, Armando Razo, and Noel Maurer (2003): *The Politics of Property Rights: Political Instability, Credible Commitments, and Economic Growth in Mexico, 1876–1929*. Cambridge: Cambridge University Press.

Hagan, Jacqueline and Helen Rose Ebaugh (2003): "Calling upon the Sacred; Migrants' Use of Religion in the Migration Process," *International Migration Review* 37: 1145–1162.

Hanagan, Michael (1998): "Irish Transnational Social Movements, Deterritorialized Migrants, and the State System: The Last One Hundred and Forty Years," *Mobilization* 13: 107–126.

Hanagan, Michael (2002): "Irish Transnational Social Movements, Migrants, and the State System" in Jackie Smith and Hank Johnston, eds., *Globalization and Resistance: Transnational Dimensions of Social Movements*. Lanham, MD: Rowman & Littlefield, pp. 53–74.

References

Hardin, Russell (2002): *Trust and Trustworthiness*. New York: Russell Sage Foundation.

't Hart, Marjolein (1993): *The Making of a Bourgeois State: War, Politics and Finance during the Dutch Revolt*. Manchester: Manchester University Press.

Hart, Peter (1998): *The I.R.A. & its Enemies: Violence and Community in Cork, 1916–1923*. Oxford: Clarendon Press.

Havik, Philip J. (1998): "Female Entrepreneurship in a Changing Environment: Gender, Kinship and Trade in the Guinea Bissau Region" in Carla Risseeuw and Kamala Ganesh, eds., *Negotiation and Social Space: A Gendered Analysis of Changing Kin and Security Networks in South Asia and Sub-Saharan Africa*. Walnut Creek, CA: AltaMira Press.

Haythornthwaite, Caroline and Barry Wellman (2002): "The Internet in Everyday Life: An Introduction" in Barry Wellman and Caroline Haythornthwaite, eds., *The Internet in Everyday Life*. Malden, MA: Blackwell.

Hechter, Michael (1987): *Principles of Group Solidarity*. Berkeley: University of California Press.

Heimer, Carol A. (1985): *Reactive Risk and Rational Action: Managing Moral Hazard in Insurance Contracts*. Berkeley: University of California Press.

Helleiner, Eric (2003): *The Making of National Money: Territorial Currencies in Historical Perspective*. Ithaca, NY: Cornell University Press.

Hirschman, Albert O. (1970): *Exit, Voice, and Loyalty: Responses to Decline in Firms, Organizations, and States*. Cambridge, MA: Harvard University Press.

Hochschild, Adam (1998): *King Leopold's Ghost: A Story of Greed, Terror, and Heroism in Colonial Africa*. Boston: Houghton Mifflin.

Hoerder, Dirk and Leslie Page Moch, eds. (1996): *European Migrants: Global and Local Perspectives*. Boston: Northeastern University Press.

Hoffman, Philip T., Gilles Postel-Vinay, and Jean-Laurent Rosenthal (2000): *Priceless Markets: The Political Economy of Credit in Paris*. Chicago: University of Chicago Press.

Hoffmann, Stefan-Ludwig (2003): "Democracy and Associations in the Long Nineteenth Century: Toward a Transnational Perspective," *Journal of Modern History* 75: 269–299.

Horden, Peregrine and Nicholas Purcell (2000): *The Corrupting Sea: A Study of Mediterranean History*. Oxford: Blackwell.

Horowitz, Donald L. (2001): *The Deadly Ethnic Riot*. Berkeley: University of California Press.

Huggins, Martha Knisely (1998): *Policing: The United States and Latin America*. Durham, NC: Duke University Press.

Humphrey, Caroline (1999): "Traders, 'Disorder' and Citizenship Regimes in Provincial Russia" in Michael Burawoy and Katherine Verdery, eds., *Uncertain Tradition: Ethnographies of Change in the Postsocialist World*. Lanham, MD: Rowman and Littlefield.

Humphrey, Caroline (2001): "Inequality and Exclusion: A Russian Case Study of Emotion in Politics," *Anthropological Theory* 1: 331–353.

Ibarra, Pedro, ed. (2003): *Social Movements and Democracy*. New York: Palgrave.

Ikegami, Eiko (1995): *The Taming of the Samurai: Honorific Individualism and the Making of Modern Japan*. Cambridge, MA: Harvard University Press.

Imig, Doug and Sidney Tarrow (2001): "Mapping the Europeanization of Contention: Evidence from a Quantitative Data Analysis" in Doug Imig and Sidney Tarrow, eds., *Contentious Europeans: Protest and Politics in an Emerging Polity*. Lanham, MD: Rowman & Littlefield.

Ingram, Paul and Peter W. Roberts (2000): "Friendships among Competitors in the Sydney Hotel Industry," *American Journal of Sociology* 106: 387–423.

Jarman, Neil (1997): *Material Conflicts: Parades and Visual Displays in Northern Ireland*. Oxford: Berg.

Jasso, Guillermina (1999): "How Much Injustice is There in the World? Two New Justice Indexes," *American Sociological Review* 1999: 133–168.

Jung, Courtney (2003): "Breaking the Cycle: Producing Trust Out of Thin Air and Resentment," *Social Movement Studies* 2: 147–176.

Jupp, Peter and Eoin Magennis, eds. (2000): *Crowds in Ireland c. 1720–1920*. London: Macmillan.

Kaelber, Lutz (1998): *Schools of Asceticism: Ideology and Organization in Medieval Religious Communities*. University Park: Pennsylvania State University Press.

Kakar, Sudhir (1996): *The Colors of Violence: Cultural Identities, Religion, and Conflict*. Chicago: University of Chicago Press.

Kalmanowiecki, Laura (2000): "Origins and Applications of Political Policing in Argentina," *Latin American Perspectives* 27: 36–56.

Kalyvas, Stathis N. (1999): "Wanton and Senseless? The Logic of Massacres in Algeria," *Rationality and Society* 11: 243–285.

Kamphoefner, Walter D. (1987): *The Westfalians: From Germany to Missouri*. Princeton, NJ: Princeton University Press.

Kamphoefner, Walter D., Wolfgang Helbich, and Ulrike Sommer, eds. (1991): *News From the Land of Freedom: German Immigrants Write Home*. Ithaca, NY: Cornell University Press.

Kanter, Rosabeth Moss (1972): *Commitment and Community: Communes and Utopias in Sociological Perspective*. Cambridge, MA: Harvard University Press.

Keck, Margaret and Kathryn Sikkink (1998): *Activists beyond Borders: Advocacy Networks in International Politics*. Ithaca, NY: Cornell University Press.

Keck, Margaret and Kathryn Sikkink (2000): "Historical Precursors to Modern Transnational Social Movements and Networks" in John A. Guidry, Michael D. Kennedy, and Mayer N. Zald, eds., *Globalizations and Social Movements: Culture, Power, and the Transnational Public Sphere*. Ann Arbor: University of Michigan Press, pp. 35–53.

Keogh, Dermot (2001): "Ireland at the Turn of the Century: 1994–2001" in T. W. Moody and F. X. Martin, eds., *The Course of Irish History*. Lanham, MD: Roberts Rinehart. 4th edn.

Kepel, Gilles (2002): *Jihad: The Trail of Political Islam*. Cambridge, MA: Harvard University Press.

Kershaw, Sarah and Monica Davey (2004): "Plagued by Drugs, Tribes Revive Ancient Penalty," *New York Times*, electronic edition, January 18.

References

Knight, Jack (2001): "Social Norms and the Rule of Law: Fostering Trust in a Socially Diverse Society" in Karen S. Cook, ed., *Trust in Society*. New York: Russell Sage Foundation, pp. 354–373.

Knoke, David (1990): *Political Networks: The Structural Perspective*. Cambridge: Cambridge University Press.

Knorr-Cetina, Karin and Urs Bruegger (2002): "Global Microstructures: The Virtual Societies of Financial Markets," *American Journal of Sociology* 107: 905–950.

Konstam, Angus (2002): *The History of Pirates*. Guilford, CT: The Lyons Press.

Koopmans, Ruud (2004): "Movements and Media: Selection Processes and Evolutionary Dynamics in the Public Sphere," *Theory and Society* 33: 367–391.

Kraska, Peter B. and Victor E. Kappeler (1997): "Militarizing American Police: The Rise and Normalization of Paramilitary Units," *Social Problems* 44: 1–18.

Krauze, Enrique (2004): "Past Wrongs, Future Rights," *New York Times*, August 10, A21.

Krebs, Ronald R. (2004): "A School for the Nation? How Military Service Does Not Build Nations, and How it Might," *International Security* 28: 85–124.

Kushner, Harvey W., ed. (2001): "Terrorism in the 21st Century," *American Behavioral Scientist* 44, no. 6, entire issue.

Lagrange, Hugues (1989): "Strikes and the War" in Leopold Haimson and Charles Tilly, eds., *Strikes, Wars, and Revolutions in an International Perspective*. Cambridge: Cambridge University Press, pp. 473–499.

Landa, Janet Tai (1994): *Trust, Ethnicity, and Identity: Beyond the New Institutional Economics of Ethnic Trading Networks, Contract Law, and Gift-Exchange*. Ann Arbor: University of Michigan Press.

Lane, Frederic C. (1973): *Venice, a Maritime Republic*. Baltimore, MD: Johns Hopkins University Press.

Lane, Frederic C. (1975): "The Role of Government in Economic Growth in Early Modern Times," *Journal of Economic History* 35: 8–17.

Laumann, Edward O. and David Knoke (1987): *The Organizational State: Social Choice in National Policy Domains*. Madison: University of Wisconsin Press.

Ledeneva, Alena (1998): *Russia's Economy of Favours: Blat, Networking, and Informal Exchange*. Cambridge: Cambridge University Press.

Ledeneva, Alena (2000): "Russian Hackers and Virtual Crime" in A. V. Ledeneva and M. Kurchiyan, eds., *Economic Crime in Russia*. The Hague: Kluwer Law International, pp. 163–175.

Ledeneva, Alena (2004): "Genealogy of *krugovaya poruka:* Forced Trust as a Feature of Russian Political Culture," *Proceedings of the British Academy* 123: 85–108.

van Leeuwen, Marco H. D. (2000): *The Logic of Charity: Amsterdam, 1800–1850*. London: Macmillan.

Lehmann, David (1990): *Democracy and Development in Latin America: Economics, Politics and Religion in the Post-war Period*. Philadelphia: Temple University Press.

Levi, Margaret (1997): *Consent, Dissent, and Patriotism*. Cambridge: Cambridge University Press.

Levi, Margaret (2003): "An Analytic Narrative Approach to Puzzles and Problems," Working Paper 2003/192, Juan March Institute, Madrid.

Levi, Margaret and Laura Stoker (2000): "Political Trust and Trustworthiness," *Annual Review of Political Science* 3: 475–508.

Levine, David (1984): "Production, Reproduction, and the Proletarian Family in England, 1500–1851" in David Levine, ed., *Proletarianization and Family History*. Orlando, FL: Academic Press, pp. 87–128.

Light, Ivan and Edna Bonacich (1988): *Immigrant Entrepreneurs: Koreans in Los Angeles, 1965–1982*. Berkeley: University of California Press.

Lindert, Peter H. (2004): *Growing Public. Social Spending and Economic Growth Since the Eighteenth Century*. Cambridge: Cambridge University Press. 2 vols.

Lis, Catharina and Hugo Soly (1979): *Poverty and Capitalism in Pre-Industrial Europe*. Atlantic Highlands, NJ: Humanities Press.

Lis, Catharina and Hugo Soly (1984): "Policing the Early Modern Proletariat, 1450–1850" in David Levine, ed., *Proletarianization and Family History*. Orlando, FL: Academic Press.

Lonkila, Markku (1999a): *Social Networks in Post-Soviet Russia*. Helsinki: Kikimora Publications.

Lonkila, Markku (1999b): "Post-Soviet Russia: A Society of Networks?" in Markku Kangaspuro, ed., *Russia: More Different than Most*. Helsinki: Kikimora Publications, pp. 99–112.

López-Alves, Fernando (2000): *State Formation and Democracy in Latin America, 1810–1900*. Durham, NC: Duke University Press.

Lye, Diane N. (1996): "Adult Child-Parent Relationships," *Annual Review of Sociology* 22: 79–102.

Lynch, Patrick (2001): "The Irish Free State and the Republic of Ireland, 1921–66" in T. W. Moody and F. X. Martin, eds., *The Course of Irish History*. Lanham, MD: Roberts Rinehart. 4th edn.

Lynn, John (1984): *The Bayonets of the Republic: Motivation and Tactics in the Army of Revolutionary France, 1791–94*. Urbana: University of Illinois Press.

Lynn, John (2003): *Battle. A History of Combat and Culture*. Boulder, CO: Westview.

MacCulloch, Diarmaid (2003): *Reformation: Europe's House Divided 1490–1700*. London: Allen Lane.

MacLean, Lauren Morris (2004): "Empire of the Young: The Legacies of State Agricultural Policy on Local Capitalism and Social Support Networks in Ghana and Côte d'Ivoire," *Comparative Studies in Society and History* 46: 469–496.

Malafakis, Edward E. (1970): *Agrarian Reform and Peasant Revolution in Spain*. New Haven, CT: Yale University Press.

Malcolm, Noel (1996): *Bosnia: A Short History*. New York: New York University Press. Rev. edn.; first published in 1994.

Marques, M. Margarida, Rui Santos, and Fernanda Araújo (2001): "Ariadne's Thread: Cape Verdean Women in Transnational Webs," *Global Networks* 1: 283–306.

Marsh, Christopher (1998): *Popular Religion in Sixteenth-Century England*. London: Macmillan.

References

Mason, T. David and Dale A. Krane (1989): "The Political Economy of Death Squads: Toward a Theory of the Impact of State-Sanctioned Terror," *International Studies Quarterly* 33: 175–198.

Massey, Douglas S., Joaquín Arango, Graeme Hugo, Ali Kouaouci, Adela Pellegrino, and J. Edward Taylor (1998): *Worlds in Motion: Understanding International Migration at the End of the Millennium.* Oxford: Clarendon Press.

Mauro, Frédéric (1990): "Merchant Communities, 1350–1750" in James D. Tracy, ed., *The Rise of Merchant Empires: Long-Distance Trade in the Early Modern World, 1350–1750.* Cambridge: Cambridge University Press.

Mayer, Arno J. (2000): *The Furies: Violence and Terror in the French and Russian Revolutions.* Princeton, NJ: Princeton University Press.

Mazower, Mark (2002): "Violence and the State in the Twentieth Century," *American Historical Review* 107: 1158–1178.

McAdam, Doug, Sidney Tarrow, and Charles Tilly (2001): *Dynamics of Contention.* Cambridge: Cambridge University Press.

McCracken, J. L. (2001): "Northern Ireland: 1921–66" in T. W. Moody and F. X. Martin, eds., *The Course of Irish History.* Lanham, MD: Roberts Rinehart. 4th edn.

McGowen, Randall (1999): "From Pillory to Gallows: The Punishment of Forgery in the Age of the Financial Revolution," *Past & Present* 165: 107–140.

Meisch, Lynn A. (2002): *Andean Entrepreneurs: Otavalo Merchants and Musicians in the Global Arena.* Austin: University of Texas Press.

Mertes, Tom, ed. (2004): *A Movement of Movements: Is Another World Really Possible?* London: Verso.

Miskimin, Patricia Behre (2002): *One King, One Law, Three Faiths: Religion and the Rise of Absolutism in Seventeenth-Century Metz.* Westport, CT: Greenwood.

Mjøset, Lars and Stephen Van Holde (2002): "Killing for the State, Dying for the Nation: An Introductory Essay on the Life Cycle of Conscription into Europe's Armed Forces," *Comparative Social Research* 20: 3–94.

Moch, Leslie Page (2003): *Moving Europeans: Migration in Western Europe Since 1650.* Bloomington: Indiana University Press. 2nd edn.

Mommsen, Wolfgang J. and Gerhard Hirschfeld, eds. (1982): *Social Protest, Violence and Terror in Nineteenth- and Twentieth-Century Europe.* New York: St. Martins.

Monjardet, Dominique (1996): *Ce que fait la police: Sociologie de la force publique.* Paris: La Découverte.

Moore, Barrington, Jr. (1979): *Injustice: The Social Bases of Obedience and Revolt.* White Plains, NY: M. E. Sharpe.

Morawska, Ewa (1985): *For Bread with Butter: Life-Worlds of East Central Europeans in Johnstown, Pennsylvania, 1890–1940.* Cambridge: Cambridge University Press.

Morawska, Ewa (1996): *Insecure Prosperity: Small-Town Jews in Industrial America, 1890–1940.* Princeton, NJ: Princeton University Press.

Morawska, Ewa (2003): "Disciplinary Agendas and Analytic Strategies of Research on Immigration and Transnationalism: Challenges of Interdisciplinary Knowledge," *International Migration Review* 37: 611–640.

Morrill, Calvin (1991): "Conflict Management, Honor, and Organizational Change," *American Journal of Sociology* 97: 585–621.

Muir, Edward (1997): *Ritual in Early Modern Europe*. Cambridge: Cambridge University Press.

Muldrew, Craig (1993): "Interpreting the Market: The Ethics of Credit and Community Relations in Early Modern England," *Social History* 18: 163–183.

Muldrew, Craig (1998): *The Economy of Obligation*. London: Macmillan.

Muldrew, Craig (2001): "'Hard Food for Midas': Cash and its Social Value in Early Modern England," *Past and Present* 170: 78–120.

Nada Patrone, Anna Maria, and Gabrielle Airaldi (1986): *Comuni e signorie nell'Italia settentrionale: il Piemonte e la Liguria*. Turin: UTET.

Naimark, Norman M. (2001): *Fires of Hatred: Ethnic Cleansing in Twentieth-Century Europe*. Cambridge, MA: Harvard University Press.

Najemy, John M. (1982): *Corporatism and Consensus in Florentine Electoral Politics, 1280–1400*. Chapel Hill: University of North Carolina Press.

Narotzky, Susana and Paz Moreno (2002): "Reciprocity's Dark Side. Negative Reciprocity, Morality and Social Reproduction," *Anthropological Theory* 2: 281–305.

National Commission on Terrorist Attacks Upon the United States (2004): *Final Report*. New York: Norton.

North, Douglass C. (1990): *Institutions, Institutional Change and Economic Performance*. Cambridge: Cambridge University Press.

North, Douglass C. (1997): "Understanding Economic Change" in Joan Nelson, Charles Tilly, and Lee Walker, eds., *Transforming Post-Communist Political Economies*. Washington: National Academy Press, pp. 13–18.

Ohlemacher, Thomas (1993): *Brücken der Mobilisierung: Soziale Relais und persönliche Netzwerke in Bürgerinitiativen gegen militärischen Tiefflug*. Wiesbaden: Deutscher Universitäts Verlag.

Oliverio, Annamarie (1998): *The State of Terror*. Albany: State University of New York Press.

O'Neill, Joseph (2001): *Blood-Dark Track. A Family History*. London: Granta.

O'Neill, Kate (2004): "Transnational Protest: States, Circuses, and Conflict at the Frontline of Global Politics," *International Studies Review* 6: 233–251.

Opp, Karl-Dieter and Christiane Gern (1993): "Dissident Groups, Personal Networks, and Spontaneous Cooperation: The East German Revolution of 1989," *American Sociological Review* 58: 659–680.

Ortega Ortiz, Reynaldo Yunuen (2000): "Comparing Types of Transitions: Spain and Mexico," *Democratization* 7: 65–92.

Ortega Ortiz, Reynaldo Yunuen, ed. (2001): *Caminos a la Democracia*. Mexico City: El Colegio de México.

Ostergren, Robert C. (1988): *A Community Transplanted: The Trans-Atlantic Experience of a Swedish Immigrant Settlement in the Upper Middle West, 1835–1915*. Uppsala: Acta Universitatis Upsaliensis.

Ostrom, Elinor (1990): *Governing the Commons: The Evolution of Institutions for Collective Action*. Cambridge: Cambridge University Press.

References

Ostrom, Elinor (1998): "A Behavioral Approach to the Rational Choice Theory of Collective Action," *American Political Science Review* 92: 1–22.

Ostrom, Elinor, Thomas Dietz, Nives Dolšak, Paul C. Stern, Susan Stonich, and Elke Weber, eds. (2002): *The Drama of the Commons*. Washington: National Academy Press.

Otterbein, Keith F. (1999): "Clan and Tribal Conflict" in *Encyclopedia of Violence, Peace, and Conflict*. San Diego: Academic Press, vol. 1, pp. 289–295.

Palmer, Stanley H. (1988): *Police and Protest in England and Ireland 1780–1850*. Cambridge: Cambridge University Press.

Pape, Robert A. (2003): "The Strategic Logic of Suicide Terrorism," *American Political Science Review* 97: 343–361.

Paravy, Pierrette (1993): *De la Chrétienté Romaine à la Réforme en Dauphiné. Évêques, Fidèles et Déviants (vers 1340 – vers 1530)*. Rome: École Française de Rome. 2 vols.

Parsa, Misagh (2000): *States, Ideologies, and Social Revolutions: A Comparative Analysis of Iran, Nicaragua and the Philippines*. Cambridge: Cambridge University Press.

Passy, Florence (1998): *L'Action altruiste: Contraintes et opportunités de l'engagement dans les mouvements sociaux*. Geneva: Droz.

Passy, Florence (2001): "Socialization, Connection, and the Structure Agency Gap: A Specification of the Impact of Networks on Participation in Social Movements," *Mobilization* 6: 173–192.

Pastor, Reyna, Esther Pascua, Ana Rodríguez-López, and Pablo Sánchez-León (2002): *Beyond the Market: Transactions, Property and Social Networks in Monastic Galicia 1200–1300*. Leiden: Brill.

Paxton, Pamela (1999): "Is Social Capital Declining in the United States? A Multiple Indicator Assessment," *American Journal of Sociology* 108: 88–127.

Paxton, Pamela (2002): "Social Capital and Democracy: An Interdependent Relationship," *American Journal of Sociology* 67: 254–277.

Piipponen, Minna (2004): "Work-Related Ties in the Everyday Life of a Russian Karelian Mill Community" in Risto Alapuro, Ilkka Liikanen, and Markku Lonkila, eds., *Beyond Post-Soviet Transition: Micro Perspectives on Challenge and Survival in Russia and Estonia*. Saarijärvi: Kikimora Publications, pp. 64–83.

Podolny, Joel M. and Karen L. Page (1998): "Network Forms of Organization," *Annual Review of Sociology* 24: 57–76.

Polletta, Francesca (1999): " 'Free Spaces' in Collective Action," *Theory and Society* 28: 1–38.

Polletta, Francesca (2002): *Freedom is an Endless Meeting: Democracy in American Social Movements*. Chicago: University of Chicago Press.

Poros, Maritsa (2001): "The Role of Migrant Networks in Linking Local Labour Markets: The Case of Asian Indian Migration to New York and London," *Global Networks* 1: 243–259.

della Porta, Donatella and Gianfranco Pasquino, eds. (1983): *Terrorismo e violenza politica*. Bologna: Il Mulino.

Portes, Alejandro, ed. (1995): *The Economic Sociology of Immigration: Essays on Networks, Ethnicity, and Entrepreneurship*. New York: Russell Sage Foundation.

Portes, Alejandro, ed. (1996): *The New Second Generation*. New York: Russell Sage Foundation.

177

Portes, Alejandro and Rubén Rumbaut (1990): *Immigrant America: A Portrait*. Berkeley: University of California Press.

Portes, Alejandro and Rubén Rumbaut (2001): *Legacies: The Story of the Immigrant Second Generation*. Berkeley: University of California Press.

Postel-Vinay, Gilles (1998): *La terre et l'argent: L'agriculture et le crédit en France du XVIIIe au début du Xxe siècle*. Paris: Albin Michel.

Postgate, J. N. (1992): *Early Mesopotamia: Society and Economy at the Dawn of History*. London: Routledge.

Powell, Walter W. (1990): "Neither Market nor Hierarchy: Network Forms of Organization" in Barry Staw and Lawrence L. Cummings, eds., *Research in Organizational Behavior*. Greenwich, CT: JAI Press, pp. 295–336.

Powell, Walter W. and Laurel Smith-Doerr (1994): "Networks and Economic Life" in Neil J. Smelser and Richard Swedberg, eds., *The Handbook of Economic Sociology*. Princeton, NJ: Princeton University Press and New York: Russell Sage Foundation, pp. 368–402.

Pretty, Jules (2003): "Social Capital and the Collective Management of Resources," *Science* 302: 1912–1914.

Proudhon, Pierre-Joseph (2003): *Qu'est-ce que la Propriété?* Antony: Editions TOPS/H. Trinquier.

Prunier, Gérard (1995): *The Rwanda Crisis: History of a Genocide*. New York: Columbia University Press.

Prunier, Gérard (2001): "Genocide in Rwanda" in Daniel Chirot and Martin E. P. Seligman, eds., *Ethnopolitical Warfare: Causes, Consequences, and Possible Solutions*. Washington: American Psychological Association, pp. 109–116.

Przeworski, Adam, Michael Alvarez, José Antonio Cheibub, and Fernando Limongi (1997): "What Makes Democracies Endure?" in Larry Diamond, Marc F. Plattner, Yun-han Chu, and Hung-mao Tien, eds., *Consolidating the Third Wave Democracies*. Baltimore, MD: Johns Hopkins University Press.

Putnam, Robert D. (1993): *Making Democracy Work: Civic Traditions in Modern Italy*. Princeton, NJ: Princeton University Press.

Putnam, Robert D. (2000): *Bowling Alone: The Collapse and Revival of American Community*. New York: Simon & Schuster.

Rafael, Vicente (2003): "The Cell Phone and the Crowd: Messianic Politics in the Contemporary Philippines," *Public Culture* 15: 399–425.

Raggio, Olsvaldo (1990): *Faide e Parentele: Lo Stato Genovese visto dalla Fontanabuona*. Turin: Einaudi.

Rapoport, David C. (1999): "Terrorism" in Lester Kurtz, ed., *Encyclopedia of Violence, Peace, and Conflict*. San Diego: Academic Press, vol. 3, pp. 497–510.

Reitz, Jeffrey G. and Sherrilyn M. Sklar (1997): "Culture, Race, and the Economic Assimilation of Immigrants," *Sociological Forum* 12: 233–278.

Rheingold, Howard (2003): *Smart Mobs: The Next Social Revolution*. New York: Perseus Publishing.

Riles, Annelise (2000): *The Network Inside Out*. Ann Arbor: University of Michigan Press.

References

Roaf, Michael (1990): *Cultural Atlas of Mesopotamia and the Ancient Near East*. New York: Facts on File.

Roberts, Kenneth and Michael D. Morris (2003): "Fortune, Risk, and Remittances: An Application of Option Theory to Participation in Village-Based Migration Networks," *International Migration Review* 37: 1252–1281.

Romero, Mauricio (2003): *Paramilitares y autodefensas, 1982–2003*. Bogotà: Instituto de Estudios Politicos y Relaciones Internacionales, Universidad Nacional de Colombia.

Rotberg, Robert, ed. (1999): "Patterns of Social Capital: Stability and Change in Comparative Perspective," *Journal of Interdisciplinary History* 29: nos. 3 and 4, Winter and Spring 1999, two entire issues.

Rotberg, Robert, ed. (2004): *When States Fail: Causes and Consequences*. Princeton, NJ: Princeton University Press.

Rothstein, Bo (2004): "Social Capital in a Working Democracy" in Fredrik Engelstad and Øyvind Østerud, eds., *Power and Democracy: Critical Interventions*. Aldershot: Ashgate, pp. 101–130.

Rubin, Jeffrey W. (1997): *Decentering the Regime: Ethnicity, Radicalism, and Democracy in Juchitán, Mexico*. Durham, NC: Duke University Press.

Ruby, Charles L. (2002): "The Definition of Terrorism," *Analyses of Social Issues and Public Policy* 2: 9–14.

Rucht, Dieter (2003): "Media Strategies and Media Resonance in Transnational Protest Campaigns," unpublished paper presented to conference on Transnational Processes and Social Movements, Bellagio, Italy.

Sanders, Jimy (2002): "Ethnic Boundaries and Identity in Plural Societies," *Annual Review of Sociology* 28: 327–357.

Sanderson, Susan R. Walsh (1984): *Land Reform in Mexico, 1910–1980*. Orlando, FL: Academic Press.

Sassen, Saskia (2002): "Towards a Sociology of Information Technology," *Current Sociology* 50: 29–52.

Saxenian, AnnaLee (1994): *Regional Advantage: Culture and Competition in Silicon Valley and Route 128*. Cambridge, MA: Harvard University Press.

Schmid, Alex P., ed. (2001): *Countering Terrorism Through International Cooperation*. Milan: International Scientific and Professional Advisory Council of the United Nations Crime Prevention and Criminal Justice Programme.

Schmid, Alex P. and Janny de Graaf (1982): *Violence as Communication: Insurgent Terrorism and the Western News Media*. Beverly Hills, CA: Sage.

Schumpeter, Joseph A. (1947): *Capitalism, Socialism, and Democracy*. New York: Harper and Brothers. 2nd edn. First published in 1942.

Scott, James C. (1985): *Weapons of the Weak: Everyday Forms of Peasant Resistance*. New Haven, CT: Yale University Press.

Scott, James C. (1998): *Seeing Like a State: How Certain Schemes to Improve the Human Condition Have Failed*. New Haven, CT: Yale University Press.

Scott, John (1991): *Social Network Analysis: A Handbook*. London: Sage.

Seligman, Adam (1997): *The Problem of Trust*. Princeton, NJ: Princeton University Press.

179

Senechal de la Roche, Roberta, ed. (2004): "Theories of Terrorism: A Symposium," *Sociological Theory* 22: 1–105.

Shapiro, Susan P. (1987): "The Social Control of Impersonal Trust," *American Journal of Sociology* 93: 623–658.

Sheller, Mimi (2000): *Democracy After Slavery: Black Publics and Peasant Radicalism in Haiti and Jamaica*. London: Macmillan (Warwick University Caribbean Studies).

Shklar, Judith N. (1990): *The Faces of Injustice*. New Haven, CT: Yale University Press.

Singerman, Diane (1995): *Avenues of Participation: Family, Politics, and Networks in Urban Quarters of Cairo*. Princeton, NJ: Princeton University Press.

Singerman, Diane (2004): "The Networked World of Islamist Social Movements" in Quintan Wiktorowicz, ed., *Islamic Activism: A Social Movement Theory Approach*. Bloomington: Indiana University Press, pp. 143–163.

Skocpol, Theda (1998): "Did the Civil War Further American Democracy? A Reflection on the Expansion of Benefits for Union Veterans" in Theda Skocpol, ed., *Democracy, Revolution, and History*. Ithaca, NY: Cornell University Press, pp. 73–101.

Skocpol, Theda (2003): *Diminished Democracy: From Membership to Management in American Civic Life*. Norman: University of Oklahoma Press.

Skocpol, Theda and Morris P. Fiorina, eds. (1999): *Civic Engagement in American Democracy*. Washington, DC: Brookings Institution and New York: Russell Sage Foundation.

Skocpol, Theda and Jennifer Lynn Oser (2004): "Organization Despite Adversity: The Origins and Development of African American Fraternal Associations," *Social Science History* 28: 367–437.

Smelser, Neil J. and Faith Mitchell, eds., (2002a): *Terrorism, Perspectives from the Behavioral and Social Sciences*. Washington, DC: National Academies Press.

Smelser, Neil J. and Faith Mitchell, eds., (2002b): *Discouraging Terrorism: Some Implications of 9/11*. Washington, DC: National Academies Press.

Smith, Adam (2000): *The Theory of Moral Sentiments*. Amherst, NY: Prometheus Books. First published in 1759.

Smith, Jackie (1997): "Characteristics of the Modern Transnational Social Movement Sector" in Jackie Smith, Charles Chatfield, and Ron Pagnucco, eds., *Transnational Social Movements and Global Politics: Solidarity Beyond the State*. Syracuse, NY: Syracuse University Press.

Smith, Jackie (2002): "Globalizing Resistance: The Battle of Seattle and the Future of Social Movements" in Jackie Smith and Hank Johnston, eds., *Globalization and Resistance: Transnational Dimensions of Social Movements*. Lanham, MD: Rowman & Littlefield.

Smith, Jackie (2004): "Exploring Connections Between Global Integration and Political Mobilization," *Journal of World Systems Research* 10: 255–286.

Smith, Jackie and Joe Bandy (2004): "Introduction: Cooperation and Conflict in Transnational Protest" in Joe Bandy and Jackie Smith, eds., *Coalitions Across Borders: Transnational Protest and the Neoliberal Order*. Lanham, MD: Rowman & Littlefield.

References

Smith, Robert Courtney (2000): "How Durable and New is Transnational Life? Historical Retrieval through Local Comparison," *Diaspora* 9: 203–232.

Smith, Robert Courtney (2005): *Mexican New York: Transnational Worlds of New Immigrants*. Berkeley: University of California Press.

Solnick, Steven L. (1998): *Stealing the State: Control and Collapse in Soviet Institutions*. Cambridge, MA: Harvard University Press.

Soto Carmona, Álvaro (1988): *El trabajo industrial en la España contemporanea (1874–1936)*. Barcelona: Anthropos.

Stanley, William (1996): *The Protection Racket State: Elite Politics, Military Extortion, and Civil War in El Salvador*. Philadelphia: Temple University Press.

Stark, Oded (1995): *Altruism and Beyond: An Economic Analysis of Transfers and Exchanges within Families and Groups*. Cambridge: Cambridge University Press.

Stein, Gil J. (1999): *Rethinking World-Systems: Diasporas, Colonies, and Interaction in Uruk Mesopotamia*. Tucson: University of Arizona Press.

Stern, Jessica (2003): *Terror in the Name of God: Why Religious Militants Kill*. New York: HarperCollins.

Tarrow, Sidney (2002): "From Lumping to Splitting: Specifying Globalization and Resistance" in Jackie Smith and Hank Johnston, eds., *Globalization and Resistance: Transnational Dimensions of Social Movements*. Lanham, MD: Rowman & Littlefield.

Tarrow, Sidney (2003): "The New Transnational Contention: Social Movements and Institutions in Complex Internationalism," Working Paper 2003.1, Transnational Contention Project, Cornell University.

Taylor, Christopher C. (1999): *Sacrifice as Terror: The Rwandan Genocide of 1994*. Oxford: Berg.

Terpstra, Nicholas (2000): "The Politics of Ritual Kinship" in Nicholas Terpstra, ed., *The Politics of Ritual Kinship: Confraternities and Social Order in Early Modern Italy*. Cambridge: Cambridge University Press.

Thompson, E. P. (1991): *Customs in Common*. London: Merlin Press.

Thompson, Ginger (2004): "Mexico's Leader to Pursue Genocide Case," *New York Times*, September 1, A10.

Thomson, Janice E. (1994): *Mercenaries, Pirates, and Sovereigns: State-Building and Extraterritorial Violence in Early Modern Europe*. Princeton, NJ: Princeton University Press.

Tilly, Charles (1975): "Food Supply and Public Order in Modern Europe" in Charles Tilly, ed., *The Formation of National States in Western Europe*. Princeton, NJ: Princeton University Press.

Tilly, Charles (1984): "Demographic Origins of the European Proletariat" in David Levine, ed., *Proletarianization and Family History*. Orlando, FL: Academic Press.

Tilly, Charles (1985): "War Making and State Making as Organized Crime" in Peter Evans, Dietrich Rues-chemeyer, and Theda Skocpol, eds., *Bringing the State Back In*. Cambridge: Cambridge University Press.

Tilly, Charles (1986): *The Contentious French*. Cambridge, MA: Harvard University Press.

Tilly, Charles (1990): "Transplanted Networks," in Virginia Yans-McLaughlin, ed., *Immigration Reconsidered: History, Sociology, and Politics*. New York: Oxford University Press.

Tilly, Charles (1992a): "Conclusions" in Leopold Haimson and Giulio Sapelli, eds., *Strikes, Social Conflict and the First World War: An International Perspective*. Milan: Feltrinelli. Fondazione Giangiacomo Feltrinelli, *Annali* 1990/1991.

Tilly, Charles (1992b): *Coercion, Capital, and European States*. Oxford: Blackwell. Revised edition.

Tilly, Charles (1993): *European Revolutions, 1492–1992*. Oxford: Blackwell.

Tilly, Charles, ed. (1995): *Citizenship, Identity, and Social History*. Cambridge: Cambridge University Press.

Tilly, Charles (1999a): "Conclusion: Why Worry about Citizenship?" in Michael Hanagan and Charles Tilly, eds., *Extending Citizenship, Reconfiguring States*. Lanham, MD: Rowman and Littlefield, pp. 247–260.

Tilly, Charles (1999b): "Power – Top Down and Bottom Up," *Journal of Political Philosophy* 7: 330–352.

Tilly, Charles (2000a): "Spaces of Contention," *Mobilization* 5: 135–160.

Tilly, Charles (2000b): "Chain Migration and Opportunity Hoarding" in Janina W. Dacyl and Charles Westin, eds., *Governance of Cultural Diversity*. Stockholm: CEIFO [Centre for Research in International Migration and Ethnic Relations].

Tilly, Charles (2001): "Do Unto Others" in Marco Giugni and Florence Passy, eds., *Political Altruism? Solidarity Movements in International Perspective*. Lanham, MD: Rowman & Littlefield, pp. 27–50.

Tilly, Charles (2002a): *Stories, Identities, and Political Change*. Lanham, MD: Rowman & Littlefield.

Tilly, Charles (2002b): "Violence, Terror, and Politics as Usual," *Boston Review* 27, nos. 3–4: 21–24.

Tilly, Charles (2003a): "Political Identities in Changing Polities," *Social Research* 70: 1301–1315.

Tilly, Charles (2003b): *The Politics of Collective Violence*. Cambridge: Cambridge University Press.

Tilly, Charles (2004a): *Contention and Democracy in Europe, 1650–2000*. Cambridge: Cambridge University Press.

Tilly, Charles (2004b): *Social Movements, 1768–2004*. Boulder, CO: Paradigm Press.

Tilly, Charles (2004c): "Social Boundary Mechanisms," *Philosophy of the Social Sciences* 34: 211–236.

Tilly, Charles (2004d): "Terror, Terrorism, Terrorists," *Sociological Theory* 22: 5–13.

Tilly, Charles (2004e): *Social Movements, 1768–2004*. Boulder, CO: Paradigm Press.

Tilly, Charles (2005): *Identities, Boundaries, and Social Ties*. Boulder, CO: Paradigm Press.

Tilly, Chris and Charles Tilly (1998): *Work Under Capitalism*. Boulder, CO: Westview.

Tishkov, Valery (1997): *Ethnicity, Nationalism and Conflict in and After the Soviet Union: The Mind Aflame*. London: Sage.

References

Tishkov, Valery (2004): *Chechnya: Life in a War-Torn Society*. Berkeley: University of California Press.

Trexler, Richard C. (1981): *Public Life in Renaissance Florence*. New York: Academic Press.

Trif, Maria and Doug Imiq (2003): "Demanding to be Heard: Social Movements and the European Public Sphere," Ithaca, NY: Working Paper 2003–06, Cornell University Workshop on Transnational Contention.

Tsai, Kellee S. (2002): *Back-Alley Banking: Private Entrepreneurs in China*. Ithaca, NY: Cornell University Press.

Turk, Austin T. (2004): "Sociology of Terrorism," *Annual Review of Sociology* 30: 271–286.

United Nations Development Program [UNDP] (2002): *Human Development Report 2002: Deepening Democracy in a Fragmented World*. Oxford: Oxford University Press.

U.S. State Department (2001): "Patterns of Global Terrorism 2000," www.usis.usemb.se/terror/rpt2000/index.html. Washington, DC: Office of the Coordinator for Counterterrorism.

U.S. State Department (2002): "Patterns of Global Terrorism 2001," www.usis.usemb.se/terror/rpt2001/index.html. Washington, DC: Office of the Coordinator for Counterterrorism.

Uslaner, Eric M. (2002): *The Moral Foundations of Trust*. Cambridge: Cambridge University Press.

Uzzi, Brian (1997): "Social Structure and Competition in Interfirm Networks: The Paradox of Embeddedness," *Administrative Science Quarterly* 42: 35–67.

Vanhanen, Tatu (2000): "A New Dataset for Measuring Democracy, 1810–1998," *Journal of Peace Research* 37: 251–265.

VanWey, Leah (2004): "Altruistic and Contractual Remittances Between Male and Female Migrants and Households in Rural Thailand," *Demography* 41: 739–756.

Varese, Federico (2001): *The Russian Mafia: Private Protection in a New Market Economy*. Oxford: Oxford University Press.

Verdery, Katherine (2003): *The Vanishing Hectare: Property and Value in Postsocialist Transylvania*. Ithaca, NY: Cornell University Press.

Vermunt, Riël and Herman Steensma, eds. (1991): *Social Justice in Human Relations*. New York: Plenum. 2 vols.

Vertovec, Steven (2003): "Migration and Other Modes of Transnationalism: Towards Conceptual Cross-Fertilization," *International Migration Review* 37: 641–665.

Volkov, Vadim (2002): *The Monopoly of Force: Violent Entrepreneurs in Russia's Emerging Markets*. Ithaca, NY: Cornell University Press.

Waldinger, Roger D. (1996): *Still the Promised City? African-Americans and New Immigrants in New York, 1940–1990*. Cambridge, MA: Harvard University Press.

Waldinger, Roger and Mehdi Bozorgmehr, eds. (1996): *Ethnic Los Angeles*. New York: Russell Sage Foundation.

Waldman, Peter, ed. (1993): *Beruf: Terrorist Labensläufe im Untergrund*. Munich: Beck.

Walter, Eugene V. (1969): *Terror and Resistance: A Study of Political Violence*. New York: Oxford University Press.

Warren, Mark E., ed. (1999): *Democracy and Trust*. Cambridge: Cambridge University Press.

Wasserman, Stanley and Katherine Faust (1994): *Social Network Analysis: Methods and Applications*. Cambridge: Cambridge University Press.

Watts, Duncan (2003): *Six Degrees: The Science of a Connected Age*. New York: Norton.

Watts, Duncan (2004): "The 'New' Science of Networks," *Annual Review of Sociology* 30: 243–270.

Weber, Linda R. and Allison I. Carter (2003): *The Social Construction of Trust*. New York: Kluwer/Plenum.

White, Harrison C. (2002): *Markets From Networks: Socioeconomic Models of Production*. Princeton, NJ: Princeton University Press.

White, Richard (1991): *The Middle Ground: Indians, Empires, and Republics in the Great Lakes Region, 1650–1815*. Cambridge: Cambridge University Press.

White, Robert W. (1993): "On Measuring Political Violence: Northern Ireland, 1969 to 1980," *American Sociological Review* 58: 575–585.

Wiktorowicz, Quintan (2001): *The Management of Islamic Activism: Salafis, the Muslim Brotherhood, and State Power in Jordan*. Albany: State University of New York Press.

Willerton, John P. (1992): *Patronage and Politics in the USSR*. Cambridge: Cambridge University Press.

Williams, Robin (2003): *The Wars Within: Peoples and States in Conflict*. Ithaca, NY: Cornell University Press.

Williamson, Oliver E. (1996): *The Mechanisms of Governance*. New York: Oxford University Press.

Woloch, Isser (1970): *Jacobin Legacy: The Democratic Movement Under the Directory*. Princeton, NJ: Princeton University Press.

Woloch, Isser (1994): *The New Regime: Transformations of the French Civic Order, 1789–1820s*. New York: Norton.

Wood, Andrew Grant (2001): *Revolution in the Street: Women, Workers, and Urban Protest in Veracruz, 1870–1927*. Wilmington, DE: Scholarly Resources.

Wood, Elisabeth Jean (2000): *Forging Democracy from Below: Insurgent Transitions in South Africa and El Salvador*. Cambridge: Cambridge University Press.

Wood, Lesley J. (2004): "Breaking the Bank and Taking to the Streets: How Protesters Target Neoliberalism," *Journal of World Systems Research* 10: 69–89.

Woolcock, Michael (1998): "Social Capital and Economic Development: Toward a Theoretical Synthesis and Policy Framework," *Theory and Society* 27: 151–208.

Wrightson, Keith and David Levine (1979): *Poverty and Piety in an English Village: Terling, 1525–1700*. New York: Academic Press.

Wrightson, Keith and David Levine (1991): *The Making of an Industrial Society: Whickham 1560–1765*. Oxford: Clarendon Press.

Wuthnow, Robert (2004): "Trust as an Aspect of Social Structure" in Jeffrey C. Alexander, Gary T. Marx, and Christine L. Williams, eds., *Self, Social Structure, and*

Beliefs: Explorations in Sociology. Berkeley: University of California Press, pp. 145–167.

Yamagishi, Toshio and Midori Yamagishi (1994): "Trust and Commitment in the United States and Japan," *Motivation and Emotion* 18: 129–166.

Yashar, Deborah J. (1997): *Demanding Democracy: Reform and Reaction in Costa Rica and Guatemala, 1870s–1950s.* Stanford, CA: Stanford University Press.

Yinger, J. Milton (1985): "Ethnicity," *Annual Review of Sociology* 11: 151–180.

Ylikangas, Heikki, Petri Karonen, and Martti Lehti (2001): *Five Centuries of Violence in Finland and the Baltic Area.* Columbus: Ohio State University Press.

Young, Iris Marion (1990): *Justice and the Politics of Difference.* Princeton, NJ: Princeton University Press.

Zablocki, Benjamin D. (1971): *The Joyful Community: An Account of the Bruderhof, A Communal Movement Now in its Third Generation.* New York: Penguin.

Zablocki, Benjamin D. (1980): *Alienation and Charisma: A Study of Contemporary American Communes.* New York: Free Press.

Zelizer, Viviana A. (2000): "The Purchase of Intimacy," *Law & Social Inquiry* 25: 817–848.

Zelizer, Viviana A. (2002): "La construction des circuits de commerce: notes sur l'importance des circuits personnels et impersonnels" in Jean-Michel Servet and Isabelle Guérin, eds., *Exclusion et Liens Financiers: Rapport du Centre Walras.* Paris: Economica, pp. 425–429.

Zelizer, Viviana A. (2005): "Culture and Consumption" in Neil Smelser and Richard Swedberg, eds., *Handbook of Economic Sociology*, revised edition. Princeton, NJ: Princeton University Press and New York: Russell Sage Foundation, pp. 331–354.

Zink, Anne (1997): *Clochers et Troupeaux: Les Communautés rurales des Landes et du Sud-Ouest avant la Révolution.* Bordeaux: Presses Universitaires de Bordeaux.

Index

Index

Index

Other Books in the Series (*continued from page iii*)